Ahead of his ti

Roy Francis and Rugby Le

Peter Lush

London League Publications Ltd

Ahead of his time
Roy Francis and Rugby League
© Peter Lush
Foreword © Jim Mills

The moral right of Peter Lush to be identified as the author has been asserted.

Front & back cover design @ Stephen McCarthy.

All photographs are from private collections unless otherwise credited to the photographer or provider of the photo. No copyright has been intentionally breached; please contact London League Publications Ltd if you believe there has been a breach of copyright.

Front cover photo: Roy Francis playing at Warrington (Courtesy *Rugby League Journal).* Back cover: 1947 Great Britain team for third test versus New Zealand (Courtesy Robert Gate)

A CIP catalogue record for this book is available from the British Library.

Published in April 2022 by London League Publications Ltd, PO Box 65784, London NW2 9NS

ISBN: 978-1-909885-29-5

Cover design by Stephen McCarthy Graphic Design
46, Clarence Road, London N15 5BB.

Editing and layout by Peter Lush

Printed and bound in Great Britain by Ashford Colour Press Ltd, Gosport, Hants PO13 0FW

Foreword

In my opinion, Roy Francis was the first 'modern' coach in rugby league. At the clubs I played for before I joined Roy at North Sydney, training sessions were some general fitness work, moves and team work. Roy concentrated on speed, even for the big forwards like me. There were a lot of sprints. He would record our times and we had to improve. It was all about fitness and developing our rugby skills. Everyone did the sprints and some of the forwards were faster than the backs, although not the wingers.

I knew Roy before he signed me for North Sydney. He had a good reputation because of his work at Hull and Leeds. I had been selected for the 1970 Lions tour when he spoke to me, and looking back, I should have gone on the tour and then gone to Australia.

Roy was a very good 'man manager'. All the players respected him and accepted that he knew what he was talking about. He lived near the Leagues Club at North Sydney, and players would come round to his house, and his wife Renee would cook steaks in the oven for us. Very nice they were too!. Renee was very supportive to me when I first came to Australia and made me very welcome. Lewis Jones was in Australia at that time and he would visit Roy when he was in Sydney. Also, the legendary Australian coach Jack Gibson would phone Roy every week. I told Roy 'He's picking your brains.' Roy knew that, but still discussed things with Gibson. The other coaches in Australia also respected Roy. He also helped some British players come to Australia.

I think the problem Roy had in his second season at North Sydney, when I joined the club, was that the team needed time to gel. We made a poor start to the season, and Roy was not given time to build a team.

I was disappointed when Roy and Renee decided to go home in 1971. I think they missed their family and there was a good business opportunity for them back in England. Roy did at times face racism in Australia – there was one journalist, Ron Casey, who he had fallen out with. One journalist said that when North Sydney had lost, 'the Black and White Minstrels trooped back over the Sydney Harbour bridge'. That wasn't nice, but I don't think Roy and Renee went home because of racism.

Another issue Roy had to deal with was Ken Irvine. He was probably North Sydney's greatest player, but he didn't accept Roy's authority as the coach. The committee backed Roy up, and Irvine left the club, but he was still very popular with the supporters.

I kept in contact with Roy when I came home from Australia. I used to meet him at the Lions dinners, and would phone him for a chat. He gave me a lot of support in Australia, and I am very pleased that this book is coming out, so that all his achievements as a player and a coach can be fully recorded.

Jim Mills

Jim Mills played in six test matches for Great Britain and in 17 internationals for Wales and was a Lions tourist in 1974 and 1979. He also played for Wales in the World Championship in 1975. He won the Challenge Cup twice with Widnes, the Championship once and played in 13 domestic cup finals.

Introduction

Roy Francis had a very full life. This book concentrates on his rugby career and activities. It does not cover his business life except where it relates to his rugby playing or coaching. Roy ran successful businesses mainly in catering and as a publican.

Roy married Irene (known as Renee) when he was 19 years old, and the couple celebrated their 50th wedding anniversary in July 1988, about nine months before he died. They had two children, Geoff and Ian. Again, there is no detailed coverage of their family life in this book except where it connected to Roy's rugby.

One important area to consider is racism. Where there were clear examples of discrimination, I have included them in the book. These include his departure from Wigan which Roy said was because Harry Sunderland did not want a black player at the club. In 1943, the gatemen at Leicester rugby club refused to believe he was an England player. The 1946 tour selection is more open to debate, and that is covered in the chapter on that period. There are also examples of racism that Roy faced in Australia when he was at North Sydney.

The period from 1948 to 1989, when Roy died, was a very important one for race relations in Britain. The growth of immigration, initially from the West Indies, and then from various Asian communities, had a major effect on British society. Rugby League, as a sport, generally had a good record in involving black players in its ranks. However, Roy had front-line roles both in rugby league and in his business activities. Renee was white, and it is inconceivable that, as a couple of 'mixed race', they did not face racism in society. Geoff Francis, Roy's son, mentioned an incident in the 1960s when the couple were not allowed to stay at a hotel in Leeds. He was not aware of any other incidents, but said that Roy was a very private man, and may not have mentioned any problems he encountered.

Anne Francis, Roy's daughter-in-law, recalls that when she had her daughter Suzi, Roy visited her in the hospital about an hour after the baby was born. She says that he wanted to see what colour the baby was and says this was "quite touching", although of course Roy didn't tell her that was the aim of his visit. To me, it is also quite sad. Anne says that he went home to tell Renee that the baby was white and that he was relieved. She says that Roy didn't want the baby to have any hassle, and that he adored her.

In rugby league circles, there was clearly respect for Roy. Racial labels were very rarely applied to him in reports and articles about the sport. In Trevor Gibbons's chapter on Roy in *The Glory of their Times*, he quotes Hull FC legend Johnny Whiteley on Roy's time in Hull: "I didn't understand racism then. Black, white, yellow it made no difference to me and he never spoke about any problems to me. But then in Hull he had such success. Roy Francis was the unofficial Lord Mayor of Hull ... It was Roy and his coaching that blended us together as that team." While at Hull, Roy was involved in the recruitment and early development of Clive Sullivan, who went on to be the first black captain of the Great Britain Rugby League team, He was also the first black British national team captain in a major sport.

In my research for this book, comments on race and racism by Roy are rare. One in his time at North Sydney stands out. After a particularly poor display, he talked to journalists about humiliation, and pointing to his arm, talked about the humiliation he faced as a black man.

He was ahead of his time in his coaching ideas, but also because the post he held meant that he was managing – and instructing – white players. The first black football manager at a British professional club was Tony Collins in 1960 at Rochdale. On the playing side, Viv Anderson did not play football for the full England team until 1977. The first black MPs in the post-War period were Bernie Grant and Paul Boateng, who were both elected in 1987,

36 years after Roy was appointed player-coach at Hull FC.

There are some issues in common faced by Walter Tull and Roy, in particular that of a black man leading and instructing white men. Walter Tull was a professional footballer at Tottenham Hotspur and Northampton Town before the First World War. He joined the Army soon after the War started. He became the first black officer to lead white troops. His appointment broke Army regulations at the time. He was killed in action in 1918 and some of his white troops, at great risk to themselves, tried to recover his body from 'no-man's land' between the trenches. That was the respect they had for him.

Roy must have instructed white soldiers in his role as a Sergeant-Instructor in the Army. As a coach, he won the respect of his players as the comment above from Johnny Whiteley shows. Overwhelmingly, players who played for Roy speak well of him.

Roy remains one of the key figures in the development of coaching in rugby league. I hope that this book adequately records his story. Roy left his last post in rugby league 44 years ago. There are few players still around who played with him. The bulk of this book is based on research using newspaper reports and the rugby league press when available. I have also looked at biographies and club histories for more information and comment. As often as possible I have used what Roy actually said at the time. Sadly, there are limitations on this. The newspaper archives in the British Library do not contain the local and regional 'football specials' that were published late on Saturday afternoons. At times when he was in Hull, Roy wrote a column in this edition of the *Hull Daily Mail*, but these were not available to me. Similarly, the national newspapers in the British Library are usually southern editions, so the Challenge Cup and Championship finals do not get the same amount of coverage as in the northern editions. Also, when Roy was at Hull in the 1950s and 1960s, the spokesperson for the club was the chairman, Ernest Hardaker. He would comment on issues facing the club, possible transfers etc. Comments from Roy at times were rare.

I hope that readers enjoy this book. I enjoyed working on it and hope that it is another small step in developing the history of rugby league.

Peter Lush
February 2022

Photo: Roy playing with his granddaughter Suzi. (Courtesy Geoff Francis)

Thank you

Many different people helped me with this book. This included providing photographs, articles and newspaper reports, sound archives, reading drafts and discussing issues. I would like to thank Geoff and Anne Francis for their support and hospitality. However, this is not an 'authorised' biography, although their input has been valuable.

Thanks to: Bill Dalton (Hull FC historian), Neil Dowson (Warrington Wolves RLFC), Harry Edgar (*Rugby League Journal*), Howard Evans, Simon Foster, Robert Gate, Alan Golding, Ian Haywood, David Hinchliffe, Eifion Lloyd Davies (Brynmawr History Society), Jim Mills, Michael O'Hare, Huw Richards, Gary Slater, Graham Starkey, Andrew Varley, Graham Williams and the staff in the Newsroom at the British Library in St Pancras. Thank you to Steve McCarthy for designing the cover and to the staff at Ashford Colour Press for printing the book. A special thank you to Rosemary for her patient support for this project.

Any errors in the book are, of course, the author's responsibility.

About the author

Peter Lush grew up in London, where he still lives. He has been watching rugby league since he went to a game at the new Fulham club in October 1980 with Dave Farrar. In 1995, with Michael O'Hare, they wrote *Touch and Go – A history of professional rugby league in London*, and Peter and Dave set up London League Publications Ltd. The company has now published over 100 books, mainly on rugby league. Peter often works on book development and design, but other books he has written or edited include *I wouldn't start from here, Tries in the Valleys, From Fulham to Wembley, The Rugby League Grounds Guide, Rugby League Review 2007, Rugby League Review Number 2*, (all with Dave Farrar), *Trevor Foster* (with Simon Foster and Robert Gate) *Peter Fox – The Players' Coach* (with Graham Williams), *Hendon Football Club* (with David Ballheimer), *Big Jim* (with Maurice Bamford). *Rugby Football: A United Game* (an historical novel), *Tries and Conversions – South African Rugby League players* (with Hendrik Snyders) and two cricket grounds guides. He was joint editor of the rugby league magazine *Our Game*, and has written for various magazines, journals and newspapers on the sport.

In recent years he has started writing about speedway, mainly focussing on the Wembley Lions team that he watched in 1970 and 1971. His books include *When the Lions Roared, Freddie Williams – Double World Speedway Champion* and *Dave Jessup – A Speedway Journey.*

In real life he works part-time at Training Link, a charity based in central London providing basic skills training to help people find work. He is also a Magistrate in East London, and sits as a member of Employment Tribunals.

Contents

Roy being welcomed to Warrington by his new team-mates, Les Jones, Harry Bath,
Harold Palin and Jimmy Featherstone.

Roy playing for Warrington against Bradford Northern at Odsal in August 1948.
(Both courtesy Geoff Francis)

1. Brynmawr

On 19 October 1968, Leeds – coached by Roy Francis – beat Castleford 22–11 to win the Yorkshire Cup. It was the first time they had won the trophy since 1958. For Roy, it had particular significance. The previous May, his Leeds team had won the Challenge Cup. Winning the Yorkshire Cup meant that as a coach he had won all five of the traditional domestic honours in rugby league. He won the Championship with Hull, and the Yorkshire League, Challenge Cup, Yorkshire Cup and League Leaders trophy with Leeds. In 1975, he added the Premiership to the list.

It was a remarkable achievement. And his rugby career had started at a small club in South Wales.

Brynmawr is a town of around 6,000 people, less than 20 miles north of Newport. It is on the Heads of the Valleys Road. It has a well-established rugby union club, founded in 1880, although the cricket club folded in 2017. In 2017–18 the rugby club won the Welsh Rugby Union's Division One East and the National Plate. As well as a senior side, they also have a junior structure. They are a feeder club for the Newport Gwent Dragons. In 2021–22, they were playing in the A1 Plate competition.

On 20 January 1919, Lionel Roy Francis was born in Port Talbot. His father, Albert Francis, had been in a relationship with a white woman called Evans. When Roy was born, she decided that she could not keep him because of the colour of his skin, so Rebecca, Albert's wife, agreed that Roy would live with them. The 1921 Census shows him listed as an 'adopted son'. Albert and Rebecca lived in Brynmawr and Roy always regarded the town as home. When he and his family lived there, it was in Breconshire. Today it is in Blaenau Gwent. It is 1,000 feet above sea level, and claims to be the highest town in Wales.

Rebecca Francis, who was black, is listed as living in Brynmawr in the 1911 Census. She also had a daughter, Olive, who was born in 1907. According to the Census, Rebecca was born in 1883. The family lived on King Street at the time of the 1921 census. Roy also had a younger half-brother who was a jazz musician and moved to London. Roy's son Geoff can remember going to the Empire (now Commonwealth) Games at Cardiff in 1958 with Roy and visiting Brynmawr. The family were part of a small black community in the town and Geoff believes that there are still relatives there today.

The town can trace its roots back to the early nineteenth century, and its development was linked to industrial development in the area. However, when Roy and his family were living there, the economic recession of the post-First World War period had a devastating effect. In the 1920s, the unemployment rate was a staggering 90 per cent. However, things improved with the 'Brynmawr Experiment'. The Quakers set up a furniture factory which provided some work. Other projects started, although some only provided voluntary work or payment by the provision of a meal. Meetings were held to organise the provision of boots for local children.

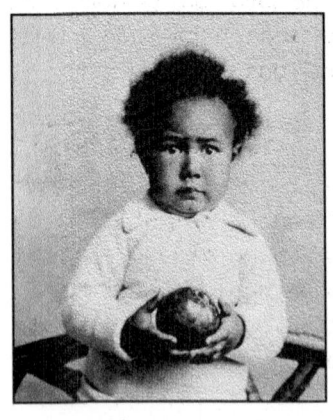

Left: A picture of Roy believed to be in around 1921, aged two. (Courtesy Geoff Francis)

Roy was clearly a talented athlete and showed his prowess in various sports from a young age. He attended the Brynmawr Elementary School and played for them. He was successful enough to be selected for a rugby union Welsh Schools Trial.

In August 1933, the *Merthyr Express* reported that Roy had won an award at the town's swimming gala. Three weeks later, the paper reported that he was third in the 120 yards open for boys aged up to 18, a very creditable result for a 14-year-old.

According to an article in the *Hull Daily Mail*, part of a 'How stars are made' series in the late 1950s, Roy's first sporting love was boxing, and he trained with an uncle who had trained the boxer Gipsy Daniels. He showed promise, but at the age of 10 became involved with sprinting. Then he changed to swimming, and was 'better then average' according to the article. He was ready to visit Cardiff for swimming training when he went to watch a Brynmawr rugby club trial. One of the teams was short of a player, so Roy played, although he had not played rugby for four years. He did so well that he was selected for the first team the following week. So, by August 1936, Roy was playing for the local Brynmawr Rugby Club.

The *Merthyr Express* said that he "showed much promise" on the left-wing as part of a young team. They had lost by six points to Risca, but the paper commented that "The committee have arranged a good side of young players ...There is every hope when these young players get more experience that Brynmawr will have a formidable side."

The next week, the *Express* reported that "Pill Harriers had a shock on Saturday, when they were defeated by 12 points by Brynmawr. The game was watched by hundreds of spectators, and the team, although the majority of them are inexperienced, held the Harriers splendidly, and there was plenty of polish on their movements. The captain. A. Davies, was the first to score with a penalty goal. and shortly afterwards Granville Watkins dropped a very smart goal. Roy Francis also scored a splendid try. There is a great future for these two lads, Francis and Watkins .... The home team continually broke up Pills's movements, and the visitors were astonished at the form of the hill lads. There was excellent cohesion, and if the team can be kept together. the prospects are rosy."

The next week, in a forward-dominated game, Brynmawr lost 9–3 at Blackwood. However, the next match, at home to Merthyr, they recovered from being 7–0 down at half-time to win 9–7. The report credits the try to Ron Francis. However, he was playing on the wing, and Roy is generally credited with four appearances for Brynmawr. Curiously though, reports usually give his full name, unlike most players who are only given an initial. Was there a Ron Francis around at this time? It is unlikely that records will be found to clarify this question.

Roy's young rugby union career was coming to an end. He is usually said to have played one game for Abertillery, who were a far more prominent club than Brynmawr. Many of their players won international honours, and they regularly played international touring teams including the South Africans in 1931. However, the *Hull Daily Mail* article says that "After four games with Brynmawr, Abertillery asked him to play for them, but before he could give them an answer, a Wigan scout came knocking at his door..." However, the article does say that Roy joined Wigan in September, which is incorrect. Local press reports in Wigan say that Roy played a couple of 'A' team games before turning to rugby league. How he kept his absence from a small place like Brynmawr is another matter.

However, on 14 November 1936, Roy signed for Wigan, and moved north to play rugby league. Today, players can switch between union and league as they choose. However, in the 1930s, even to speak to a league scout could result in a life ban from the 'amateur' union code.

All the major rugby league clubs had scouts in South Wales. If recognised, they were thrown out of rugby union grounds and treated with hostility. Roy was very young to be turning professional. However, the signing on fee would have been helpful to him and his family. The scout must have seen the potential Roy had for rugby league. However, it was a gamble on Roy's part. Once a player had turned professional, there was no going back to 'amateur' rugby union.

He was not alone in being tempted to 'go north'. Even before the formation of the Northern Union in 1895, Welsh players had been tempted to join the larger, more commercially run rugby union clubs in Lancashire and Yorkshire, competing in county cups and leagues. The offer of a signing on fee as well as regular income for playing rugby was important for many players in these economically depressed times.

Gareth Williams, a well-known union historian, comments in *1905 and all that* how 150 Welsh internationals 'went north' in the first 100 years of the WRU's existence. Sixty-nine of these were in the inter-war period, reflecting the economic crisis that hit South Wales. Williams continues: "... we can never know how many hundreds of ordinary, unemployed club players were lured north by a persuasive agent offering anything from £300 to £500 down, £4 for a win, £3 draw or lose, and the promise of a job. It would soon become apparent that some of these acquisitions, like Jim Sullivan and Gus Risman, were far from ordinary." Rugby league historian Robert Gate has calculated that more than 900 players 'went north'. It is not known whether Roy was working or not when he was offered the chance to turn professional by Wigan.

In a chapter in *The Global Sports Arena*, Williams says that it was "... the western valleys of Monmouthshire and the eastern valleys of Glamorgan, highly dependent on iron and coal, that bore the brunt of the recession." He then outlines the very high unemployment rates in different towns, including 74 percent of the male workforce in Brynmawr in 1934. He continues: "These areas were rich pickings for rugby league: in November 1936 Brynmawr lost to Wigan the 17-year-old Roy Francis, sensationally good as a threequarter and later as coach..."

In the same piece, Williams outlines how certain clubs attracted Welsh players. He says that "The list of Wigan's recruits would have to be headed by Jim Sullivan and the speedy Johnny Ring who joined in 1922 for the then record [signing-on] fee of £800, and of the side that won the Lancashire Cup Final in 1922, only two had not been recruited from South Wales. What gave Wigan its 'particular mania' for raiding the Welsh market was its readiness to find positions for many of the new arrivals as ground staff and pay a small wage for odd jobs like boot repairing on top of match payments." Maybe this was another factor in Roy's decision to change codes and turn professional.

Another factor that may have been considered by Roy was race. There were black players established in professional rugby league during the 1930s. Wigan stand-off George Bennett played three times for Wales, including in their first-ever match against France. Oldham loose-forward Alec Givvons played six times for Wales's from 1936 to 1939. In 1937 Jimmy Cumberbatch was the first black player to play for England. His brother Val played for Barrow and also was capped by England.

The Cumberbatch brothers played for England 40 years before Viv Anderson became the first black player in Association Football to play for England.

Every Welsh rugby union player aspired to play for the national team, but it was not until the 1980s that a black player was selected for Wales. It was an open secret that black players would not be chosen for Wales at this time. So, Roy's future lay at Wigan and Central Park.

2. Wigan

At the age of 17, with only a handful of club rugby union games under his belt, Roy had clearly been signed by Wigan on the basis of his potential, to learn his trade in the 'A' team. However, he did have some advantages. Of the all the positions, switching codes for a winger was probably one of the easiest. There was the basic skill for a player new to league from union of learning the 'play-the-ball' and not to release the ball in the tackle. Tackling was certainly tougher in league than union, and the need to protect oneself was always there. However, for a forward there were more differences, with no lineouts. There were differences in the scrums as well, with only six forwards in a league scrum compared to eight in union.

In moving to Central Park, Roy was joining the most famous rugby league club in Britain. Although people from St Helens may disagree, ask any casual sports fan for the name of a rugby league club, and Wigan is most likely to be the reply.

The first rugby club in Wigan was founded in 1872. However, that club collapsed in 1878, and Wigan Wasps was set up in 1879. In 1881, they changed the name to Wigan. They were founder members of the Northern Union in 1895. When Roy joined, they had won the Challenge Cup twice – the second time in the inaugural Wembley Final. They had won the Northern Rugby League Championship four times, most recently in 1934. In Lancashire competitions, they had won the Lancashire League 10 times and the Lancashire Cup six times. They played at the huge Central Park stadium.

However, Roy was joining a club with a considerable Welsh presence. At full-back, Jim Sullivan had joined Wigan from Cardiff in 1921, also at the age of 17. He became one of Wigan's greatest ever players. Also in the team at this time at stand-off was another black Welsh player, George Bennett. He was from Newport and played for Risca before signing for Weston-Super-Mare in 1929. His father had come to Wales from South Africa as a child; his mother was Welsh. He played for Monmouth at rugby union, and for Wales in league. He left the club about a year after Roy joined Wigan. He had lost his first team place to Jack Garvey, and joined Bradford Northern. Apparently, he was "affectionately known as 'Darkie'" according to Graham Morris in his *100 Greats* book about Wigan RLFC.

In his *Illustrated History* of the club, Jack Winstanley mentions five other Welsh players who were signed during Roy's time at Central Park. However, none of them were wingers. However, Roy was seen as much as a centre as a winger at Wigan.

Roy faced considerable competition for a first team place. On the right wing was Jack Morley, who had joined the club from Newport Rugby Union in 1932. In 1936 he toured with the British Lions, and also played for England and Wales. He made almost 300 appearances for Wigan, scoring 223 tries. On the left wing, Alf Ellaby was the regular incumbent. He spent most of his career with St Helens, but had moved to Central Park in 1934, because St Helens had major financial problems. He was another British Lion, having toured in 1928 and 1932. However, he was now aged 34, and returned to St Helens at the end of Roy's first season.

A third player in contention for one of the winger places was Eddie Holder. He had joined Wigan from Streatham & Mitcham as the London club gradually collapsed during the 1936–37 season, eventually withdrawing from the league in February 1937. Before switching codes, he had won 10 caps for the All Blacks. He played for Wigan until the Second World War, when he went back to New Zealand, and was re-instated into rugby union after the War.

On 17 November 1936, the *Wigan Observer* reported that "Lionel Roy Francis, and W. Brown" had been signed by the club. The report said that Roy was a "centre threequarter, who have been given a number of trials with the 'A' team. Francis is a convert from Brynmawr RUFC. In his trials he has shown promising form. He is not quite 18 years of age, stands 5 feet 10 inches and turns the scale at 12 stones 4 pounds. Both players are included in the 'A' team to play Rochdale Hornets at Central Park this Saturday." It is interesting to consider how Roy kept his trips to Wigan to play for the 'A' team as a trialist secret in a small close-knit community like Brynmawr. Even for playing in a trail match as an amateur he would have been banned from rugby union by the authorities if they had found out.

Wigan's 'A' team were starting a long unbeaten run. In Roy's debut, Alf Ellaby also played. Roy was always named in the 'A' team squads, and seems to have played regularly. On 12 December, they played a Lancashire Junior League select. One suspects this gave the Wigan officials the chance to look out for new talent. The 'A' team won 40–5, and scored 10 tries. The *Observer* said that "the tenth try was gained by Francis after a brilliant individual effort." There was no time off for Roy over Christmas – on 19 December the 'A' team beat Broughton 15–0 in front of 2,000 fans at Central Park. They then beat Salford on Christmas Day and St Helens on Boxing Day. To start the new year, Roy scored against Castleford at Central Park.

Two weeks later, they beat Warrington's 'A' team 17–11 at Wilderspool. A 10,000 crowd saw Australian Dave Brown make his debut for the Wire. A week later, Eddie Holder made his Wigan debut for the 'A' team, against a Manchester Junior League Select. Roy played on the right wing, and was "prominent". The *Observer* reported that in the first half: "Francis came into the picture with a burst along the touchline, but Seeling missed his inside pass." It added: "Early in the second half, Meadows dribbled through and Francis took the ball over the line to score." Later in second half, "Meadows came away from a scrum and sent Francis over to score behind the posts". Wigan 'A' won 24–0.

The next week, Roy played at left centre in a 16–6 win over Oldham. The report said that "After 20 minutes Francis deceived the opposition to increase Wigan's lead with a splendid try." Roy also had a try disallowed for a forward pass. Against Halifax the next week: "Constructive play by the home threequarters resulted in two tries by O'Sullivan from passes by Francis." Roy added another try. The 'A' team were unbeaten since October. They were coached by Wilf Hodder, a former Wigan and Wales forward.

A couple of weeks later, Castleford were beaten 31–5. Wigan scored nine tries and "Francis ran through the defence for the second try." A week later, 7,500 came to Central Park for the match against Liverpool Stanley, who were also at the top of the table. Eight players were sent off, four from each side, and two went off injured. Roy managed to stay out of the mayhem, and scored a try in Wigan's 24–2 win.

With a lot of fixtures to be played at the end of the season, Roy made his debut for the first team at left centre. He was thrown into the deep end on Good Friday, 26 March 1937, in the usually ferociously competitive derby match against St Helens at Central Park. Wigan won 16–3 against a Saints side who were struggling in the bottom half of the league.

Roy (second from left) with Jim Sullivan (centre) during his time at Wigan.
(Courtesy *Rugby League Journal*)

He marked his debut with a try in front of 10,000 fans. Snow and 'atrocious conditions' probably reduced the size of the crowd. The *Observer* reported that "Wigan rested Gwynne Davies and introduced Francis, the 'A' team centre, and considering the mud which lay inches deep everywhere he made a good impression. He handled the ball well and gave Morley a service far better than he has had in many games this season. He did not wait until the Welshman was on the fringe of the touchline to give him the ball and had the day been anything like Morley in all probability would have turned some chances that came his way to account."

Roy kept his place for the Easter Saturday match against Leigh, again at Central Park. Wigan won comfortably, 51–10 against opponents who finished the season in 28th place with just 14 points. Roy scored a hat-trick of tries, but Alf Ellaby overshadowed him with five. The *Observer* said that Wigan practically fielded a reserve team. It commented that "Francis ... was a star number. He played a tireless game and looked as fresh at the end as he did at the start, and he certainly gained the confidence of the crowd even if the opposition was weak. Despite the heavy going he showed plenty of speed, and was thrustful at all times, and the manner in which he drew his opposite number was a feature of his play. He looked for openings to get the best out of Morley, timing his passes judiciously. In defence he also showed some effective work and Wigan should have little fear of including him in their side against the bigger 'shots' of the rugby league."

Roy was not selected for the next two matches, but returned to the team against York, again at Central Park, and this time in the right centre position, with Eddie Holder on the wing. He scored three of Wigan's six tries in a 20–5 win, with Jim Sullivan only kicking one goal. Gee sent Roy over for an unimproved try; Jim Sullivan sent him over for a try just before the interval and a 'crisp' passing movement gave Francis his third try.

Roy again kept his place for a home match with Leeds, which Wigan won 8–2. The *Observer* reported that "Francis, who was given another chance with the seniors to the exclusion of G Davies, did well to a point, but in this match, he seemed rather hesitant on several occasions. Several of his efforts, however, were cleverly executed and he impressed the crowd with his free action once he got into his stride. That Wigan have a useful centre in the making is obvious and with a little more experience he cannot remain out of the league side as a regular very much longer."

His final appearance of the season was away to St Helens Recs. Wigan lost 20–10, with their points all coming from the boot of Jim Sullivan. Roy was not mentioned in the *Observer's* match report.

Roy, who had turned 18 in January 1937, finished the season with seven tries from five appearances. Wigan finished the season in fifth place, three competition points away from the Championship play-offs. The 'A' team won the Lancashire Combination.

Roy could look back on his debut season with pride – he had broken into the first team, and could hope to challenge for a regular place in 1937–38. Away from the rugby pitch, Roy played cricket for a team of Wigan rugby league players against Platt Bridge Methodists. It is not known if he played cricket regularly in the off-season.

For the new season, 1937–38, the departure of Alf Ellaby back to St Helens saw Jack Morley and Eddie Holder become the regular wingers. In the first public trial match, Roy "did a lot of useful work" for the Blues against the Cherry & Whites. At the end of August, the *Observer* printed a list of the Wigan players for the new campaign. Roy was listed as a centre, along with Gordon Innes, Charlie Banfield and Dennis Williamson. Seven wingers were included. He started the season in the 'A' team, and "tackled effectively" and set up two tries against Oldham. He scored the next week against Liverpool Stanley, and a couple of weeks later against Huddersfield. However, a regular first team place did not come.

Roy made just three appearances in the first team, two of them at centre. On 13 November he played against Barrow at Central Park in a 9–5 defeat. The *Observer* wrote that "Francis, playing his first game in the League side this season, made mistakes that were costly. Once in the first half, when he distinguished himself with a strong run, he wasted a scoring chance when he forgot that there were others on the field to support him. He created an opening which had the Barrow defence well and truly beaten, but instead of passing the ball when he was challenged by Blackburn, he tried to go through and was tackled. Another mistake on his part followed on the interval when he passed the ball rather than go down with it when the Wigan defence was all out of position. His pass went astray and Barrow took advantage of the mistake and scored from it."

In January 1938, Edward H (Ted) Ward, a 20-year-old centre, was signed from Llanelli RFC. Roy was named in the first team squad for the match at Halifax on 15 January, just after Ward had been signed. However, he was unable to play due to a carbuncle. Ward made his debut the following week. He kept his place for the rest of the season and went on to play 213 games for Wigan. He played for the club until 1953.

Back in the 'A' team, Roy played against a Lancashire Federation team and "outpaced the opposition and scored a magnificent try" in a 51–16 win. In early February, Gordon Innes joined Castleford, reducing the competition for centre and wing places. Away to St Helens Recs 'A', Roy "ran the full length of the field to score a fine try for Wigan." Roy scored again at home to Hull, at Rochdale, twice at home to St Helens Recs, at Leeds and at home to a Manchester League side, when he "ran almost half the length of the field." At home to St Helens on 2 April, Roy dribbled the ball three parts the length of the field, but it ran dead. Earlier, he "...cleverly outwitted three opponents and ran down the middle to gain a try behind the posts."

Roy finally got another chance with the first team on East Saturday at Leeds in a 21–9 defeat. Ward and Williamson were unfit, so Gwynne Davies and Roy played. The *Observer* said that "It was unfortunate that Francis failed to produce his 'A' team form but that being so it would be unfair to offer a severe criticism. It was something of an ordeal for Francis to be banged into the side against a team of Leeds' calibre and expect great things of him and it was evident that because he did not make a good impression, he was left out of the Wigan side on Easter Monday. He was, however, not the only flaw in the Wigan attack." Roy had missed a pass from Emlyn Jenkins that was a scoring opportunity.

He played on the wing in the final match of the season, a 19–8 win against Widnes at Central Park and scored: "after a passing movement which culminated in a brilliant try...".

Roy had now played one and a half seasons of rugby league, mainly in the 'A' team. However, he faced the dilemma of many young players at a top club – they lack opportunities because new 'ready-made' stars can be signed. Roy had only played a handful of club rugby union matches before joining Wigan, but had now clearly got to grips with the rugby league code. However, the team – by Wigan's standards – had not been particularly successful, finishing ninth in the league, four places lower than the previous season. Part of this was due to fixture congestion, but if he could not get a regular place when the team was not doing well, when would he?

On 23 July 1938, Roy married Irene Austin. She was usually called 'Renee' and was the daughter of the family he lodged with. They were married for over 50 years. In 1939, the couple had their first son, Geoff.

Roy was selected for the first game of the 1938–39 season, and scored in a 15–11 win against Wakefield Trinity at Central Park. However, his next first team appearance was on 19 November. He had a run of three matches on the left wing, but did not score. Two of the games were lost, but his last first team match for Wigan was won, 7–4 at Watersheddings against Oldham.

First team opportunities for Roy at Central Park were clearly limited. However, according to Robert Gate, who interviewed Roy, he believed that Harry Sunderland, an Australian who was appointed as Wigan Secretary-Manager in September 1938, was racist, and that this was the reason for his departure. Sunderland had undertaken initiatives to develop the sport, and Robert Gate says in *Gone North* that he "... is now held by many to have been one of the game's great visionaries. When it came to Roy Francis, however, his vision must have been impaired for within a couple of months of his taking control at Central Park he had transferred the blossoming wing star to Barrow...".

Left: Roy and Renee with Geoff in 1939. (Courtesy Geoff Francis)

In his obituary of Roy in *Code 13* (issue 11) Robert Gate says that "In an interview with me in 1985 Roy made it clear that Sunderland obviously disliked the colour of Roy's skin."

Although he remained living in the town for some years, the end of his Wigan career came in January 1939, when he was transferred to Barrow. In 12 official first team appearances he had scored nine tries. However, not everyone was happy about Roy being sold. A letter in the local paper, from 'Shareholder' said: "Will you allow me a small space to vent a grievance not only for myself but for hundreds of other supporters of the Wigan Rugby Club. Why has Francis been transferred? Next to Morley he was considered by hundreds to be the best threequarter the club had, and he had not had a real chance. Other men have been kept on the team who have never shown the ability of Francis. After the election of the Board of Directors with the new blood last June, everybody thought the club would 'sail along' but I am afraid it has done the reverse." In fact, Wigan finished the season in ninth place in the league, the same as in 1938–39.

A small article in the *Wigan Express* of 24 January 1939, after Roy had returned to Central Park with his new team, said that a writer in the *Barrow News* had asked "Why have Wigan parted with him [Roy]?" The writer continued: "and on the way to the game on Saturday I was taxed with a similar question. I am still wondering, for the boy has unusually good football in him.

Another season and Lionel Roy Francis is a star. He gave a display that delighted me. Cumberbatch, fed at the right time and receiving the ball at the correct height, gave his best display of the season. Francis, at 20, has many years of football in him. He is a stylist and can exploit his ability. What impressed me most was the way in which he drew men to him to transfer at the right time and to a most unexpected quarter. Lovely, skilful play, and he has set a standard the crowd likes. They gave him a great ovation and he earned it."

10

3. Barrow 1939 to 1944

Barrow by road is around 86 miles from Wigan. Roy was still living in Wigan. It is safe to assume that Roy did not always make this journey, by car or train, twice a week for training and to play in home games. When the part-time players of this era transferred to another club some distance away, they often continued to train one evening a week with their original club or another local team.

He was joining a club that had been founded in 1875, and joined the Northern Union (NU) for the 1897–98 season. They had had limited success since joining the NU, but in 1937–38 had reached their first Challenge Cup Final, losing to Salford 7–4 at Wembley. They had also played in their first Lancashire Cup Final in the same season, losing to Warrington.

Barrow's right winger was Val Cumberbatch, who was one of the early black players to represent England. His brother Jimmy was the first, having been capped in 1937. He was then playing for Broughton Rangers, and scored two tries on his debut against France at Thrum Hall on 10 April 1937.

Val won international honours in 1938. As a Barrow player he made his debut for England on 20 March in Paris. He scored a try in a 17–15 victory.

Their father was from Barbados and their mother from the Isle of Man. Jim Thornburrow was the regular left-winger, so Roy made his debut in the centre for Barrow on 14 January 1939. He played in every game for the rest of the season, with the last eight being on the left-wing.

In the *Barrow News* (*The News*), *Sentinel* reported that Barrow had been negotiating with Roy for a fortnight about joining the club, and he had finally signed on 12 January. Warrington had also been interested in him. The report said that Wigan wanted £450 for him, and the actual amount, while not revealed, was close to that. The paper said that Roy had "the reputation of a promising young player who is regarded as equally at home at centre or stand-off half." In fact, Roy had little experience at stand-off, although he did play at centre as much as on the wing for Barrow in his first campaign.

Roy made his debut at home to Hunslet two days after signing. Barrow won 20–2, and *The News's* headline said "New man's part in big victory". *Sentinel* wrote that it was "a wise move" to include Roy in the team. The club "attracted a big 'gate', strengthened a threequarter line that had been weakened by the absence of Gummer and found they had a new player of undoubted merit."

Sentinel wrote in his report: "I like Francis. This Welsh-born lad had good stuff in him. From his play on Saturday, I take it that he will be equally at home at stand off as well as centre. He has the build; he knows the tactics and he can get his man. A compliment to his team-mates for giving him the 'big hand'. It must have meant a lot to him to come on the field for the first time and find his colleagues ready to help and congratulate him. The crowd, too, showed their appreciation for his smart work in no uncertain way."

Roy started well, and *Sentinel* said that "Francis, ever on his toes, was early astir and as he went to work in fast style, he almost had Cumberbatch over for a try near the corner." He also reported that it was Roy's long, high pass that created a try for Cumberbatch in the corner. Later in the game, Roy set up a try with another high pass for Thornburrow. It was clearly a satisfactory debut.

Having seen off the champions, Barrow's next match was a trip to Roy's old stamping ground, Central Park. Barrow lost 7–0, and the match report said that Roy "was accorded a fine reception on entering the ground to oppose his old colleagues, was never in the picture. He had a very poor match." The report said that the conditions were not good for 'spectacular' rugby and maybe Roy was nervous about returning to Wigan so soon after his transfer.

Roy's first try for Barrow came on 4 February, at Halifax in the Challenge Cup. Barrow lost 8–3, but the report said that their challenge was "virile" and that the game was never safe for Halifax. Roy scored from a pass by Higgin, and he "gave the dummy and went over." The report added that he showed "power in attack as well as defence."

Roy's defensive play was much in evidence over the next month. In four games, Barrow scored two tries, both by Cumberbatch. At Salford, in a 19–0 defeat, *The News* reported that "Francis, Higgin and Thornburrow performed wonders in defence." On a heavy pitch, Leeds were beaten 3–0 at Craven Park, but *Sentinel* wrote that "the experiment of Francis on the wing had not much chance of proving anything under the conditions."

Roy's second try came on 25 March in a 9–0 home win against Halifax. This time, *Sentinel* said that "Playing Francis on the wing was a distinctly successful experiment, and the speedy Hickey was often falling victim to the Barrow winger's tackles. He tackled fearlessly and always for the feet. Two such efforts in the second half saved the day for Barrow when the situation looked very menacing." Roy's try was Barrow's third and sealed their victory.

At Leigh, Roy scored twice for the first time for Barrow. He and Cumberbatch were said to be "very fast on the wings". Barrow won 20–5, the first time they had scored double figures since Roy's debut. Roy scored in the next two games, at home to Liverpool Stanley, and at Oldham. Both were won.

Against Salford, in a narrow 3–0 home win, "Francis played a grand game, tackling Hudson every time he threatened danger." Roy's final two tries came at Belle Vue in a 15–6 defeat against Wakefield Trinity. He could have had a hat-trick; *The News* outlined that "The greatest disappointment was when Francis outdistanced Teall in a race for the ball but unluckily stepped on it in his efforts to regain possession."

Barrow won 10 times in Roy's 18 appearances, with two draws. He scored eight tries, mainly when he played on the wing. Even in his limited time at the club, he finished joint third highest try scorer, behind Val Cumberbatch and fellow Welshman George Gummer. Barrow finished the season in eighth place, seven points away from the play-offs.

In May 1939, the Military Training Act was passed. It introduced conscription to the Armed Forces for young men aged 20 and 21. When the War started, this was changed to 18 to 41 and then in October 1939, men between the ages of 20 and 23 were required to register. Roy came into this category

Training for the new rugby league season started for Barrow at the end of July. The club said that 37 players attended. *The News* published a list of two full-backs, 14 threequarters – including Roy, four half-backs and 14 forwards. A couple of trial matches were played before the league matches started on 26 August. Roy scored a couple of tries in the first match.

Barrow started the 1939–40 season with a win against Liverpool and a draw at Widnes. Roy played in both games, but then the War against Germany was declared and the Northern Rugby League competition was abandoned.

Unlike in the First World War, the government recognised the impact sport could have in helping keep civilian morale up. After a three-week break, Barrow resumed playing, in the War Emergency League Lancashire section. The Rugby League Council confirmed that the New Zealand tour was cancelled, and that matches would resume at the end of September in county-based leagues.

Roy played six more games, all on the left wing. On 7 October, he played for Barrow in a 22–14 win over Oldham at Craven Park. *Sentinel* reported that "If Saturday's game at Craven Park represents war-time football, give me more... It was a tonic, and Francis's passage over the Oldham line for a try brought the crowd to their feet. That picture try will live in the memory. Francis had been awaiting his chance all afternoon; eager and ready it came, he was off from the word go, and Davies, Mitchell and Griffiths gave up the chase. Along the wing, up the centre and under the posts Francis went. No wonder the crowd were spontaneous in their plaudits."

Roy scored again in his next match, at Leigh, when Barrow lost 11–8. Barrow were now able to announce their Lancashire League fixtures until February. However, Roy was called up to the Army the week after the Leigh match. The paper later reported that six Barrow players, Alex Troup, George Gummer, Tom Barr, Tom Whyte and W. Oxley as well as Roy were now in the Forces. Roy had joined the RASC, the Royal Army Service Corp.

Roy played against Warrington on 2 December when he was on leave. His last appearance was on Boxing Day, away to Widnes. Barrow lost 18–5. The day before, he had scored a hat-trick of tries, as did Cumberbatch, at home to Broughton Rangers. Barrow won 26–7. Overall, he played eight games and scored five tries.

Barrow finished seventh out of 12 teams in the 1939–40 Lancashire section of the War Emergency League. They won 10 games and drew one of their 22 fixtures. However, they then withdrew from the competition for the next three seasons. Travel difficulties may have been a reason for this, as well as work commitments for the players in the local shipyards.

It is interesting to note that the Government remained in favour of sport being played, The Ministry of Labour sent a message to the Rugby League Council meeting on 7 August 1940 urging the clubs to play as much football as possible, so that the workers had recreation and relaxation.

Roy was aged 20 when the War broke out. Like many professional sportsmen, he lost opportunities because of the War. However, when he joined the Army, he became a Physical Training Instructor, and after initially being based in Aldershot – his second son Ian was born there in 1941 – spent most of the War based in Yorkshire. His family returned to Wigan when he was posted to Yorkshire.

Roy remained on Barrow's books, but mainly played for Dewsbury. Barrow did not play in the War Emergency League again until 1943–44, when Roy played twice, in away matches in Yorkshire, scoring two tries. Barrow finished in ninth place in the league, with 11 wins and 11 defeats.

Roy did not play for the club in 1944–45. He broke his leg in August 1944, and although he was playing in an Army rugby union game in October, and was listed as playing in previews of a couple of other matches, does not seem to have played any rugby league that season. Possibly military commitments also cut across this. Travelling to Barrow from his base in West Yorkshire may also have been an issue. Barrow improved on their performance the previous season and finished in fifth place, with 15 wins and a draw from their 23 matches.

Roy's next match for Barrow was in 1945.

4. Wartime rugby 1940 to 1942

The government faced the task of getting thousands of new recruits physically fit. One resource the Army used was professional sportsmen who had joined up. One new recruit to the Army was Joe Mercer, who went on to have a distinguished association football career as a player and then a manager. In his autobiography, *The Great Ones*, he outlines that Sir Stanley Rous, the FA Secretary, had sent round a circular saying that footballers with coaching experience were encouraged to join the Army Physical Training Corps, where "we would be able to keep fit and would be made sergeant-instructors immediately." It turned out that Sir Stanley had been mistaken, resulting in a near-mutiny by some of the footballers. As a compromise they were made temporary sergeants while they took a course. Mercer outlines that he played a lot of football during the war, while doing his job in the Army. His chapter in the book concludes "... don't think that we footballer-P.T. instructors regarded our service as just a giggle. That was far from the case. We were not born soldiers but we took our job of making the fighting men fit seriously and, I feel, we did not do it too badly."

In his biography. Trevor Foster outlines that after three months basic training, he applied to become a PT Instructor: "I was accepted to go into the gymnasium and excused any further military duties. I was keen on physical fitness and spent the next nine months in the gym." After a posting to Aldershot, Trevor 'passed out' as a Sergeant-Instructor. One of the people on the same course was Roy. Trevor recalls that he and his fellow Welshman who had also 'gone north' were good friends. Several other league players joined the Army as non-commissioned officers as physical training instructors. However, promotion above the rank of Sergeant was rare.

Trevor had become 25 years old in December 1939. He had enjoyed a good rugby union career in South Wales before joining Bradford Northern in October 1938. He had considered going to Wigan with Roy, but had changed his mind and stayed in South Wales for another 18 months. Roy had been in rugby league for longer than Trevor, but his first team experience was a dozen games with Wigan, and two half-seasons with Barrow. In January 1940 he had become 21. He was also black British, and there were relatively few black British soldiers in the Army at this time. There were no records of ethnicity kept by the Armed forces.

One estimate puts the Black British population in 1939 at 8,000. Another says 15,000. Either way, the number eligible for military service must have been fairly small. As the War went on, more troops were recruited from the Empire, so the Armed Forces became more ethnically diverse. In Stephen Bourne's study of black servicemen and women in the Second World War, *The Motherland Calls*, the *In Memoriam* postscript includes three people who were born in Cardiff and one in London. The rest were born in the colonies.

Roy was based in the south of England for the first part of the War. His son Geoff had been born in 1939, and Geoff recalls that his younger brother Ian was born in Aldershot in 1941. His mother Renee later took the children back to Wigan where they stayed for the rest of the War.

Roy must have impressed the Army authorities for someone of that age and ethnic background to become a Sergeant-Instructor. Arguably, it was to change his life.

Another change for the rugby league players was that, in matches playing for a military team, they were allowed to play rugby union. For some Welsh players, this was the chance they had sacrificed by turning professional, to wear the red shirt of Wales in their original code.

As the War went on, there was more flexibility in rugby league about player registrations for clubs. Some clubs had closed and their players could play for other teams as 'guests'. Later in the War, if a team were short of players, they could borrow from another club to be able to field a side. Dewsbury, whose manager was a young man developing his rugby league career called Eddie Waring, took advantage of this relaxation of the rules. That they were near major Army camps also was to their advantage. In Association Football, Aldershot Town FC suddenly found that they had international players available to them from the major army camps in the town, unheard of for a club from the lower reaches of the Football League.

Tony Hannen, in his biography *Being Eddie Waring*, says that "Clearly, teams located near to military bases such as Leeds, Bradford and Halifax now held a colossal advantage. Even so, few, if any, were swifter on the uptake than Eddie Waring. As a wartime wheeler-dealer, he knew no equal. Paying particular attention to the Caulms Wood army camp, he set about putting together a side..."

In the first part of the War, Roy's role was getting the troops fit. As the War went on, it changed to rehabilitation of injured soldiers. He was based at Overton, near Dewsbury. Again, he seems to have applied the lessons he learnt from this experience to coaching later in his life.

Roy's first match for Dewsbury was on 12 April 1941. He scored a try in a 13–9 win at Oldham. One of his team-mates that day was the Welsh rugby league legend Jim Sullivan, who had also gone north at a young age, to join Wigan. The *Dewsbury Reporter* outlined that "Last minute negotiations saw Dewsbury include Harrison of Wigan at stand-off, Roy Francis (Barrow) and R Kenny, the Salford loose forward."

The reporter believed that Dewsbury could have had another 10 to 15 points: "Tom Kenny threw away three points with Francis unmarked, Francis hesitated once, probably thinking he was offside, when a straight run would have given him a try... In the second half Francis came more into the picture and when Royal had his kick charged down, and was palpably obstructed, Francis gained possession and simply refused to be held, dashing over for a brilliant try which Sullivan improved."

Dr John Schleppi, from the University of Dayton in Ohio, interviewed Roy for his academic research on rugby league during the Second World War. He also wrote articles on this subject for *Code 13*. He looked at the problems players experienced physically getting to matches. He says that Roy recalled his trip from Salisbury Plain to Dewsbury: "First, he went to the station on foot, then by delayed train to suburban London, by motorbike into London, truck to the station and finally by train to Dewsbury. Almost 15 hours one way!" It is inconceivable that Roy did this every week.

Dewsbury finished the 1940–41 season in 10 place in the 14-team Yorkshire section of the Wart Emergency League. They won six and drew two of their 23 games. The difficulties facing the sport's organisers were shown when Dewsbury arrived at the Boulevard five players short. They recruited two players who had turned up to watch, and borrowed three from their hosts so that the game could go ahead.

1941–42

The following season, 1941–42, Roy played in 27 out of Dewsbury's 30 fixtures. As well as Sullivan, another Welsh league legend to line up beside Roy was Salford's Gus Risman. Roy finished as top try scorer, with 29 tries. Despite – or maybe because of – fielding even more guest players, Dewsbury won the League Championship.

Dewsbury had finished top of the 17-team league, with 19 wins and a draw from their 24 matches. The teams did not all play the same number of games, so a percentage system decided the league table. Dewsbury were top on 81.25 percent.

The part Roy played in Dewsbury's Championship success is shown in the *Dewsbury Reporter's* (*The Reporter*) coverage of the team.

Roy made his debut in the second match of the season, a 34–8 win over Broughton. "Great display by Francis" was the headline of the Reporter's coverage. *Onlooker* wrote: "The 'star' of the game was undoubtedly Francis, the winger whom Dewsbury have secured from Barrow. Francis gave a clever display in the cup tie at Oldham last year, but last Saturday he eclipsed that effort. His bag during the game was four tries, the third being a perfect gem of quick thinking, timing and resolution, and it was not surprising that he soon established himself as a great favourite. He was a real bag of tricks when in possession and if he can play as regularly as is hoped, he should collect a bagful of tries this season." The report continued: "But before the interval Francis came into the picture with a couple of tries, one a very spectacular effort, which must rank as one of the best scores seen at Crown Flatt for some time, for he beat the opposition entirely on his own." Dewsbury had Jim Sullivan and Gus Risman playing, so Roy was playing in the same team as Welsh rugby league legends.

The following week against Wigan: "Edwards and Francis … were quick into their stride and it needed all Wigan's defensive efforts to check them." Dewsbury took the lead when: "Tom Kenny intercepted a passing movement and when the ball travelled to Francis, it was apparent that a try would be scored. The wingman took the ball cleverly and ran over for an excellent try."

The last game in September was the local derby at Batley. There has always been an interchange of players between the two close neighbours, but '*Observer*', who covered Batley noted that in Dewsbury's 5–4 win there were three Dewsbury men in the Batley side and three in the Dewsbury side. He said that all the backs in the Dewsbury team were "foreigners". He noted that "Francis is a potential match-winner if given the latitude".

The next week, Leeds were the opposition. *Onlooker* reported that "… in a minute or two of time, Towill, Edwards, Hudson and Francis combined in a spectacular effort which ended in a brilliant try for Francis which sent the crowd of 5,000 into raptures. Francis … showed himself a dangerous raider"

On 11 October, Roy's try-scoring run came to an end against Bradford Northern at Odsal. The report noted that "Francis was so neglected that he had to run into the middle to seek the ball in about the only chance he had."

17

Despite all the stars in the team, *Onlooker* wrote that "Without the inspiration of Francis, I doubt whether Dewsbury could have beaten Featherstone Rovers at Crown Flatt on Saturday ... I think that Francis turned the scale when the Rovers seemed likely to get the upper hand."

Certainly, Featherstone had given Dewsbury a hard game. *Onlooker* said in the second half: "Then Francis came into the picture. First, he shot up the centre of the field, turned into the middle, and when outnumbered, put his foot to the ball, which bounced awkwardly, and before Parkin could recover, Towill was at hand to dive for the ball in such a position that Sullivan had no difficulty with the goal. But better still was to follow, for Francis, getting the ball well inside his own half a few minutes afterwards, made a glorious run in which he beat four opponents entirely on his own, and scored as fine a try as has been seen at Crown Flatt for some time, and again under the posts ... That try undoubtedly settled the result, for afterwards Dewsbury were all over their opponents and, to crown his display, Francis came again and when the Rovers were all out to stop him, he coolly bluffed them to send Miller over for a try in the corner. Thus, by taking a great part in producing three clever tries, all the result of quick thinking, speed and elusiveness, he completely changed the game. It was not surprising that he received generous applause."

The next two matches were against Castleford in the Yorkshire Cup. In an 18–2 defeat at Weldon Road, "Francis never had the chance to show his worth for the ball rarely came to him when he had room to work in." A week later, Dewsbury improved enough to win the second leg 8–5. However, "Francis missed a glorious chance when he failed to retrieve the ball in a great individual effort."

Back in the league, Dewsbury beat Keighley comfortably away and then at home. In the first match,
"Francis, always a live wire, opened with a couple of tries." A week later, "In the second half, a smart move by Francis paved the way for a try by Bradbury."

Dewsbury suffered a rare league defeat on 22 November at Hull. The team had to travel by train and change in a public baths near the ground. Roy is not mentioned in the report and failed to score.

The end of November saw the return match against Batley: "Francis brilliantly intercepted a slow Batley passing round, just managed to evade Thomas, shook off the challenge of Farrar and then dashed away for the line to score a brilliant try after a run three parts the length of the field." However, later in the game, "Risman, Francis and Edwards made a terrible mess of a glorious chance." Dewsbury won 13–4.

Roy missed a 37–0 home win against York. He had received a head injury while doing physical jerks. He was back in action in a 5–3 defeat at Featherstone. He was "just caught by the ankle when about to finish off a great run." As in 1939, when he was at Barrow, there was a full fixture list over the Christmas period. Against Wakefield on Christmas Day: "Francis put on speed to follow a cross kick and touch down in the corner." He got another in the second half.

Two days later against Bramley, "Risman and Francis were in sparkling form" according to *Onlooker*. Roy scored four tries in a 45–8 win. A successful Christmas ended on 3 January 1942 with a narrow win at Oldham: "Roy Francis got hold of a loose ball and, eluding a number of opponents, raced away to score the winning try." A Lancashire sports writer was quoted by *Onlooker*: "The ball was flung out high and wide and in came the dusky Francis, lithe and eager to snatch it with a leap. Defenders dived for him, but he seemed to slip through their fingers. As he emerged into the open, to scamper the last 15 yards to the line, a profound and melancholy silence fell over the scene." *Onlooker* himself commented. "This, of course, was not the first time that Francis has proved himself a match winner since joining Dewsbury." It is interesting to note that the Lancashire sports writer comments on Roy's race, which did not happen in the Dewsbury paper's reports.

The nature of war-time rugby league was shown in the next couple of matches. Vic Hey was suddenly recruited to the Dewsbury ranks to play St Helens. Roy was injured after 15 minutes following a heavy tackle. "Francis's dazzling runs and entertaining play were missed," according to *Onlooker*.

The next week, Dewsbury had no match, so Roy and other players were given permission to play for different clubs. Roy was available for Batley, but their match against Hull was postponed. "Francis is recovering nicely from the concussion and ankle injury he sustained last Saturday," it was reported.

Postponements meant that Dewsbury's next match was against Castleford on 14 February: "But once again Roy Francis showed himself to be a match winner. In the first half he paved the way for the try by Miller, he had saved a certain try by tackling the redoubtable Batten, when the winger was well set for a score, but he came still further into the limelight by two brilliant tries in the second half, which showed his real genius. He was operating at centre, a new position for him, but his quick cut throughs and elusiveness were a treat to watch." Two weeks later, against Halifax, "Francis, although not at his best, proved his worth." He scored yet another try. He missed out against Bradford at Crown Flatt, when he rarely saw the ball in the second half.

Representative honours also came Roy's way. On 21 March he played for Northern Command against a Rugby League XIII at Thrum Hall. A 6,000 crowd saw his team win 22–18. Roy scored one of his team's four tries from the unfamiliar position of stand-off.

A week later, he played for Lancashire against Yorkshire. He qualified for selection as a Barrow player. Yorkshire won 13–2 at Crown Flatt with Roy playing on the wing.

In April, the *Reporter* outlined that a ban on travelling by service players could be a problem for Dewsbury. Against Hull, the paper said that "It was fortunate for Dewsbury that Francis was in the side, for not only did he score as spectacular a try as has been seen at Crown Flatt for some time – one of his best – but he came to the rescue of Dewsbury again and again by his speed and was an inspiration to his colleagues."

Two days later, on Easter Monday, the Dewsbury players travelled to St Helens in the guard's van. The game was delayed and kicked off close to 4pm. Dewsbury had to borrow two players to field a full side. They won 9–2 and "Francis completed a smart passing round by crossing for a try."

The second weekend of April saw the Championship play-offs start. Dewsbury beat Hull 32–18. The report outlined that "Francis ... had two tries, one a brilliant affair through the middle, in which he eluded two men almost miraculously while his other score revealed his genius on the touchline."

The final was played at Headingley on 18 April, and the Dewsbury side makes interesting reading. All the backs, except Roy and Dewsbury's Harry Royal, were Salford players, as was stand-off Tom Kenny. Also, the pack included two Salford players and one from Broughton. The RFL introduced a rule for the following season that players had to play four games as a guest for a club before they could play in the play-offs. Bradford, meanwhile, only had one guest, Ken Davies from Keighley, who was playing because regular scrum-half Donald Ward was injured.

Bradford were seeking their third consecutive championship. An 18,000 crowd saw a scoreless first-half. With 15 minutes left, the game was still poised at 0–0. A 40-yard drop goal broke the deadlock, before Barney Hudson touched down to put Dewsbury 5–0 ahead. Graham Morris writes that after Hudson's try: "Another assault [by Dewsbury] soon followed, Hudson running into a gap inside his centre, Edwards, to take the ball up before handing on to Risman who, in turn, fed Roy Francis, the left winger flying into the corner before the defence could get across." Risman's successful conversion made it 10–0, and Kenny scored in the last couple of minutes to complete Dewsbury's 13–0 win.

The Reporter said that the gate receipts were £1,100. On Roy's performance, the report said that "Francis was over [for a try] before the defence could reach him" and "Francis was a dangerous raider with half a chance."

It was Roy's first winner's medal in senior rugby league. The Challenge Cup was played at the end of the season. Dewsbury lost in the second round to Wigan 6–4 at Central Park, and 14–12 at Crown Flatt. In the first game, the report says that "Francis actually spent most of the game acting as policeman to Lawrenson instead of raiding the Wigan line."

Even after the Wigan games, the season was not quite over. Dewsbury played Huddersfield twice over the next two weekends. Roy scored twice in the first, a 23–9 win at Fartown, but missed the second, a comfortable win at Crown Flatt.

As well as his success with Dewsbury, Roy could reflect on his first representative honours, for Lancashire and Northern Command. Another honour was to finish top of the national try scorer's list – his 29 tries for Dewsbury and one for Northern Command giving him 30 for the season. Surely a Welsh rugby league cap would come soon.

Roy had a reputation as one of the fastest players in the game. Trevor Foster recalled to his son Simon how Roy would train in spikes to increase his speed, and how he had an 'obvious love of athletics'. Robert Gate wrote in *Gone North* (Volume 1) that Roy was "possessed of a fine physique he was a powerful runner with a rare turn of speed, having performed less than evens for the 100 yards…". In 1942, he won the Army sprint championship, although it has not been possible to find details of this achievement.

5. Wartime league and union 1942 to 1944

At the start of the 1942–43 season, Castleford and Bramley withdrew from the War Emergency League. They were soon joined by Hunslet, who said they could not commit to three trips to Lancashire. Only three Lancashire teams were left in the competition – Wigan, Oldham and St Helens. Again, the league was decided on a percentage basis. Teams played between 15 and 19 fixtures.

Dewsbury continued to be one of the top teams. They fielded 30 guest players during the season. Roy managed to make 17 appearances, scored 19 tries and even kicked a goal against Wigan in the Yorkshire Cup. The three Lancashire teams had been allowed to enter the Yorkshire Cup.

Dewsbury's league matches started on 5 September. Roy did not play, and on 12 September, the *Reporter* said that "There have been many enquiries concerning Roy Francis, the League's leading try scorer last season, but at the moment I am afraid I have no information about him." However, Roy returned to action in the local derby with Batley on 19 September. *The Reporter* commented that: "The Dewsbury supporters had a pleasant surprise awaiting them when they learned that Roy Francis was playing. He signalised his return to the side with two tries. His first was a grand individual effort, while he was often in the limelight with his speed and tricky running." Dewsbury won 29–2.

The preview of the match against Bradford at Odsal said that the Dewsbury team's strength would depend on which of the "services players can get away." Roy missed the game, and was also unavailable for Dewsbury the following week because he was again selected by Northern Command to play against a Rugby League XIII at Hull. He played at centre in a 14–10 win.

Roy had a regular run of games for Dewsbury until the new year. The Yorkshire Cup dominated Dewsbury's fixture list from October to early December. Each tie was played over two legs. Dewsbury beat Leeds 25–20 on aggregate after losing the first leg at Headingley. On 17 October, *Candidus* said in *The Reporter* that Roy had been on an Army course, but would definitely play against Leeds at Headingley. The report of the home match said that "Francis was better than Batten, who found the Dewsbury winger too fast for him"

In the second round Dewsbury lost by two points at Hull before winning 23–7 at Crown Flatt. *The Reporter* outlined that at The Boulevard "Francis scored a lovely try in the corner, but the referee, who was fully 40 yards from the scene, said that the Dewsbury player had not grounded properly, yet Francis had simply to drop on the ball." In the second leg, "Francis was another who was on top form. He put everyone in a good humour in the early stages with a 'Francis special'. From the halfway he beat three men with very little room in which to work. His general play was good and he was always dangerous. He scored three tries and later in the game when he went to stand-off, he showed thrust and ability in this position."

Wigan and St Helens had been given byes in the first round, and then faced each other in the second. In the semi-finals, Dewsbury beat the Central Park side 11–3 at home and won 6–0 in Lancashire to reach the Final. In the first match, "Roy Francis opened the scoring with a dropped goal from 40 yards out. He took a clearing kick and in a position which he could do nothing else, he put in a drop kick which hit the cross-bar and bounced over." He also scored a try. In the second leg, "Francis was suffering badly from a cold, but he had not much of the ball. In possession he spelt danger."

Dewsbury had last won the Cup in 1927–28. An 11,000 crowd squeezed into Crown Flatt to see them beat Huddersfield 7–0 in the first leg of the Final. Dewsbury fielded eight guest players, including Roy, who scored the only try.

The *Huddersfield Daily Examiner* report described Roy's try as follows (from *Gone North*, Volume 1): "The try was a brilliant affair, and quite a bolt from the blue. It came after a scrummage near the Dewsbury line by the right touchline. The ball came out on the Huddersfield side and one of the attackers threw out a wild pass. If the ball had been taken there was a chance and the crowd was on its toes, but the pass fell short, and Francis, the Dewsbury right-wing, got to it, picked it up smartly, cut inside and ran almost the length of the field to score on the left wing without a Huddersfield defender being able as much to lay a hand on him."

The Reporter said that "The highlight of the game was a wonderful try by Roy Francis in the last minute." He scored from the halfway line. It was "A most thrilling try", "Hats were thrown in the air" and "The spectators gave the winger a great ovation.".

The Huddersfield team had nine guests, including three forwards from Castleford in their pack. A 6,252 crowd at Fartown saw the home team win 2–0, but Dewsbury, including Roy, won 7–2 on aggregate. *The Reporter* commented that: "Francis never received an opportunity but his tackling was of the highest order."

On the Saturday before Christmas, Dewsbury beat Batley 28–8. Roy again tormented Dewsbury's local rivals: "Francis set the seal on victory with three tries in the first half. His best was his third, when he ran through a crowd of opponents. with beautiful sidestepping movements. Francis ran very fast for his first try when he outpaced both home and visiting players. Actually, the Dewsbury winger is tremendously fast when at his best, and he is beginning to show his best speed due to extra track training."

Roy was now clearly pressing for more representative honours. He was again chosen for Northern Command to play against Dewsbury on 2 January. The match raised money for the Red Cross Prisoners of War fund. Northern Command won 21–10. Roy played at centre with St Helens' Jimmy Stott. *The Reporter* said that "Both he (Stott) and Francis are only 23 years of age, so they will form a tremendous force in after-war football."

For Dewsbury, Roy turned out at Headingley to play against Leeds. Dewsbury won 22–8 and "Francis was the star performer with four tries to his credit."

Roy was also busy off the pitch. *The Reporter* reported that Eddie Waring and Roy addressed a large gathering of boys at the YMCA on rugby tactics. Sargent Francis spoke on "the necessity of fitness and the methods of training." They both answered many questions.

Roy's next representative match was on 23 January 1943 at Headingley, but this time playing rugby union. A Northern Command Union XV faced a Northern Command League XV. It is interesting to note that the league team was composed entirely of players from the ranks, with the most senior being Sergeants, three of whom, including Roy, were Sergeant-Instructors. Eight players were league internationals.

The union team included four internationals and every player was from a senior club. There was one Private in the pack, and a couple of Corporals. The match programme declared that "This is the first time a Representative Rugby Match has been played between a team of Amateurs and a team of Professionals." It attracted a crowd of 8,000.

Some of the league players had played union again in the Army. However, as soon as they had turned professional their peace-time union days were over. The League team won 18–11. *The Times* reported that "The Rugby Union side gave a fine display until they lost Cowie at a vital stage in the second half when they were leading by 11 points to nine. From that moment the League team gained complete control and doubled their score. There was some superb passing by both sets of backs, but the League players carried out their movements more quickly and were more accurate…" Roy did not score, but must have been pleased to take part in a memorable occasion.

Although the English and Welsh rugby unions had adapted to including rugby league players, the Scottish Union had not. Always staunch defenders of 'amateurism', they sent a telegram saying that no players who had played league should be included in the Union side. As it happened, the Union side was made up of only peace-time union players, including eight who were Scottish or played for Scottish clubs. The Scottish Union subsequently demanded that the Northern Command Union team to play against them not include any league players. The Northern Command, which included RFL Secretary John Wilson on their committee, refused to agree and the fixture was cancelled.

Given Roy's try-scoring with Dewsbury, it should not have been a surprise when he was chosen for the Wales rugby league side to face England at Central Park on 27 February 1943. However, the Army intervened. Roy was also selected for the England Services rugby union team to play against Scotland on the same day, and a senior officer said that this must take precedence over the league fixture. So instead of heading to Wigan, where his family lived, he joined the England team travelling to Inverleith in Edinburgh, to face Scotland.

There were four league players in the England team. Presumably the Scottish RU did not object to their presence. As well as Roy, Ernest Ward played at full-back, Wigan's Johnny Lawrenson was at centre and Ted Sadler in the pack.

The report in *The Times* said that "The English forwards were much the better throughout the game and gave their backs every opportunity to give of their best … the powerful running of Francis on the wing had much to do with England's large score." England won comfortably 29–6. In the second half, all England's points were scored by rugby league players. As well as Roy's try, Lawrenson with three and Sadler touched down. Ernest Ward kicked three goals to add to the one he scored in the first half.

The week after his international debut, Roy returned to Dewsbury and scored two tries in a 15–9 win against Huddersfield at Fartown. The *Reporter* outlined that "Francis scored two tries, the first when he snapped up a wild pass and raced away to ground behind the posts, and the other in the second half when he went over at the corner to run right behind the posts. Francis likes to score behind the posts and on Saturday many other wingers would have grounded in the corner."

Two weeks later, on 20 March 1943, he kept his place in the England rugby union services international team to, ironically, face Wales.

An 18,000 crowd watched the match at Gloucester's Kingsholm Stadium. Ward, Lawrenson and Sadler were all in the England team with Roy, except Ernest Ward was now selected at centre. Wales included five league players, Alban Davies (Huddersfield), Alan Edwards (Salford), Syd Williams (Salford), WTH Davies (Bradford Northern) and Trevor Foster (Bradford Northern). Les Thomas went north to rugby league after the War and Joined Oldham.

Wales won comfortably, 34–7, their fourth consecutive win against England. *The Times* said that "Francis and Unwin made the most of their few chances for England." Roy scored a try for England in the second half.

Three weeks later, Roy was again selected for England, this time on 10 April against Scotland at Leicester's Welford Road. For someone whose senior rugby union was a game for Abertillery, playing at these famous venues in international matches must have been a surreal experience for Roy.

However, he experienced some problems when he arrived at Welford Road. Dr Schleppi wrote in *Code 13:* "He [Roy] arrived at the Leicester ground early in the afternoon for the game against Scotland. There he encountered two elderly gentlemen who enquired 'What do you want?' 'I would like to go into the ground', replied Francis. 'But we don't open until two', explained the two gatemen. Francis tried again 'But I've travelled a long way and would like to rest in the dressing rooms.' Surprised, they responded, 'What do you want in the dressing rooms?' 'I'm playing for England', Francis exclaimed. Whereupon one of the gentlemen turned to the other, leaning against the wall and with peals of laughter said 'Hey, Charlie, this is playing for England.' It was only after nearly one and a half hours and the persistence of the England manager that Francis was admitted to the ground." It is interesting to note that the gatemen would not even believe the English manager that a young, black soldier could be playing for the England Rugby Union Services team. Without in any way excusing their behaviour, it should be pointed out that no black player had played for the full England team since before the First World War, and it would be the 1980s before another one did.

Later in 1943, Sir Learie Constantine experienced a similar incident in a London hotel. Having told the hotel that he and his family were black when booking his room, the manager initially refused to admit them when they arrived, and then said that they could only stay for one night. The reason Constantine was in London was that he was playing cricket at Lords, captaining the West Indies team. Constantine took the hotel to court and won his case.

Anyway, England with Roy having been admitted to the ground, won 24–19. Once again, there were four rugby league players in the team. Jimmy Stott replaced Ernest Ward. Roy continued his scoring record for England, and "ran away for the final England try" according to *The Times*.

Although the British Army was integrated, although black officers were very rare, the American Army was segregated. As more American troops came to Britain, race issues could arise if American soldiers objected to the presence of black people in a bar or restaurant.

Peter Fryer outlines the problems that black soldiers faced, both from white American troops and when a 'colour bar' was implemented by British run establishments. The issue became more serious as the number of black troops from various parts of the Empire who were coming to Britain grew. It is unlikely that Roy was not affected by these problems.

Dewsbury were enjoying the best season in their history, mainly due to the 'guest' players recruited by Eddie Waring. Roy played regularly in league matches, but in March 1943, the Barrow secretary-manager, Mr E Senior, said that because Barrow were entering the Challenge Cup, Roy could not play for Dewsbury in the competition. Barrow lost in the first round to St Helens, but the ban remained in place. On some of the Challenge Cup dates he was playing in Services rugby union internationals anyway. The dispute with Barrow was resolved.

In April, Roy's progress was highlighted by Eddie Waring. In *The Reporter,* the Dewsbury manager said: "One of the results of his wholesale borrowing of players has been the making of a new star, Roy Francis, whom Wigan allowed to go to Barrow before the war. Francis, under Mr Waring at Dewsbury, has become one of the best wingers in the game, an achievement which has been crowned with selection for England in two services rugby union internationals."

Over the Easter weekend, Dewsbury won the Challenge Cup, beating Leeds 16–15 on aggregate. Roy returned to the team for the Championship semi-final against Bradford. The Odsal side won 8–3 at Crown Flatt, but were then disqualified when Dewsbury protested that Wakefield's Sandy Orford had not played the four league games necessary for him to play in a semi-final. Their protest was upheld, so Dewsbury qualified for the Final, where they played Halifax. Roy only played in the first leg, an 11–3 win over the Thrum Hall side. Dewsbury were 3–0 down approaching half-time, when Halifax's "Millington almost went under the posts ... but Roy Francis appeared from 'nowhere' to take 'man and ball to earth' in a tackle that probably changed the outcome of the match" according to Graham Morris.

In the second half Dewsbury were playing with the slope, and Charlie Seeling put Roy in for their second try. Morris adds that "Dewsbury got a third when, with Seeling again providing the pass, the home fans were treated to a 'Francis special' as the winger cut inside to fly past two defenders and finish behind the posts."

A week later, Dewsbury recovered from being 8–6 down at half-time to win 22–13 and claim the title with a 33–16 win. Or so they thought. Roy missed the match because he was playing rugby union for the West Riding in a Northern Command Sevens tournament at Headingley. Presumably Roy would have preferred to play in a Championship Final rather than a meaningless sevens tournament. but the Army authorities decided that the union tournament should take priority. Often in union matches in league areas, the well-known league players were selected because they were a big attraction and drew in the crowds.

On 23 June, Bradford got their revenge for their semi-final disqualification. They complained that Castleford's Smith had played in the semi-final when he was ineligible. The RFL decided that he had only played three league games for Dewsbury, not the required four, and decided not to award the title that season. Smith had in fact played 15 first team games for Dewsbury before the ill-fated semi-final, but 12 were cup ties.

There had even been controversy before the semi-finals, when Leeds tried to play a match on East Monday morning, hoping to win to reach the top four, despite the fact that they were playing in the Challenge Cup Final second leg in the afternoon. The RFL did not allow the extra fixture to go ahead. No medals were awarded, the players were given War savings certificates.

Roy finished the season as Dewsbury's joint top try scorer with 19 from 18 games. Overall, 200,000 fans had seen Dewsbury play in the 1942-43 campaign.

1943–44

The War Emergency League grew to 16 clubs, including Barrow. The competition was still mainly based in Yorkshire, with the only Lancashire clubs being Barrow, Wigan, St Helens and Oldham. Due to the ongoing wartime travel restrictions, York and Hull did not have to travel to Lancashire. Barrow's home games were arranged around the work schedules at the local shipyards. The guest player system continued, but clubs were only allowed no more than six players from any non-playing club of their choice, and no more than three from any other non-playing club.

Dewsbury continued to use a large number of guest players – 35 all told. The rules were enforced – Gus Risman was home on leave from Italy in January, but was not allowed to play for Dewsbury because they already had six Salford players on their books. The club was also censured for playing Wigan's John Clinton without permission.

Roy continued to mainly play for Dewsbury, made a couple of appearances for Barrow, and played services union as required. It is hard to find all the records of the services union games, which may explain why on some Saturdays he was not playing rugby league.

Due to travel difficulties, it was not practical for Roy to play for Barrow in home matches. He played twice in away matches in Yorkshire. Barrow seemed to have a relatively settled side, probably of locally-based players.

Roy made 11 appearances for Dewsbury, including the Championship Final. He did not play in the Challenge Cup or the Yorkshire Cup, but otherwise played reasonably regularly.

His first appearance of the season was on 18 September. He marked it with a hat-trick in a 48–15 win against St Helens. *The Reporter* said that all three tries were "Francis specials". The report said that "He is one of the outstanding wingers playing football today." The paper also said that he had been selected to play rugby union for South Wales in a match raising funds for charity, but preferred to play for Dewsbury.

The following week, in a narrow win at Hunslet, Roy "never received a pass." However, "His defence was sound." In November, Dewsbury lost 4–2 at home to Wakefield Trinity. The match report said: "Even Francis, of whom much had been expected, failed to rise to the occasion, due, I rather think, to lack of match practice. The rugby union games he is getting are not doing him any good."

That weekend, 20 November, three Dewsbury players, Roy, Alan Edwards and Syd Williams were all in Swansea for a services rugby union international. The following week, reporting on Dewsbury's 16–3 win over Oldham, the report commented: "Francis had a run in the centre. He scored one try, but is not yet running like he did last season..."

On 4 December 1943, Roy could not travel with Dewsbury to York, so instead played his first game for Barrow since 1939. He scored twice in a 15–10 defeat at Halifax. Roy did turn out twice for Dewsbury against Batley over Christmas. Dewsbury won narrowly at Mount Pleasant and comfortably at home. Roy scored in both games.

In the second half of the season, rugby union commitments meant that Roy only played five times for Dewsbury, and once for Barrow – a 21–3 defeat at Odsal.

His next Dewsbury appearance was in a 6–5 win over Hunslet on 19 February. The report said that "Francis made an unexpected appearance but was not outstanding." On 10 April, he helped Dewsbury to a 9–2 win over Wakefield Trinity at Belle Vue: "Francis made a dazzling touch line run to ground in the corner. The touch judge ruled that he had stepped in touch and this was a matter of opinion."

Roy's last three appearances for Dewsbury were in the Championship play-offs. Dewsbury had finished fourth in the league table, a couple of percentage points ahead of Halifax. In the semi-final at Wakefield on 6 May, *The Reporter* said that he was "outstanding", and that his "speed and power caused grave concern to the home team. He scored only one try, but was often dangerous and kept his opponents constantly guessing."

Wigan beat Hull 27–10 in the other semi-final, so Dewsbury would face the Central Park side in the Yorkshire club's third consecutive Championship Final.

Jim Sullivan, at the age of 40, came out of retirement to play at full-back for Wigan. A 14,000 crowd saw his team win 13–9 to take a four point lead to Crown Flatt the following week. In the second match, an early move by Charlie Seeling and Roy almost created a try for Joe Gardner. A Seeling penalty gave Dewsbury, who included eight guest players, a 2–0 lead. A try by Fleming pegged them back, but Seeling created a try for Roy just before the break to make the score 5–3, and cut the aggregate deficit to two points. However, it was not to be. Sullivan kicked two penalties and a last minute try by Joe Egan, converted by Sullivan saw Wigan win 12–5 on the day, and 25–14 on aggregate.

Roy continued to play for England in the rugby union services internationals. The first was at Swansea on 20 November. Wales fielded six rugby league players – four backs, Davies at half-back and Trevor Foster in the pack. For England, Ernest Ward was at full-back, Stott and Lawrenson at centre and Roy on the wing.

England lost 11–9, having "surprised everybody, including probably themselves, by leading a well-established Welsh team at half by six points to three" according to *The Times*. In the second half, Ward missed a conversion and a penalty that could have earned England at least a draw for their efforts. A crowd of 25,000 squeezed into the Swansea ground, including several thousand American soldiers.

A week before Christmas, Roy was listed in the programme to play for a Northern Army XIII against a Rugby League XIII at Halifax, but did not play. Whether this was because of injury, military commitments or travel problems Is not known. Some players either arrived late or not at all.

In January, he played for a Northern Command XV against a Civil Defence XV at Castleford. What the local rugby league followers made of this union fixture is not known, but these games were important fundraisers for wartime charities and boosted both civilian and military morale.

27 February 1943: Roy's debut for the England Services Rugby Union team. They beat Scotland 29–6 at Inverleith with Roy scoring a try. (Courtesy Geoff Francis)

A Dewsbury team in 1943, having won the League and Yorkshire Cup in 1942, and the Challenge Cup in 1943. Eddie Waring is in the centre of the front row, next to Roy.
(Courtesy Geoff Francis)

Trevor Foster, Ernest Ward, Roy and Jim Stott in London before playing for the Army against the RAF at Richmond in January 1944. (Courtesy Simon Foster)

The Army rugby union team that beat the RAF. (Courtesy Geoff Francis)

Above: Action from the match, against an Irish XV in 1944, with Roy on the left.
(Courtesy *Rugby League Journal*).
Below left: Roy played regularly for the British Army XV in matches that raised funds
for war-related charities.
Below centre: The programme from the 1944 match at Odsal.
Below right: Rugby union at Wheldon Road. (All courtesy Simon Foster)

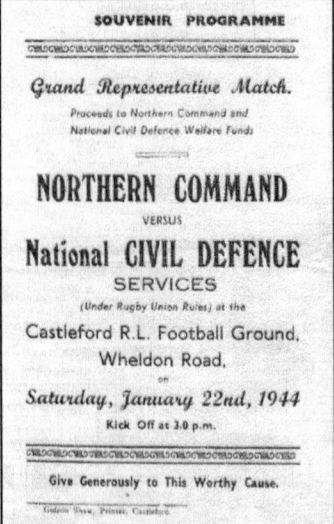

England Services team that beat Scotland 23–13 at Murrayfield on 12 February 1944.
Back: L/Cpl Ernest Ward, Sq/Ldr Jim Parsons, Cpl Joe Mycock, Lt James B Doherty Schoolmaster
(Navy), Fl/Lt R H G (Bob) Weighill, Cpl A Gordon Hudson; seated: LAC Johnny Lawrenson,
Lt Gerry Hollis, CFN Jimmy Stott, Capt Robin E Prescott (captain), Cpl Raymond J Longland,
Sgt/Instr Roy L Francis, Sgt Gerald T ('Beef') Dancer; front: F/Sgt Ian H Dustin, Lt Peter R Hastings.
Ian Dustin was killed in RAF action over Norway 11 April 1945.
(Courtesy Howard Evans)

British Army XV versus South Wales, 21 October 1944 at Swansea RFC. (Courtesy Robert Gate)

One appearance he did make, just before Christmas, was at a meeting of the Earlsheaton Army Cadets. Accompanied by Trevor Foster and Eddie Waring, they were asked to discuss which was the better game of the two codes. Both players chose rugby league, although Trevor said that it was a harder game. The two players, and Eddie Waring, answered questions about sport as well.

In February, March and early April, Roy played the XV-a-side code. He was part of a British Army XV that beat an Irish XV 15–0. Two weeks later, he turned out for England against Scotland at Murrayfield, the first time he played at this major international rugby union ground. One of his team-mates this season was Bob Weighill, who after a distinguished career in the RAF later became secretary of the RFU. His war-time experiences of playing with the rugby league players did not persuade him that there should be free passage between the codes. England won comfortably 23–13. The next week, Roy turned out for a Northern Command team which beat the Scottish Services 37–5 at Headingley. Roy touched down twice.

Two weeks later, he faced Scottish opposition for the third time in the return international at Leicester. An 18,000 crowd saw England win 27–15. Roy scored twice, and *The Times* said that "Francis, who was about the fastest man in the match, could have got over more than twice with better luck."

The international services internationals concluded on 8 April. England finally beat Wales. A 15,000 crowd at Gloucester saw a 20–8 victory for the home team. *The Times* reported that "Lawrenson and Francis made some final individual efforts". In the second half, "…. A typical breakthrough by Lawrenson resulted in Francis gaining a try."

A couple of days later, on Easter Monday, Roy returned to action with Dewsbury, touching down in a 9–2 win at Wakefield.

Rugby league followers had enjoyed Northern Command's rugby league XV's win at Leeds the previous season against their rugby union colleagues. Now there was to be a clash between the two codes –under union rules of course – at Combined Services level. It was played at Odsal on 29 April 1944. George M Thompson, writing in the *Bradford Observer*, said that the match "must rank as the outstanding match in the history of rugby football." Maybe – both sides had problems due to service commitments and injuries. The Union side were 10–0 ahead at half-time, as it took the league forwards some time to re-familiarise themselves with the rules. Both sets of players were good at the skills their code used, although *The Times* said that the league players were "not so sure as league players usually are in handling the ball, being hustled out of their accuracy by the quickness of Tanner, Gray and Sullivan…" The report continued that "the league men were masters in quick restarting, instantaneous formation and regrouping when the wing's way was blocked."

The league side levelled the scores early in the second half with two converted tries. *The Times's* ruby union correspondent said that they were "a trifle lucky to snatch a win." In the *Bradford Observer,* George M Thompson wrote that "…the winning score did not come until three minutes before the finish, and what a thriller it was! In an almost now-or-never effort, Brogden got the opposing defence twisted. Francis dashed in from the wing, gave the reverse pass to Brogden, and the last named went through a gap for the line in a manner which left friend and foe gasping."

Sadly, this was the last time such a game was staged. After union went open in 1995, Wigan and Bath played two matches, one in each code. Bath were run ragged in the league clash. In the union one, Bath won primarily because of their forward play, which even the Wigan players with some union experience could not challenge. When Wigan got the ball, they showed some great handling skills. The wartime rugby experience is interesting because the England side consistently selected league players in the back positions, despite the wide range of union talent that was available to them.

The Championship Final was the last professional rugby league match that Roy played during the War. He also did not add to his seven rugby union services international appearances. On 23 August 1944, a short report in the *Halifax Evening Courier* said that Roy was in a north-eastern hospital, with a broken leg and torn ligament. The report does not say how the injury occurred – it could have been in rugby playing or training, or possibly in his Army role, or in an accident. Whatever, he recovered enough to play rugby union for an Army team in October 1944. He may have played for Northern Command and Army teams, but the line-ups for these matches are difficult to find. Often it depended on who could be released from their military duties, or could overcome the travel obstacles that were widespread at that time. There were reports of him being selected for other Army rugby union matches in the autumn of 1944, but it is not known if he actually played.

Roy was selected for a short rugby union tour of Germany in November 1945, and would not have been selected unless he was still a serving soldier. He missed a couple of Barrow matches to play. Roy seems finally to have been 'demobbed' from the Army in the spring of 1946. He played in a representative charity rugby union match in March 1946.

Roy could look back on his wartime rugby record, in both codes, with some pride. Also, the experience he had in the Army was important for his future development as a coach. However, before that phase of his life, he would resume his career with Barrow in 1945.

Wales team versus England at Swinton 12 October 1946. A 20,213 crowd saw Wales win 13–10. (Courtesy Robert Gate)

The Wales players before a match in 1947. (Courtesy Geoff Francis)

6. Back at Barrow 1945 to 1948

The War in Europe had finished in May 1945, and the use of atomic bombs by the Americans in Hiroshima and Nagasaki forced the Japanese to surrender on 15 August.

The Northern Rugby League competition resumed with 27 clubs on 25 August 1945. Workington Town had joined the competition; Leigh did not return until the following season. Roy missed Barrow's first game, but went on to play in 25 out of Barrow's 43 matches. Barrow went on to finish fifth in the league, three points behind Bradford Northern in fourth place. They were also runners-up in the Lancashire League behind Wigan. They made less impact in the Lancashire Cup, beating Warrington over two legs before losing 6–0 at Widnes. In the Challenge Cup, they beat Rochdale in both legs of their first round tie, beat Bradford Northern 5–0 at home in the second before losing at home to Wigan in the third round.

The backs were particularly strong. At full-back was Joe Jones. James Lewthwaite had joined the club from a local Association Football club in 1943. He went on to make 500 appearances for them, mainly on the wing, scoring 354 tries. Val Cumberbatch, who was primarily a winger, was still with the club, although he moved to Liverpool Stanley early in 1946. Another centre was Bryn Knowelden. He had joined Barrow from a local works team in 1943. And Willie Horne, one of the legends of rugby league in Barrow, featured regularly at stand-off. In the pack, one regular was Welsh international Fred Hughes, who had joined the club in 1936. In January 1946, he was transferred to league's newest professional club, Workington Town.

For most of the season, Roy was still in the Army. The *Barrow News* noted that four players would be missing on 24 November. Fred Hughes, Joe Jones and Willie Horne were all involved in the Wales versus England rugby league international, and there was "further distinction for the Barrow club in the selection of Francis for the Services team which will be touring Germany for the next 10 days." Roy played for Barrow on 10 November, but was not in action again until 22 December.

Roy made 22 of his 25 appearances on the left wing, and three on the right. He scored 16 tries, including four against Rochdale in April, when the team played nine matches in a month, and a double against St Helens on 30 March.

Roy missed Barrow's first match, but then had a run of eight consecutive appearances. He had not played professional rugby league since his finale at Dewsbury in 1944, a period of over a year. In a 12–11 win over Halifax, *The News* said that "The return to Barrow ranks of Roy Francis, the war-time international improved the attack, and he and Knowelden were the best wing on the field and together produced some thrilling moments." In the return at Halifax a week later, *The News* reported that Roy "impressed along with Knowelden and Bowker. The next week saw the first cup-tie of the season. Barrow beat Warrington 18–8, and *The News* said that Barrow's backs "When they settled showed up the poverty of Warrington's set. Francis and Knowelden were the better pair..." Roy did not score a try, but "picked up smartly to drop an unexpected goal."

Barrow went through to the next round of the Lancashire Cup by five points. The reporter in *The News* picked out Jones as the key defender, but said that Roy was "full of resource".

Barrow lost their next two matches, including at Widnes in the Lancashire Cup. Roy was next mentioned in a report of their 9–5 win at Warrington. Barrow had little possession from the scrums, but launched a "sudden raid". The report said that "Francis snapped up a loose ball near his own '25' and cutting through the middle had only Belshaw to beat." Roy passed to Cumberbatch who scored the try that gave Barrow victory. Roy played the following week in a 3–3 draw with Broughton. His next Barrow appearance was on 10 November, in an 8–8 draw at Odsal. The report says that "Francis was able to arrive from Headingley in time to play and Bowker also made a long bus journey after being demobilised. Francis was not well used, being short of passes as was the other wing. But Francis scored a try from a kick in the first half."

So, what was Roy doing at Headingley? From October 1945 to March 1946, a New Zealand Army rugby union team toured the United Kingdom and France. That day, they played Northern Services at Headingley. The home team contained 10 rugby league players. Ernest Ward came into the side as a late replacement, and presumably Roy was on standby as well. The New Zealand team won 14–7. Roy was in the original selection for the British Army XV to play the New Zealanders on 1 December at Bristol, but did not play.

He was "unable to turn out" against Wakefield the following week, and his next appearance for Barrow was on 22 December. He scored against Warrington, then touched down again on Christmas Day at Craven Park against Workington. Barrow's "star threequarter" missed the return match on Boxing Day.

Roy played on New Year's Day in a 31–2 trouncing of Batley at Craven Park. *The News* commented that "Francis is an outstanding player, and the 7,897 spectators were treated to some more of his smart side-stepping and good play." In a narrow defeat at Oldham, he made a rare error when he failed to touch down properly after crossing the try line, and the referee disallowed his try.

Barrow beat Widnes at home 20–14. Roy scored a try and *The News* said that he "...was the finest player on the field. His corkscrew run, beating his opponents before passing to Knowelden to score, was a brilliant piece of work." At Widnes at the end of January, Barrow faced a tough away match without five players who were on county championship duties. Roy was one of three players who "made brilliant efforts in the first half", and then Roy touched down from a Higgins pass in the second half. Noall converted to secure an 8–8 draw.

The following week, Roy's try away to Liverpool Stanley "crowned a great run" as Barrow won comfortably. The second of February saw the start of the Challenge Cup. Barrow won their first-leg match at Rochdale. Roy's scoring run continued as he "showed a clean pair of heels to score another try." He missed the return match at Craven Park, but was back in action against Dewsbury in the next league match. Barrow won 10–0, and Jack Bowker set up an easy try for Roy in the last minute.

The following Thursday, a 17,500 crowd squeezed into Craven Park and saw Barrow beat Bradford 5–0 to reach the third round of the Challenge Cup. Nine days later, 20,475 fans paid record receipts of £1,549 to see Wigan in the next round of the Challenge Cup. Barrow missed Jones at full-back and went down 13–3. *The News* said that "Barrow were not classy enough, and though the brilliance of Francis gave them a try – and the lead – after 20-odd minutes, Ratcliffe had Wigan level within two minutes and Ward's goal put them ahead." Wigan scored a converted try in the last minute to seal a 13–3 win.

Roy missed an easy home win against Broughton, but returned for an exciting 30–22 win at St Helens, and contributed two tries. His form "caused much comment" according to the report. Three days earlier, Roy had been playing ruby union at Headingley. JM Kilburn in the *Yorkshire Post* reported that: Rugby League and Rugby Union players will be seen together at Headingley this afternoon when an Army Physical Training Corps XV play Army XV for the benefit of the APTC Benevolent Fund. AJ Risman, captain of the rugby league side to tour Australia, leads the APTC XV and has with him other rugby league internationals in Francis, GS Brown, Prosser and Tattersfield. Of the rugby union players Trott has played full back for Wales and AA Brown in the England pack." The APTC won 21–16 in an open game, in reality an exhibition match.

In April, Roy returned to his wartime club, Dewsbury with Barrow, and had to play at centre after Woods was injured and "occasionally came into the picture in a 12–3 defeat. In a midweek match at Wigan, Roy "tackled valiantly but was never given a chance as a fast winger" as Barrow lost 16–2.

Roy's last game of the season was at home to Rochdale Hornets on Good Friday. Barrow won 34–18 and the report was headed "Francis in top form". The report said that he was "outstanding" as he scored four tries. He missed the last four matches.

Towards the end of the season there was a report in *The News* that Halifax were interested in signing Roy. The fee was £750. Dewsbury were also interested but were not sure that they could meet the fee. Roy had originally been priced at £1,200 which was then reduced to £1,000 and then to £750.The matter was first reported in the Yorkshire Post on 20 March. The report said: "Halifax are one of several Rugby league clubs interested in Roy Francis, the Welsh international winger, who has asked to leave his present club. Barrow. Francis, Army physical training instructor, stationed at Ovenden Convalescent Camp, Halifax. It said that he wishes go to a Yorkshire club. He leaves today for France with the rugby league [Welsh] international team. Halifax are to lose the services of their right winger. Daniels, who has been called for service with the Forces." However, Halifax subsequently signed Walter Dockar from Hull who was a winger. The move did not happen and Roy was still at Craven Park for the 1946–47 season.

Roy was not eligible to play in the County Championship, but did finally play in an international for Wales, having played against Wales in the wartime services rugby union matches. He made his debut at Bordeaux on 24 March, playing on the right wing in a 19–7 defeat by France. He did not play for Wales in their first match in the European Championship against England on 24 November. However, he did not play for Barrow that day, so may have been injured, or had Army commitments.

With a tour arranged for the British Lions to Australia and New Zealand in the summer of 1946, two tour trial matches were held, one in January at Central Park, and the second at Headingley three weeks later. Surprisingly, Roy was not given a chance in either match. On 5 January, *The News* reported that Lewthwaite, Knowelden and Hughes had been chosen for the tour trial match. The report said that "many were wondering" why Willie Horne was not included, but did not mention Roy. In February, the paper reported that Trevor Petcher was selected for a tour trial, the report again expressed surprise that Willie Horne was not chosen. However, Petcher scored two tries in the match and was not selected, while Willie Horne was.

The Lions tour went on to be one of the most famous – and important – in the sport's history. It re-established international rugby league for the post-war era. The Lions, who won the Ashes, became known as the Indomitables – they travelled to Australia in a ship called The Indomitable, which was mainly taking troops home.

Was the colour of Roy's skin an issue? Australia had a 'whites only' immigration policy at this time as they tried to attract British – and to some extent European – workers to emigrate. However, Roy did not want to emigrate down under, and the tour was very important to the Australian authorities. Their foreign minister helped facilitate it, and *The Indomitable* was an Australian ship. Would they have challenged Roy's selection?

Robert Gate certainly believes that race did play a role in Roy's non-selection. In his obituary of Roy in *Code 13* (issue 11), he writes: "Racism raised its ugly head on more than one occasion in Roy's career ... Most damagingly it deprived him of a place on the 1946 Lions tour. There were clearly no four better wings than Roy in the British game yet he was left out of the squad for political reasons. Australia still operated a colour bar and the British selectors were not brave enough to push the Australians into a corner."

Huw Richards, in a 2022 paper for the British Society of Sports Historians conference, says that the issue has been more widely debated than any other aspect of the tour. He makes the valid point that the Australians had accepted Maori players as members of New Zealand teams, and 'non-white' cricketers from the West Indies in 1930, India in 1947 and the Nawab of Pataudi in 1932 who played for England. In 1949, they welcomed a New Zealand All Blacks side which included Maori players who were not allowed to play in a simultaneous tour of South Africa.

However, the Australian government had initiated the idea of the tour in September 1945, and were keen for it to go ahead. Would they have tried to pressure the selectors not to pick Roy? Maybe words were said behind the scenes, as happened with Basil D' Olivera's non-selection for the England cricket tour to South Africa in 1968? On the other hand, Roy only played 12 games for Barrow in the first half of the season, scoring three tries. His form improved in the second half of the season, but by then the choices for the trial matches and ultimately the touring party had been made.

As well as concerns about the reaction in Australia or by the Australian Government to a black player representing the British Lions, there may also have been racism among the selectors. No black player had played for Great Britain, although they had represented England and Wales.

The Lions selected four wingers to go on the tour. Scoring tries is not the only criteria, but is an essential part of a winger's game. The tour party was selected on 11 March. The four chosen were: Eric Batten who was an established international and the game's top try scorer that season with 35; Roy's clubmate Jim Lewthwaite who scored 28; Arthur Bassett who had international experience, but only scored 14 tries in 19 games for Halifax; and Albert Johnson, who scored nine tries in 19 games for Warrington, but had played for England and

Lancashire that season. He had also scored a hat-trick of tries against France. Roy had scored 16 tries in 25 games, more than Bassett and Johnson, and arguably had more international experience than Johnson, depending on how much weight is given to his wartime rugby union games. Robert Gate believes that Roy should have been in the touring party ahead of Johnson.

The *Yorkshire Post's* report, on 12 March, on the touring party said that there were four notable omissions: Ledgard of Dewsbury, Huddersfield's Anderson, Rookes of Hunslet and Wakefield Trinity's Wilkinson. Roy is not mentioned. The writer does say that "Barrow have played little football in Yorkshire this season, and their men are not well known on this side of the Pennines." Maybe he was excusing his own lack of knowledge of the form of the Barrow players, but four were in the touring party. Alan Edwards is also generally believed to have been unfortunate to miss out, although he was named as a reserve for the tour.

It is also possible that there was a certain amount of horse-trading among the selectors. Barrow had four players in the Lions squad: Horne, Lewthwaite, Jones and Knowelden. Bassett was the only Halifax player involved.

Bassett scored 18 tries in 11 games on tour, including a hat-trick in the crucial second test win in Brisbane. Johnson scored 15 tries in 17 games, but did play in three of the four tests. Lewthwaite scored 25 tries in 15 matches, but did not play in any of the test matches. Eric Batten scored 17 tries in 13 matches.

1946–47

This season will always be remembered for one of the most bitter winters in living memory. With limits put on midweek sport due to concerns about falling industrial production, the season was extended to the end of May. In February Barrow only played once.

Barrow found both the cup competitions and the league more challenging in the second season after the war. Compared to the previous season, they conceded just eight more points. However, their scoring rate fell from 535 points to 385. They won four less games than in 1945–46, and fell from fifth place to 12th, 12 points away from the play-offs. In the Lancashire Cup they lost to Widnes over two legs early in the season, and in the Challenge Cup lost both matches to Leeds, failing to score a point.

Despite playing for a slightly less successful **team**, Roy thrived. He played in 33 of Barrow's 40 first team matches, and scored 28 tries and a goal. He scored two hat-tricks, at home to Rochdale and Leeds. He also scored two tries in a match eight times. Near the end of the season, he played a couple of games at centre, but otherwise was on the left wing.

Barrow's season opened with a home victory against with Salford. In *The News, Sentinel* said that "There can be no doubt that Roy Francis contributed a good deal to the home side's victory. His undoubted skill has well earned him favour with the Barrow crowd ... he was behind all the scoring moves, but his own try brought him a great ovation, and well he and Petcher – who combined so neatly with him – deserved those cheers." He concluded: "To Francis goes a big bouquet. His tactics at times bewildered even his own men, and his try came after he had eluded every one of the opposition. It was the outstanding feature of a mediocre game."

The players line up before the France versus Wales match in Marseille. (Courtesy Geoff Francis)

Coming onto the pitch before the France versus Wales at Marseille 18 January 1947.
France won 14–5.
(Courtesy *Rugby League Journal*)

The Lancashire Cup provided a tough two-leg first round clash with Widnes. Roy gave Barrow's fans one of their few good moments of a 26–5 defeat at Naughton Park. *The News* reported that "...whenever Francis was in possession, three or four Widnes players were after him. Yet he scored the try of the match after intercepting, side-stepping and tearing a great gap in an outpaced defence."

Barrow won the return leg 10–3, but this was not enough to take them through. *Sentinel* commented that "Francis, apparently injured, was not much in the picture, but he was unlucky not to get a try after a thrilling race to ground the ball." Barrow were still missing their members of touring party. The final game without their international contingent was a 23–5 defeat at Salford. Barrow made little use of what possession they did have. *The News* outlined that "The one exception was when Roy Francis took a pass inside his own half and after leaving Rogers, the Salford full-back standing, scored the try of the match..."

After scoring a hat-trick at home to Rochdale Hornets, Roy injured his thigh in a 20–10 defeat at Odsal, and missed a 0–0 draw with Widnes because he was playing for Wales. Roy was back on the score-sheet with two tries against Liverpool Stanley. *Sentinel* said that "The running of Francis was again a feature, and his great solo effort to give Barrow their first try brought the crowd to their feet." At Warrington, in a 12–6 defeat, Roy had a try disallowed "after a dash over the home line".

Roy scored his second hat-trick of the season in a comfortable home win over Leeds. *Sentinel* wrote that "So far as the home men were concerned, Francis and Horne must be acknowledged as the men who seized opportunities when they saw them and tuned them to full use." He continued "But it was Horne and Francis who had the major share in Barrow's victory. I heard a Leeds supporter sighing for a pair like that to help them in their team building."

Roy missed a 19–6 defeat at Huddersfield, but was back in action on 16 November for the return match, having been dropped by Wales who were in action that day. He scored twice in an 8–7 win. *The News's* reported asked "Did the Welsh selectors though engaged at Swansea hear the terrific ovation given Francis at Craven Park on Saturday when he scored his second try of the Barrow-Huddersfield game and gave the home team the lead. If they did, then they must have wondered – with most of the 6,451 Barrow crowd – however they came to overlook him for the international. The player is obviously the most entertaining wing threequarter seen for seasons and the second of his two tries on Saturday was a picture – the long run along the touchline; a short kick to elude Leake; and a final dash to regain possession and touch down."

Whatever the Welsh selectors thought about Roy – he had played for Barrow two days before he was not chosen for the Wales side, so presumably was fit – was not reflected in what the Barrow fans made of his efforts. The *North-Western Evening Mail* published an appreciation of Roy on 11 December 1946. It is worth reprinting in full: "When Wigan transferred Roy Francis to Barrow before World War II, they could hardly have been expected to know that they were parting with the most entertaining wing-threequarter in the Rugby League today. Nor could they have known that omission of his name from the Welsh Rugby League team would cause a commotion down Swansea way. The fact remains that they transferred him and that their loss has been Barrow's gain. Happily for Barrow, some disagreement between club and player has been satisfactorily settled and the Furness club retain the services of a skilled player who has rapidly become a Craven Park idol.

With a style of his own and an uncanny ability to outwit opposing players, Francis has come right into the front rank this season – witness his chasing Ashcroft for the honour of being the League's leading try scorer. While on Army service he was frequently chosen for big Services games, and played in excellent company. His return to Barrow ranks was very welcome. As unassuming off the field as he is clever on it, Roy Francis is deservedly popular. Dewsbury were most anxious to secure his services when a transfer was mooted and there are always many keen and critical eyes watching his style, his zig-zagging and his tricks wherever Barrow play.

The ovations which have rewarded his scoring efforts at Craven Park are surely evidence of his popularity. He is one of the stars in a team which can accomplish big things."

Roy's good scoring run continued at Hunslet. In a rare Yorkshire visit, Barrow won 15–3, and according to *The News:* "Twice Francis outpaced all opposition to score in spectacular style."

This win was followed up by a 15–3 triumph against another Yorkshire team, this time Bradford Northern at Craven Park. *Sentinel* reported that "This form will take the team to the top of the league tree. Lewthwaite scored a try in the 20th minute and Francis added two more in the second half..." A 10–10 draw away to Liverpool Stanley, where "Francis never had a chance", and then Warrington were beaten 5–4 at Craven Park. Roy made Parker's try with a kick through after a move involving Horne, Knowelden, Parker and Roy. The Barrow centre beat Brian Bevan to the ball to touch down.

Roy missed the Christmas Day home defeat to Workington, but returned to action on Boxing Day in the return match which Barrow lost 11–9. Their poor run continued with a 10–3 loss to Wigan at Central Park. Things improved on New Year's Day, when Roy scored twice against Hunslet in a comfortable win. He followed this up with two more tries in a 13–7 win at Rochdale. A week later, Roy scored at home to Leigh. A 3–3 draw at Belle Vue, which Roy missed because he was playing for Wales, was followed by the same result at home to Oldham. From singing the team's praises a few weeks before, the report by *Sentinel* was pessimistic about Barrow's chances in the Cup. He did say that "Francis, who scored Barrow's try in the seventh minute of the game, was easily Barrow's best."

Sentinel was proved correct. A 17–2 defeat at Leigh, where "Two or three times, Francis on the wing, had scoring chances but he invariably found himself alone way up-field when he wanted to part with the ball." In the Cup, Barrow were drawn against Leeds. A 12–0 defeat at Headingley, followed by a 6–0 loss the following week ended Barrow's cup hopes. The second leg was also played at Headingley due to the state of the Barrow pitch.

Roy missed a 5–2 win at Crown Flatt, and the return match the following week. At Oldham on Easter Monday, he touched down twice in a 22–15 defeat. Oldham concentrated their attack down Lewthwaite's wing to avoid "the elusive Francis", who "severely marked" the Oldham winger Evans. The following Saturday, Wigan came to Central Park as league leaders, but lost 8–7 to four goals by Willie Horne. To catch up with the fixtures, the rugby league season dragged on to June.

In a 16–12 defeat at Leeds, despite injuring his knee, Roy "dropped a spectacular goal" and "scored a magnificent try as a fitting reward for his enterprise in attack, and as he nearly won the game for Barrow in the last minute he had a field day... Francis was the star."

Roy scored in a win at Swinton before the season ended in defeat at St Helens. Roy finished fourth in the national try scorers table with 29, 28 of which were for Barrow. It was his best season for the club. Barrow finished 12th in the league, with 18 wins and four draws from their 36 matches, 12 points behind Leeds who were fourth and qualified for the Championship play-offs.

On the international front, there was no touring team, but the International (European) Championship as played. England, Wales and France played each other home and away, so there were some international opportunities for Roy. Wales began their campaign with a win, 13–10 against England at Swinton. Roy scored one of Wales's three tries in front of a crowd of over 20,000. He was not selected for the next game, on 16 November at Swansea. Arthur Bassett took his place, and England won comfortably, 19–5. On 18 January in Marseilles, Roy returned to the team, but Wales went down 14–5 to France. He was then not selected for the return match in Swansea on 12 April. Wales won 17–15 to finish the season with two wins and two defeats.

1947–48

Rugby league was still attracting large crowds, as the post-war boom in sports attendances continued. Interest in the sport was heightened this season by the New Zealanders touring Great Britain and then France. It was the first time they had toured France, and before they crossed the Channel had a full schedule. Their first match was on 25 September at St Helens, and they completed the first leg of their tour at Odsal on 20 December. While not as famous as the 'Indomitables' tour, this was the first tour from 'down under' after the War.

Barrow did not have a great season, finishing 21st in the table. Undoubtedly, the highlight of Roy's season was on the international front. He was not selected for Wales's first two matches, but did line up against England at Swansea on 6 December. Two days earlier, he had played for Barrow against the Kiwis in a 2–2 draw, in front of a Thursday afternoon crowd of 5,565.

Great Britain won the first test against the Kiwis 11–10 at Headingley on 4 October. A month later, on 8 November, New Zealand won 10–7 at Swinton in front of a 29,031 crowd. So, the final test at Odsal on 20 December would decide the series. It was the first time that the massive Odsal bowl had staged a test match, and 42,685 fans came on the Saturday before Christmas. Roy had been playing as much at centre as in his usual place on the wing. He had scoring fairly consistently for a Barrow side who struggled to score tries. After the defeat at Swinton, the British selectors chose Roy ahead of Eric Batten on the right wing. Albert 'Massa' Johnson kept his place on the left wing. Black players had played for England and Wales before. However, Roy became the first black player to represent Great Britain. He was, however, the only Welsh player in the team – Trevor Foster was a reserve. His Barrow team-mate Willie Horne was chosen at stand-off.

The Great Britain players in a meeting before the New Zealand test match. (Courtesy Geoff Francis)

The Great Britain players training at Odsal before the New Zealand match.
(Courtesy Simon Foster)

Meeting the guest of honour, Lord Calverley, before the match. (Courtesy Geoff Francis)

Roy about to catch the ball playing for Great Britain against New Zealand. Harold Palin is the Great Britain player behind him. (Courtesy Robert Gate)

Action from the match (Both courtesy Geoff Francis)

Robert Gate in his *Rugby League Lions* book says that "This historic occasion was graced with a superb game of rugby with Great Britain playing brilliantly to beat a tenacious Kiwi side ... after some beautiful inter-play between Tommy Bradshaw and Martin Ryan, Roy Francis swept over for a try near the posts, which Ward converted ... From a scrum Bradshaw, Willie Horne and Ward cleverly sent Francis over for his second try, again goaled by Ward. Two minutes later, a perfectly executed move between Francis and Harold Palin sent Ward 40 yards straight up the field. Palin took a return pass and crashed over at the corner. Ward kicked a wonderful conversion and Great Britain led 17–2."

The Kiwis pulled a try back before half-time, but in the end Great Britain won 25–7. Sadly, for Roy, it was the last test of the season, so he did not have the chance to consolidate a place in the Great Britain side. He did, however, earn £10 – worth £394 today – the payment to the British players for a win. He did experience international rugby again in March, turning out for Wales at Swansea in a 20–12 loss to France.

Roy was asked to write about 'The high spot of my career' in the *Rugby League Gazette* in October 1949. He chose his Great Britain debut for the article: "If you were to ask a Welshman who had ever represented his country: 'What do you consider the highlight of your career,' you would undoubtedly be told 'The day I wore the old red jersey,' for that is every Welshman's ambition.

I was fortunate to realise that ambition, and in a way improve upon it. This happened when the selectors of the Great Britain team to meet New Zealand in the Final test at Bradford on December 20th, 1947, deciding I was the man to fill the right-wing position. I was the only Welshman in the team. So, in saying that the match was the high spot of my career, I can still claim allegiance to the declaration of all Welshmen.

This being a 'decider' I was with class company – the best. Ryan, 'Massa' Johnson, Ashcroft Ernie Ward, myself, Horne and Bradshaw, Gee, Egan, Curran, Len Aston, 'Chalky' White and 'Moggy' Palin were the team, with Russ Pepperell and Trevor Foster as reserves. Dai Rees of Bradford as manager, and Mr Tom Brown of Wigan in charge.

After a four-day preparation of hard training and marvellous food we arrived at Odsal with no illusions as to the immensity of our task. A great crowd of 45,000 people who had paid a record £6,000 had assembled to witness this struggle. It was our intention to keep the 'Ashes' or bust and with this foremost in our minds we went down those endless steps to Bradford Northern's ground.

Our introduction to Lord Calverley over, Pat Smith and Joe Egan decided on ends, and we ran to our positions. As we went Ernie Ward, my centre, said to me: "Well, Roy, this is it." Ernie had been experiencing a rough time with his form, due to illness and business and this match meant much to him. Being in my first test match, it meant a heck of a lot to me too, and we were kindred souls.

Smack! Little Tommy Bradshaw kicked off and nerves, qualms, prayers, went by the board as they always do when you kick off. Away went our forwards like greyhounds coming out of a trap. What a game! Many have said it was the finest game seen in years.
Each player striving his hardest, for the stakes were high. Five minutes play and Ernie Ward kicked a penalty. That put him on his mettle and us right on our toes. Martin Ryan got the ball, and as only he can, came side-stepping up field from his own '25', working towards me

he dummied and then beat another man, gave the ball to me, and I just managed to come inside Warwick Clarke and over in the corner. The first try of the match, in my first test, in the first eight minutes – I was tickled pink. But lady luck hadn't finished with me. Ernie Ward came into his own and started a run from about 50 yards out, beating his centre and the cover defence; he drew Warwick Clarke and Forrest out of position and gave it to me; over in the corner I went to score my second try.

Ernie kicked the goal and at half-time Ernie and I had two tries and four goals between us. It seemed as if we couldn't go wrong. But don't think it was easy, those Kiwis were tough nuts to crack. As for our side, who couldn't play with our six forwards running like stags, and Joe Egan getting the ball from the scrums? No pack playing cold have held our pack that day. Horne and Bradshaw were pulling all their tricks out of their bag. 'Massa' Johnson and his sidestep were playing havoc on the left wing with big Ernie Ashcroft bustling the Kiwi centres around. It was great football which had the crowd screeching with delight. It was all Great Britain.

Later in the second half the Kiwis decided it was time to do some bustling on their own account and they gave us a hectic and shaky half an hour. Fast running and wonderful handling was their speciality and they certainly brought them to bear That was when Martin Ryan especially stood out. He brought off tackle after tackle, as the last line of defence; first in one corner, then in the other. He played a wonderful game.

And so, the 'Ashes' stayed with us, and the memory of a super game. It was a grateful and happy Roy Francis who climbed back up those steps."

Simon Foster, Trevor Foster's son, comments: "In the lead up to the big games they played in, through the week before when players were together, Roy was always the 'smart one' in the sense that his meticulous preparation shone through. He would often train in light athletic shoes or spikes and work on his own after a training session was completed. Trevor saw him, for example in 1947, before the New Zealand test match, on the huge cinder surfaced car park at Odsal, doing repeated 50-, 60- and 110-yards sprints. Some of the players would stand together and watch him working. He had an obvious love of athletics. Roy was at that time very interested in learning about the psychology of sport, particularly through his experience in the Army. Trevor said he was always asking people about the physical training side of things. Both Roy and Trevor had been Army PTIs and shared many thoughts and ideas about rugby football."

As mentioned above, Barrow had a poor season, slipping to 21st place in the league. They had little joy in the Cups as well. They lost to Belle Vue Rangers over two legs in the Lancashire Cup. In the Challenge Cup, they beat Halifax, also over two legs, by one point on aggregate, but then lost 6–2 at home to Keighley.

Roy played 26 times for Barrow, 16 games at centre, nine on the left wing and one at stand-off. He scored 12 tries, but his last one for the season was away to Liverpool City on 13 December. Barrow played 41 matches in the season, and failed to touch down 15 times.

The season opened with a home win against Halifax. Roy scored a try, and *The News* reported that "Barrow's attacks were mainly engineered by Francis and Knowelden." The report also said that "The old forward trouble is still with us." The next week, Roy touched down twice to help Barrow to a win against Belle Vue Rangers in the Lancashire Cup, but 10 days later in the midweek return leg, Barrow lost 37–2 to finish their interest in the competition. Remarkably, the score was 2–2 at half-time, but after conceding an early try, Barrow fell apart. Unusually, Roy played at stand-off in the second half, with the injured Parker a passenger on the wing. *The News* commented that "There were occasional flashes from Francis and Lewthwaite but they never really got a sporting chance of a try.

Between the two Lancashire Cup ties, Barrow lost at home to Huddersfield. Another defeat came at Widnes after the rout at Belle Vue. Roy was unfit for a home win against Hunslet, but returned to the side to score their only try in a 9–5 defeat at Rochdale. However, the big event for the club was the arrival of Australian second-rower Harry Bath. He was 22 years old, and *The News* said he was an "outstanding forward". Barrow lost at home to Warrington, and in the next two matches lost at Oldham and at home to Wigan, when Bath made his debut. Roy missed the game because he was a reserve for Wales in an tour match against the New Zealanders.

Barrow ended their poor run with a win at Central Park, only their third since 1901. Barrow won 13–11, and according to *The News*, "Barrow's tries by Francis, Trelore and Jones were the outcome of tricky, classy football which had the defence well beaten." Barrow now hit a winning streak. Away to Hull KR, *The News* said that "Barrow had Francis at left centre and Trelore on the wing to him, and while the former was in his most impressive form, the display of the young Askam winger was one of the bright spots of the afternoon." Roy scored twice in Barrow's 23–12 win.

Roy scored again in a win away to Liverpool Stanley, but *The News* notes that understanding between him and Trelore was very good, with a "model pass" from Roy setting up a try for his winger. Despite two away wins, a poor crowd was at Craven Park to see a 41–8 win over York. The report in *The News* said that "Francis was in rare form at centre and the entire threequarter line worked well."

Roy did not claim one of the Barrow's nine tries, but did score in the return match with Hull KR, which Barrow won 11–10. *The News* outlined that it was a "thriller" and that "Francis, again in outstanding form at centre, scored the first try…".

Roy scored in a defeat at Swinton, and then played in a midweek 2–2 draw against the New Zealanders. Roy and Joe Jones missed the next match at home to Swinton because they were playing for Wales. Willie Horne was playing for England in the same match, and on 13 December, *The News* reported that he and Roy had been selected for Great Britain in the final test against the Kiwis on 20 December. Between the two international matches, Roy played for Barrow in a 30–0 win at Craven Park against Liverpool Stanley. He scored twice, but did not know at the time that they would be the last tries he scored for Barrow.

Their defeat against Warrington was the start of a run of six Barrow games when they did not score a try. The last two were 0–0 draws, a relatively unusual result even in those days of lower-scoring matches. The team's form recovered somewhat with an 18–4 win over Halifax in the first leg of the Challenge Cup first round tie. However, a 17–4 defeat at Thrum Hall the following week saw Barrow through by the narrowest of margins. A defeat in the league at Salford was followed by a 6–2 defeat at Craven Park to Keighley in the Challenge Cup. Harry Bath asked for a transfer, and played his last game for Barrow on 6 March. He joined Warrington six days later. Trevor Petcher also asked for a move, and did not play for the first team again. Jim Trelore also asked for a move, but he stayed with the club and eventually retired in 1956.

It is not clear whether this upheaval at the club had any effect on Roy's decision to ask for a move at the end of March. *The News* reported that "The fee which Barrow are asking for this brilliant player has not been divulged." Three weeks later, *Sentinel* reported in *The News* that "The Rugby League has reduced the transfer fee asked by Barrow for the services of Roy Francis, international wing or centre threequarter, from £2,000 to £1,250. This follows an appeal by the player." The report continued: "Although some clubs made inquiries when Barrow announced that Francis had been placed on the transfer list, it was obvious that the high figure asked for his services would not encourage business. It is now likely that two clubs, at least, will make fresh endeavours to obtain the player from Barrow, and it is understood that Francis himself desires a position as player-coach."

To put Barrow's original valuation of £2,000 into context, the record transfer fee at the end of the 1947–48 season was £2,650 which Leigh paid Dewsbury for Jim Ledgard. Roy was aged 29 when he asked for his move.

It was a sad end to his Barrow career. While he had only played three complete seasons for the club, along with two half-seasons in 1939, Barrow had seen him develop to become a Great Britain player. However, in July 1948, Warrington offered Barrow £800 for Roy and he signed for the current rugby league champions. He would face strong competition for a regular team place at Wilderspool.

Roy had continued to live with his young family in Wigan, where they had a men's clothing business. Possibly the reduction in travel was a factor in his move. He was now 29 years old, and had considerable experience as a rugby player. Maybe it was the fact that he could play at centre as well as on the wing that the directors at Warrington found attractive. New challenges would await him.

It is interesting to note Roy's ambition to be a 'player-coach'. Some clubs had 'trainer-coaches in the pre-War era, but it is unclear how much coaching they actually did. There had been a handful of player-coaches before the War, including Harold Wagstaff for his last season at Huddersfield. At Wigan, Jim Sullivan had been 'captain-coach' during Roy's time at the club, but it is not clear how much coaching he actually did. After the War, when Sullivan had retired as a player, he became a coach, at Wigan and then at St Helens, although he opposed the introduction of coaching qualifications.

The RFL were on the verge of appointing Trevor Foster as the sport's first national coach. Unusually, in Roy's Great Britain appearance, both sides had coaches – Bradford Northern's manager Dai Rees for the home team and Tom McClymont for the New Zealanders.

How much Roy considered the state of coaching in rugby league at this time is not known. However, he was clearly drawing on his wartime experience in both fitness training and rehabilitation, and again – ahead of his time – could see the potential for coaching. He wanted a future in the game after his playing career and coaching could provide that.

7. Warrington 1948 to 1949

Roy was aged 29 when he was signed by Warrington for a £800 transfer fee in July 1948. To put that price in context, the record transfer fee went from £2,750 to £4,000 in the 1948-49 season. The former was for Ike Owens's moves from Leeds to Castleford and then to Huddersfield; the latter for Stan McCormick's move from Belle Vue Rangers to St Helens.

In moving to Wilderspool, Roy was joining the sport's reigning champions. Warrington had won the title for the first time in the 1947-48 season, having been runners-up three times. In the Challenge Cup, they had won the trophy twice, both times before the First World War.

Roy would face more competition for a first team place than he had at Barrow. On the right wing, Brian Bevan was the regular selection. In his first full season, 1946-47, he scored 48 tries, and in 1947-48 57, more than one a game. On the left wing, Roy was competing for a place with Albert Johnson, one of the wingers who had been chosen ahead of him for the 1946 Lions tour.

On 10 July, the *Warrington Guardian* (*The Guardian*) reported that Roy had signed for the club: "...the Directors will not begrudge the four-figure fee they have paid Barrow for the dusky South Walian. Now the club has an array of threequarters – Bevan, Albert Pimblett, Bryn Knowelden [a former colleague of Roy's at Barrow], Stan Powell, Johnson and Francis. So, each player will have to play for his place. In any case, it is a wise move, to have first-class men ready to fill the place of an injured comrade or deputise for a player on county or international duty." The report noted that Roy had joined the Warrington players for training on 8 July.

The following week the paper had a photo of Roy being welcomed to the club by captain Harold Palin, Harry Bath [another former Barrow team-mate], Les Jones and Jimmy Featherstone.

It is interesting to note the use of the term 'dusky' to describe Roy. The *Barrow News* had not referred to his ethnicity when he signed for Barrow, maybe because they had already fielded Black British players. Warrington had had a Maori playing for them, Richard Papakura in 1911, but it is believed had not had a Black British player before Roy. However, the use of the term 'dusky' was not unusual at the time, although was rarely used about Roy.

Roy made his Warrington debut in the pre-season Wardonia Cup match against Wigan at Central Park. He scored in an 18--8 win in front of a massive 31,960 crowd. The game is best remembered for Brian Bevan's sensational 'try of the century'. *The Guardian* commented that "Francis took a risk and was unlucky. Still, if he can score a try while partially crippled, we can expect much better things." The paper said that Roy was injured, but would still be considered for selection for the first league match at Halifax. Roy did play and scored in an 18–2 win. Jack Steel – the pseudonym used by *Guardian* writers such as Cyril Briggs – said that Roy made a defensive error, along with Palin and Bevan, but said that Roy "came from nowhere" to score his try. In poor conditions, he said that "Bevan and Francis will show up better than this." Five days later, Roy touched down again in a comfortable 40-2 win away to Liverpool Stanley. Steel noted that Roy had scored in every appearance so far for the Wire, and said that "when Francis is really fit he will score many tries."

Warrington continued their winning run at Odsal where Roy had a try disallowed. Steel outlined that he "... shot to the line, grounded short but managed to pop the ball over the line. No try." He again also noted an error by both wingers: "Slips by Francis and Bevan presented Bradford with a scoring chance which they failed to utilise." He concluded in his 'player-pointers' that "Francis is not perfectly fit; better form is on the way."

Roy then faced his old club, Barrow, twice in four days in the first round of the Lancashire Cup. Warrington won the home leg 30-8, and then won 7–4 at Barrow to comfortably qualify for the next round. In the first match Roy played at centre and Knowelden at stand-off, but Steel commented: "Flashes of brilliance maybe from Knowelden and Francis, but Knowelden is essentially a centre and Francis a wingman." He added: "As for Francis – well he was never really happy and, although I must admit all passes to him were not well directed, he made many mistakes in catching. Even when he did hold the ball, it was not taken cleanly." At Barrow, with Roy back on the wing, Steel said that several Warrington players were "ineffective". He added: "Francis put in two or three good runs down the touch, but he was not a dangerous winger."

Roy scored two tries in a 17–7 win at Rochdale. Steel outlined that "It was championship form, however, when a concerted method led to Francis running from near halfway – he was the odd man over – to score his first try, while it was play with a punch which resulted in him carrying the ball over the line a second time." He added: "I am glad to report an improvement to Francis's form. He appears to be running faster, and while his handling is not perfect – yet – it should be remembered he has already scored five tries."

Five days later, a record attendance of 24,285 at Leigh saw the Wire win 15–10 to reach the Lancashire Cup semi-final. Roy did not score, and Steel noted that he and Bevan saw little of the ball. It was a move by Roy out to the wing, when two Leigh players moved to watch him, that created the space for Warrington's first try.

Warrington then beat Leeds comfortably at Wilderspool, running away with the game in the second half. Steel noted "unorthodox play by Francis". Another Yorkshire team came to Wilderspool and were well beaten when Huddersfield lost 35–2. Steel's report refers to the "crippled left wing" of Knowelden and Francis, without explaining what injuries they sustained. Both missed the Lancashire Cup semi-final when Oldham were easily beaten three days later. Knowelden did not play again until January.

Albert Johnson took Roy's place on the left wing, and Roy did not play again until 20 November. Previewing Warrington's match with Rochdale on 23 October, Steel said that both players were still injured.

The following week, when the Warrington first team played – and beat – the Australian tourists, Roy was chosen for an 'A' team friendly at Widnes. Knowelden was also playing, but went off after 10 minutes with a pulled muscle, so Roy moved to play at left centre. This is probably the first 'A' team game he had played since his time at Wigan 10 years before.

Roy missed the Lancashire Cup Final defeat against Wigan, but returned to the Warrington team to face Salford on 20 November. Warrington won narrowly, and Steel commented that "Johnson will always be the first candidate for the left-wing position providing Francis continues to reveal in and out form." He also said that apart from Bevan and Powell, the backs were "mediocre".

Roy played on the left-wing against Salford, but moved to left centre for the next four games. At Swinton, Warrington had five players missing on international duty, but won comfortably 21-7, with Roy contributing two tries. Warrington had been expected to lose their unbeaten record, but Steel said: "It was a case of well played Warrington with a chunk of praise to Francis (two tries and a hand in two others) ...". He continued: "The tries came through Francis, who thought and acted quickly, first by dodging three men and secondly by finding a wide open space by beating a man. Bevan raced through to secure the touch after Francis had put in a 'grubber' kick. The result left Warrington on top of the Northern Rugby League table with 14 wins from 14 games, and top of the Lancashire League.

Against St Helens, Warrington's backs were all internationals except Brian Bevan. Steel said that the crowd enjoyed "the Francis burst". He also noted "typical Francis tackling (which not only stops the man but any ideas of a quick pass) ...". Roy set up a try for Bevan with a 'cut out' pass, and Warrington won by 10 points.

A visit to Fartown was Warrington's next fixture, and they anticipated a much closer game than the 25–2 win at Wilderspool in September. The Wire were 9-3 down at half-time, but fought back to win 11–9, and Roy scored the final – and crucial – try. Steel said that "As for Francis, well his try when the score stood at 6–9, was well worth the journey over the Pennines or any other range of hills for that matter." His report also included a pen-picture of Roy, saying that he was an "Unorthodox player who has a fine 'football brain.'"

Warrington faced three matches in four days over Christmas. Roy scored a hat-trick at Widnes on Christmas Day, missed the home match with Leigh, but then returned to action at Headingley on the left-wing, when he touched down again.

The Guardian had a table of Warrington's scorers up to the Christmas break. Bevan was top with 33; the next highest was Harry Bath. Roy was joint fifth with eight tries, including his debut one in the Wardonia Cup.

Steel reported that at Widnes "The match was a triumph for Francis, who got three good tries, but he had to thank Jack Fleming for two of them." He added: "Francis's third try followed an interception near halfway and for the last 20 yards to the posts he merely trotted along." He also noted that Bevan was sent off in the last minute. On 28 December, Warrington won 14–0 against Leeds. Steel wrote that "The movement which brought Francis' try followed a wide throw by Ike Fishwick. Powell ran close to Bevan, slipped a pass in the opposite direction and Knowelden's expert hands and brains made the score for Francis."

Roy's skills were not confined to the rugby pitch. On New Year's Day, the Wire won 3–2 at Whitehaven. Steel outlined that "The team had a homely reception at Kendal, where a stiff-shirt hotel dance was one of the town's events. ... [the players had] a spot of ballroom hopping, with Roy Francis making himself one of the most popular visitors by leading a sequence dance."

Bob Anderton, the club secretary, wrote in the next Warrington programme: "At the end of the Whitehaven game both sets of players were caked in mud and frozen stiff and, seeing the state of them, it was small wonder that good football had been at a discount. To add to the players' discomfort at the end of the game the bathing facilities were very primitive.

The Warrington team that played Wigan in the Wardonia Cup on 14 August 1948. A crowd of 31,960 saw Warrington win 18–8, with Roy scoring a try. (Courtesy Neil Dowson)

1948–49 Warrington team. (Courtesy Neil Dowson)

Meeting the Earl of Derby before a match against Huddersfield in September 1949. Bryn Knowelden is on Roy's left. (Courtesy Geoff Francis)

The 1949–50 Warrington team. (Courtesy Neil Dowson)

Left: Roy being tackled by Price and Pimblett of Belle Vue while playing for Warrington. (Courtesy Neil Dowson)

It is worth recording though that our players did not lose their noted sense of humour for as they crowded together under the showers, looking like the *Kentucky Minstrels,* they gave a rendering of *April Showers* in real Al Jolson manner."

Again, this would be unthinkable today. The *Kentucky Minstrels* was a popular series of BBC radio programmes broadcast between 1933 and 1950. It featured white entertainers blacking up their faces and pretending to sing like slaves on old plantations. It was a more extreme version of *The Black and White Minstrel Show* that ran on BBC television from 1958 to 1978 and again featured white entertainers blacking up their faces and singing slave songs. The entertainer Al Jolson has been described as "the king of blackface performers" such was his reputation for singing with a blacked-up face.

Brian Bevan was given a two-match suspension for his sending-off, so Roy made two rare appearances on the right wing. The first was in a 29–7 win over Workington. Steel outlined that: "It must now be realised that Pimblett ... Johnson and Francis are dangerous men to stop ... Francis's unorthodox play not only bluffed the opposition and the crowd, but had a touch of humour about it. A warning about overdoing the running closer to the posts idea. Roy must remember his experiences at Leeds when he crossed the line on three occasions without getting the approval of referee Railton." The following week, Workington got their revenge with an 11–6 win. So, the Wire lost their unbeaten league record. Steel reported that "Had the ball reached the wingers – remember Francis and Johnston got the tries – there is no saying what might have happened...".

Bevan's return saw Roy move to left centre at home to Wigan, then right centre the following week, then two games on the left wing before another move to left centre. Warrington's form showed a brief decline. A record 34,304 crowd saw an 8–4 defeat for the Wire, which was followed by an 11–6 loss at Belle Vue. Steel commented that "Francis and Bath came near to saving the game."

A 29–5 win over lowly Liverpool Stanley saw Roy score one of the Wire's seven tries, although the often-critical Steel said that "Knowelden and Francis did not consistently show that form which gained them honours."

In the Challenge Cup, Warrington were drawn against Hull KR. Steel wrote about the first leg at Wilderspool: "Johnson fans will be wondering why he is not playing. Personally, I think he should be included with Francis at centre in place of Knowelden." Warrington won by 10 points, a good lead to take to Humberside. A letter in the *Guardian* from a supporter asked "What Warrington supporters want to know is why Bevan is 'starved' for passes, and why Francis is chopped and changed and not given the chance to settle down in one position?"

Back at left centre, Roy helped Warrington win 28–5 at Craven Park. Steel reported that the "last try came through a Francis piece of bluff. He roared 'right' but the ball went to the Bevan wing instead of the left."

Roy missed a comfortable win over Oldham, but was recalled for a shock 8–3 Challenge Cup defeat at Belle Vue. He was "completely off form" according to *The Guardian*, and was dropped for the league match at Hull. Roy himself felt that he needed a break from first-team and 'A' team action and so told the directors, who still picked both teams. The match programme on 19 March reported: "Roy feels that of late he has not been producing that form which he believes himself capable and has asked the directors not to consider him for either team for a time. He has no quarrel – indeed he is still attending to his training daily – but he feels that a complete rest from actual play for a few weeks will put matters right for him." The directors agreed and were rewarded as Roy scored seven tries in the last six first-team games of the season.

First, on 7 April he scored two tries for the 'A' team against Wigan, and returned to first team action against Widnes on Good Friday. He scored then and added another against Bradford Northern on Easter Saturday. Against Hull a week later he contributed a hat-trick to a comfortable Warrington win, with Steel saying that his form was one of the features of the match." Warrington finished top of the table with 31 wins in their 36 matches, and also won the Lancashire League. In the Championship semi-final, they beat Barrow 23–8, with Roy on the left-wing. *The Guardian* noted that "Francis must have wondered what had happened when he failed to hold a pass with a sure 'walk in'."

The Final was at Manchester City's Maine Road ground, with a huge record crowd of 75,194. They faced Huddersfield, who had finished third in the league and won at Wigan to reach the big day. The official programme for the match (priced six pence in old money) had Francis and Johnson bracketed together for the number five jersey but when kick-off arrived it was Roy who was selected on the left wing. Huddersfield were on top in the first half and went ahead with a try from John Daly, converted by Pat Devery. Their Australian winger Lionel Cooper added a second to give the Fartown side an 8–0 lead. After the break Devery touched down and converted his own try to take his team's lead to 13–0. Warrington had a try by Bevan disallowed before Roy 'rolled over' in the corner, although there were claims that he had dropped the ball. Steel said that "Francis struggled over for what was easily the luckiest try of the season." He added that "Bill Jackson and Francis failed to show anything like cohesion."

Palin had been injured, so Bath kicked the goal. With seven minutes left, the score was 13–7. Warrington scored again through Jackson, Bath again converting, but there was not enough time left for the Wire to snatch a winner. Even the *Warrington Guardian* accepted that "It would have been an injustice had Huddersfield lost the lead in those vital last seconds." However, Roy had played in his first major peace-time final.

Apart from the six-week spell from the end of September to mid-November, Roy played fairly regularly. Of his 29 appearances, 17 were on the left wing, two on the right wing, 10 games at centre, two on the right and eight on the left. Johnson only played on the left wing and scored 19 tries in 25 appearances. Roy scored 22 tries, including hat-tricks at Widnes in December and at home to Hull in April. He scored two tries three times. He finished 11th in the national try-scorers list. However, he was not chosen for Wales this season.

Roy's first appearance for Warrington in the 1949–50 season came on 7 September. He was named as reserve for the Wardonia Cup match with Wigan, a sign of the strength of Warrington's backs. On 7 September, he scored against Bradford Northern in a 30–7 win. However, Steel commented that Roy "must learn to take the ball on the run."

He had a run of five games on the wing, then played a couple at centre. The week after the Bradford game, in a 45–7 win over Belle Vue Rangers, Roy touched down twice. Steel said that "Francis, in particular, got in an almost impossible pass, which produced five points. The left-winger's form was the best for a very long while and he was speedy in try line dashes." On 8 October, away to Hull, the Wire won 18–5. Steel wrote that "In the first 40, Ron Ryder, Francis and Bevan partially penetrated the defence and it was only split-second tackling that saved Hull. Francis, in particular, was inches short, but he once threw out a poor pass with Bevan well placed."

The next week, Warrington beat Huddersfield 36–9. Steel outlined that: "I am now convinced that Francis is purely a winger and not a centre. His unorthodox play does not always fit in and playing alongside a player of Bevan's calibre, one cannot expect the best possible results. There are times when Francis likes to carve his own openings and should be given every encouragement to do so. What wing he will play on when Bevan is back I cannot at the moment visualise."

Roy played in Bevan's place away to Belle Vue Rangers when Bevan was on international duty. The Wire lost 14–5. Steel reported that: "Men who deserved to be on a bonus despite defeat were Brian Bevan's deputy Roy Francis and big-hearted Bob Ryan. Francis did 75 per cent of the work which preceded a try which won't be bettered this season; and was always a menace until he was unaccountably starved in the second half.

And what a try it was when it did come. Francis collected the ball in his own half, exchanged passes with Fleming and gradually got hemmed in, overcame two tackles, recovered magnificently when practically grounded by a third and made 50 yards before transferring to Ryan who gave Fishwick a blueprint final pass."

However, Roy was dropped for the next week's match at Swinton. *The Guardian* said that this "caused much comment in view of the fact that he was one of Warrington's very few stars in the defeated side at Belle Vue." Roy asked to go on the transfer list. A week later, he was signed by Hull. He was living in Wigan, and had recently opened an outfitting business. No fee was disclosed, but it was a 'satisfactory' deal for both clubs.

Roy had scored five tries in eight appearances in his final season at Wilderspool. Hull FC paid £1,200 for Roy to join them. It was seen as quite a high fee for a player who was nearly 31. However, it proved to be money well spent and an important move for Roy's future.

8. Hull 1949 to 1952

Hull FC is one of the oldest ruby league clubs, having been formed in 1865. They moved to The Boulevard in 1895, and also that year became a founder member of the Northern Union. Along with their neighbours – and rivals – Hull Kingston Rovers, they were an eastern outpost for the sport in the United Kingdom. One advantage that both clubs had was that Hull City Football Club were usually in the lower depths of the Football League, and therefore not a great competitor for any 'floating' supporters. However, the clubs did try to avoid direct fixture clashes where possible, particularly if cup-ties were involved.

Hull had enjoyed some success in the past. They won the Championship in the first two seasons after the First World War, and again in 1935–36. They won the Challenge Cup in 1913–14, and when Roy joined them five times. However, since the end of the Second World War, their only Final had been in the Yorkshire Cup in 1946–47. They had finished outside the top 10 in the league every season since the War. The Boulevard had suffered some bomb damage during the War, which did not help their cause. The club's centenary history brochure says that despite signing three Australians and three other players, 1947–48 was "only a moderate season". The brochure says that 1948–49 was "disappointing", but in both campaigns the 'A' team had been successful, so maybe there was potential at the club.

Roy signed for Hull FC in November 1949, but continued to live in Wigan. *Kingstonian* wrote in the *Hull Daily Mail (The Mail):* "Twenty-four hours after the Warrington Rugby League club had acceded to his request to be placed on the open-to-transfer list, Roy Francis, Welsh international centre-threequarter and wing-man, was snapped by the Hull club. The Wilderspool directors invited offers and, I am told, the deal, which was announced in the *Hull Daily Mail* extra edition yesterday, was completed at figure satisfactory to all concerned. The Hull club this morning described the fee as 'substantial.' Mr Pattison left Hull for Lancashire early yesterday morning in an attempt to be first in the field. At least four other clubs were of the same idea, and it was not until after 5 o'clock in the afternoon that a decision was reached. Francis chose to come to Hull, and so the lengthy Boulevard search for a high calibre centre-threequarter [concludes] ... Francis, a married man with two children who lives in Wigan, and owns an outfitting business, will train at Wigan."

A feature in *Rugby League Review* said that "Great hopes are held out by Hull for their latest capture, Roy Francis from Warrington. Francis, it is anticipated, will provide the ideal 'feed' for Ryan."

His first season was very disappointing for the Hull fans, who must have wondered if the £1,250 transfer fee for a 30-year-old had been well spent. He made his debut at Keighley on 12 November. The match was abandoned at half time with the score 0–0. The weather conditions were "atrocious" according to the *Mail's* report.

He played at home to Halifax, again at left-centre, the following week in a 14–5 win. He partnered Australian winger Bruce Ryan, a combination that Hull had great hopes in. The *Mail* reported that "Francis seemed a little over anxious during the game; apparently too eager to please. It is obvious that he was unable to dovetail with Bruce Ryan in their first game together. A number of his moves, however, were those of the reputable centre he is. and a pointer to things to come."

However, Roy injured his knee against Halifax, and withdrew from the Airlie Birds next match at Leigh. The *Mail* commented that "Francis' inability to play is most unfortunate, for much was expected him in tomorrow's match." On 8 December, the paper reported that "Roy Francis will not play for the Boulevard Club until the New Year. He has a twisted knee tendon and has been ordered a rest from the game."

He made a comeback for the 'A' team in mid-January and set up two tries. He was hoping to make a come-back at Odsal on 21 January, but broke down in training the day before. On 26 January, the *Mail* outlined that "Hull FC centre, Roy Francis, may have to go into hospital for an operation. This is indicated by the specialist's preliminary reports. A cyst has developed on the player's cartilage. This probably means that Roy will not be seen in the Hull line-up again this season."

Two weeks later, this news was confirmed. On 10 February, the *Mail* reported that Roy was going "... into St Christopher's Nursing Home. Wigan, on Monday to have a cyst removed from a cartilage. The operation will be performed on Wednesday morning. Officials at the Boulevard are not without hopes that Roy will be seen in action again this season, however, and it is a sure thing that all the Hull well-wishers will keep their fingers crossed for a rapid recovery for the player."

This operation means that for Francis things will be reversed. During his war-service he was an instructor with the Army Physical Training Corps attached, to a remedial centre catering for former victims of cartilage trouble. He therefore knows the procedures thoroughly and this knowledge no doubt, will be a valuable asset him on his road to recovery."

Hull finished the season in 19th place in the Northern Rugby League. The *Centenary Brochure* again noted that the 'A' team was successful. Apart from Roy, two other Welsh players were recruited, one of whom, Tommy Harris, made a huge contribution to the club's later successes. However, Bruce Ryan left to join Leeds, so the partnership between him and Roy never happened.

1950–51

The report of the club's Annual General Meeting said that "Referring to the £1,250 paid in transfer fees another shareholder said that the club had made a 'good buy' in Roy Francis from Warrington." This was despite Roy making such a small contribution on the pitch due to injury. The club showed its faith in Roy when he was appointed as captain. The *Centenary Brochure* says that in this season there was "nothing of note to report from a playing point of view." What was significant was some of the new recruits – Colin Hutton, Johnny Whiteley and Jim Drake were all signed. Bill Drake, Jim's twin brother, was signed a year later.

Roy played 29 games for Hull, 22 at left centre and seven on the left wing. Ivor Watts or Emlyn Walters, who joined the club in November from Bradford Northern, were usually his partner when he played at centre. In the first league game of the season, at home to Bradford Northern, Roy was partnered by former Barrow team-mate Jim Trelore, who was having a trial; with Hull. *Kingstonian* wrote in the *Mail* that "Hull will make their task easier if they will give full play to the wings. Last season the Boulevard wingers got far too few opportunities, but with the experienced Francis in the centre with Turner we can hope to see a more thoughtful distribution of the ball across field."

Hull won 18–10, and *Kingstonian* commented that "Roy Francis lived up to the highest hopes of him and thrilled the crowd with his dash in the centre. He needed only half a chance to put Northern's line in danger, and there was class the way he ran in two opportunist tries." At Bramley, Roy set up one of Hull's tries in a defeat, and missed the goal-kick. He was only a very occasional kicker and the third player to try to kick a goal in this match. A further defeat followed away to an in-form Keighley side. *Kingstonian* said that Roy "lacked virility in the centre."

Hull won the forward battle against Wakefield at the Boulevard, and the game, but again *Kingstonian* was critical of Roy, saying that he "rarely revealed the qualities expected of him." Hull beat their first visitors for the season from Lancashire, Widnes, 5–3, but *Kingstonian* reported that "There was insufficient punch in the middle. Turner played a strong centre's game and did well, but Francis was again unable to reveal the forcefulness and determination inside-back's position demands. I doubt if he will ever shine in this position as he did when playing wing."

A 10,000 crowd saw the second leg of the Yorkshire Cup clash with Dewsbury. Hull faced a 14–2 deficit from the first leg, and could only draw 2–2. *Kingstonian* commented that "Early in the second half another golden opportunity for Hull was absolutely thrown to the winds. A breakaway by Jackson won the Airlie Birds a strong position, and brilliant handling by half-a-dozen men took the ball clean from right to left.

It only remained for Francis to draw the defence's last man and Trelore was over, but when the centre's pass came it was four feet too high ... There was another near miss when Francis broke away for 40 yards after intercepting. A colleague in support could have taken the ball and scored as full-back Thompson, the only man to beat, closed for the tackle, but Francis had left everyone behind and Dewsbury breathed again as the centre failed to beat his man." He also said that Roy "made errors he will want to forget."

The Hull directors decided not to sign Jim Trelore, and instead moved Roy to the left-wing to face Leeds. *Kingstonian* wrote that "Perhaps the most important change affects the captain, Roy Francis. An effort is being made to let him find his form in his old position—left-wing—and the centre position he vacates is given to Stan Shaw ...". Hull lost to the Headingley side by six points, but the change in position seemed to work for Roy. *Kingstonian* was more positive about his performance and the two tries he scored: "I don't think anyone else in the side but Francis — a lot of his old smartness back — could have capped the moves which led to him scoring."

For Hull's visit to Castleford, *Kingstonian* said that "Francis has shown himself to be a strong scoring power back in his wing position, and if openings can be created there may be more points coming his way."

Hull lost 15–3, and Roy missed the next match, at home to Dewsbury, another defeat. *Kingstonian* reported that "Although changes were expected for the weekend's game, there may be a certain amount of surprise at the form they have taken. Captain Roy Francis after appearances on the wing and an afternoon on the bench last week returns to the centre with Ivor Watts coming in on the left-wing. It will be the latter's first senior appearance since injuring a shoulder last May."

The team's performances were clearly upsetting the supporters. A letter in the *Hull Daily Mail* denounced the directors' team selections. The writer's proposed team did include Roy on the wing. He also pointed out the need for a new coach. However, things improved with a win at Wakefield, Hull's first double of the season and away win. *Kingstonian* was more positive about Roy, saying that "Francis had ideas in attack..."

Roy touched down in a comfortable home win against Rochdale Hornets, but missed a win at Featherstone through stomach trouble. He got his place back the following week, and kept it, despite receiving a shoulder knock against Huddersfield.

Hull lost at home to St Helens, and *Kingstonian* said that "Francis, at left-centre, is never at his best in defence, and unless Walters proves effective in checking the man against him, the left flank will need a lot of watching." Roy missed the return match against Huddersfield.

An article in the *Mail* pointed out that Hull were a 'cosmopolitan' side, with only five local players in the squad of 15 to face Keighley. It said that Roy was living in Lancashire, which could be seen as 'cosmopolitan' in Hull terms. In fact, he moved to East Yorkshire the following year.

On Christmas Day, Roy had his first experience of a Hull derby match, when Hull KR visited the Boulevard. He scored Hull's only try in a 3–3 draw. In Michael Ulyatt's history of the derby match, he quotes Johnny Whiteley saying that "Roy Francis in pre-match team tactics talk didn't speak of merely 'a game' but more of 'a war' that was going to take place." Roy went on to play in another seven derby matches, scoring another three tries. The return match, at Craven Park in March, was not a good day for Hull, Rovers winning 21–4.

At home to York, just after the Hull KR match, *Kingstonian* wrote that Roy "was excellent in attack, but how much sooner would opposition attacks come to grief if he could curb his appetite for interceptions." Roy scored twice in a comfortable home win. In early February, in a defeat at Widnes: "Roy Francis was in excellent form at centre and with his wingman Emlyn Walters, was dangerous with half a chance. The threequarters had few opportunities, however."

In the Challenge Cup, Hull faced a tough draw against Roy's old club, Warrington. The Wire won both games, 25–9 at Wilderspool and 5–3 at the Boulevard. *Kingstonian* reported in the match at Warrington: "Just exactly what Roy Francis had to say to his Hull teammates at half-time at Wilderspool on Saturday I do not know, but the pep talk the players smiled about later apparently had a great effect.

Warrington piled up the points before the interval. Then came Francis's talk and the whole-hearted application of rehearsed tactics by the Hull team." He continued: "Francis was again in good form, covering well in defence and a schemer in attack."

On the home match against Bramley, the *Mail* said that: "Had it not been for Hull's all-Welsh left wing, Emlyn Walters and Roy Francis, the referee's final whistle would have been practically the only real finish in the game at the Boulevard on Saturday." The report added: "Well timed passes by Francis sent Walters in for two tries ..."

1951–52 Hull team with Roy as captain. (Courtesy *Rugby League Journal*)

Rugby League Review from November 1950, saying
that Hull was an 'outpost' for the sport. (Courtesy Peter Lush)

On 27 February, the paper reported that: "Hull FC's captain, Roy Francis, is due to become a much-travelled man. Roy, who lives and has a business in Wigan, will be visiting Hull once a week to supervise Hull's new field training programme, under which local and out-of-town players will get together. When the travelling time for this new commitment is added to games, he will be spending a good many hours per week moving to-and-fro across country. I happen to know that the frequent journeys will not trouble him, however. Roy told me some time ago that his ambition was to make headway in a direction that would keep him in the game when his playing days were over – not that he expects them to end for quite some time yet. In fact, it is not long since I heard him say jokingly 'I won't give up on my own accord; I'll have to be thrown out!' Can it be that Roy's coaching duties with the Airlie Birds have set his feet on a new path to tread when he puts his boots away."

At St Helens in early March, Walters and Roy swapped positions. The paper commented that: "Roy Francis, playing in his old international position on the wing, had a good day. Emlyn Walters, in the centre, however, was never given the room to apply the directness in the middle for which the left-wing switch was designed." The same week, Colin Hutton was signed from Widnes. It was a very significant move that gave Hull more options at full-back and in the threequarter line. Meanwhile, Roy had an ankle injury that saw him miss the return to another of his old clubs, Dewsbury.

In early April, Roy injured his ankle training in Wigan. The club doctor advised him to see a specialist as there was a potential ligament problem. He was named as the extra back for the final game of the season at Hunslet, but did not play.

Hull finished the season in 18th place in the league, one place higher than the previous season, but with one less competition point. Roy had scored 10 tries in 29 appearances for Hull. However, despite the team's lack of improvement, there clearly was potential in some of the younger players who were finding success in the 'A' team. Some had also played for the first team. Tommy Harris was established at hooker, and Johnny Whiteley had made some appearances in the second half of the season.

1951–52

This season started the transformation in Hull FC's fortunes. Roy had temporarily become player-coach in July, At the Hull FC AGM, the *Mail* reported on 8 August that "Mr E Hardaker, chairman, said that 'organisation had been made for Roy Francis to continue coaching well up to the end of the light nights.' Mr Jack Murray, who has been re-engaged as trainer-masseur, said that "he had never seen Francis so fit." However, the club's financial position was "desperate" according to a former board member, with a loss of £1,768 the previous season. However, the club now owned some houses.

The report also said that "A shareholder thought that Roy Francis had 'done a wonderful job.' He had seen the team training and he thought Francis had got them in good shape. Prospects this season were bright." The next day, the *Mail* had a photo of Roy giving advice to some of young players at the Boulevard for trials with Hull FC.

Hull started the new season with five straight wins in the league, the only disappointment was being knocked out of the Yorkshire Cup by Wakefield Trinity over two legs. The season opened with a win at Barrow. The *Mail* reported that "…Then Roy Francis, playing his best game since joining Hull, set an example with his lightning handling and tackling, and the Airlie Birds fell in line with him to make certain of a great victory in the second half."

The report continued: "Hull scored five tries, every one a good one and some of them brilliant. If one could be mentioned apart from the rest, it would feature Roy Francis either his own following a wily interception, or the one he gave Gittoes after completely baffling the opposition with a run that left Barrow open mouthed. Whichever way you looked it was Francis's game…".

Roy scored again in a home win against York, and then Hull won 31–10 away to league newcomers Cardiff – a rare visit to South Wales for Roy. In their report on a 29–0 win against Bramley, *Kingstonian* said "… Foreman and Francis who so far this season have been the 'brains' of the team" Roy missed the first leg of the Yorkshire Cup match with a back injury, but returned for the second leg. Hull were top of the league when Huddersfield came to the Boulevard. *Kingstonian* wrote that "One could also sense the inspiration which Francis was affording. The first try-scoring movement started with him and after he had crossed himself later it was tough luck that a further try was denied him."

Marksman, in the *Mail's* 'sports gossip' column, looked at Hull's potential on 11 September: "Today, when Hull FC are top of the Rugby League, the only remaining 100 percent Yorkshire club and at the outset of what appears to be a big revival, I think it is as good a time as any to recall a conversation I had with Roy Francis, the club captain and temporary coach, some seven months ago, in which he forecast how such a revival could come about. It was when the Hull team were staying at a Blackpool hotel before meeting Warrington in the Rugby League Cup that Roy told me of his belief in his fellow players, and that if their efforts were directed into the proper channels, they could get among the leaders. During the close season, with a month before the start of next season for training and tactics, and then make a winning start, Roy said that 'you would not recognise this team.

For a beginning,' Roy continued 'it would be important to have the edge on everyone else for fitness, which would be vital to secure a winning start. Confidence would grow, and once a team get a strong belief in themselves, that's half the battle.' Well, things have happened more or less just like that. The coaching scheme Francis envisaged materialised. He was appointed to supervise it by the club, and we have all seen the results. Real team-work and spirit is the essence of the side's winning start and if progress is maintained Hull are certain to become a power in the Rugby League."

Roy's temporary position as coach soon became permanent. On 15 September, in the 'sports gossip' column, *Marksman* wrote: "We may see a development at the Boulevard shortly to the Roy Francis training scheme which I mentioned earlier this week, for after the initial success of the scheme, the Hull club are hoping to engage Francis as player-coach for the remainder of the season. Hold-up at the moment is a domestic one. Francis's home and business are in Wigan, but there are strong hopes that he will find it possible to travel to Hull on training days and continue to operate a full-scale organised training and coaching plan for the Hull players."

Three days later, the *Mail* reported that Roy had been engaged for two years as player-coach to the club. "Chairman E Hardaker said today their negotiations with Francis had been completed and for the time being Francis would travel from his home in Wigan and stay in Hull during the midweek training period." The report said that during the close season Francis had been charge of training and coaching for senior and junior players. It concluded: "Although Mr JE Murray was engaged as trainer to the team last season, Hull FC had no official coach until Francis took over last July."

Although it was not acknowledged at the time, this is believed to be the first time a black coach had been appointed in a major sport to coach a professional team. Even today, black head coaches are not that common; in the early 1950s there were only a few black British players in rugby league, let alone coaches.

It should be pointed out that during his time at Hull, it was still the directors who picked the team, and also controlled recruitment both through transfers and signing young players or players from rugby union. How much Roy was consulted is unclear.

Distinguished rugby league historian, and also a Hull FC fan, Raymond Fletcher, said of Roy's move to Hull: "Although he was past his peak, Francis still retained much of his class and individual style. His keen anticipation made him an expert at intercepting passes and his dummies could mesmerise the best of defenders. He was also an inspiring captain and during the 1951–52 season Hull appointed him player-coach."

Roy had one of his best seasons on the pitch. He played in 36 of Hull's 42 matches; 31 at left-centre, usually partnering Ivor Watts, four on the left wing and one on the right wing. He scored 16 tries, three behind top scorer Watts. Hull won both derby games, and Roy scored in both, an 18–10 away win on Christmas Day, when the team were "intelligently led by Francis", according to *Kingstonian*, and a 9–5 home win in April on Good Friday. This match was a tactical battle between former Warrington team-mates Roy and Bryn Knowelden, who was Rovers' player-coach. Roy clinched victory in the last minute; the *Mail* reported that "Rovers defended grimly until Francis snapped up a Hutton pass in the 79th minute to score."

Roy's influence as a player comes through in the match reports in the *Mail*. At St Helens in October: "Hutton and Francis had a much better day in the centre, and it was a brilliant interception by Francis that rounded off an excellent first half for Hull..." Hull won 15–10. In November against Batley: "The first try was one of those kick-and-follow-up efforts which usually result in the defence winning by inches. This time though, Francis, a perfect judge of his kick, landed it in an ideal spot for fleet footed Watts to touch it." The next week, at York: "Francis, who scored one and had a hand in the other two ... played [his] part well." A couple of weeks later at Keighley: "Welshmen Turner and Francis from whose wing four of Hull's five tries came..." On 15 December against Leeds, "Francis worked a try for Coverdale and scored two himself." At home to Hunslet on Boxing Day, "Francis intercepted, set off downfield at full speed and timed his pass to Whiteley beautifully so that the young loose forward cum centre had no trouble in dashing the remaining 20 yards to score."

On 1 January 1952, the *Mail* noted that Hull were top of the NRL table, and added that it was 16 years since they had won the title. Roy missed a couple of games just after Christmas through injury. He had hurt his back on Boxing Day, and was also consulting an eye specialist. Hull supporters will have welcomed the news – in the *Mail's* sports gossip section – that Roy was planning to move with his family to Hull. The report said: "His intention to live in Hull is

66

a decision he cannot have taken lightly, because of the business he has been running at Wigan, but in a couple of months or so, Roy and his family should be in the act of settling down here. While he has made up his mind that he is definitely moving, the man who has done so much to take the Hull club to the top of the Rugby League is no yet sure what he will do besides his football interest when he arrives. I understand he may consider opening a business, or he may take a business appointment. Whatever he does in a private line, Hull rugby league fans will welcome his decision to settle here. The closer Francis is to the Boulevard, the better the fans will like it– they cannot be blamed for thinking the destinies of man and club are closely linked."

His importance to the team was shown in their home win against Barrow in January. The *Mail* reported that "Hull might have thrown themselves at Barrow's defences all day if, just before the halftime whistle, Roy Francis had not shown them how to put their impeccable handling to best use. The captain, seeing his forwards battering on Barrow's line to no effect, moved in significantly to act as half back. He was not spotted. A prefect long pass to Lawrenson near the right wing and Nutland did the rest with a try which gave Hull an interval lead."

The sports gossip column added that "Roy Francis, Hull FC's captain and trainer-coach adds another official 'title' to the list tomorrow when he takes on the job of master of ceremonies at the supporters club annual dance for the first time." It was noticeable throughout his time in Hull that Roy and Renee were involved in the social side of the club.

The success Hull were enjoying was seen by a 20,000 crowd squeezing into the Boulevard for Hull's match with Bradford Northern. After their 12–8 win, the *Mail* reported that Roy said that Hull were pretty certain of a place in the championship play-offs. "Pointing out that nine of his side are under 25, Roy says they are a 'young team, a good team and a happy team.'"

A couple of days later, the *Mail* had a rare interview with Roy. *Kingstonian* wrote that the team had to prove their staying power, according to Roy. He said "Roy Francis, who between last season and this seemed to work a miracle at the Boulevard, told me last night 'Anything can happen at this stage of the season. This is where those who have no staying power drop out of the running. We have to prove that our success has not been a flash in the pan.'"

Pointing out that Roy had travelled hundreds of miles between Wigan and Hull, *Kingstonian* said that for Roy, "success ... has been hard earned." Roy outlined that team spirit "was behind everything" and that "the team include the directors, staff and all the players on the books." He stressed the importance of the board: "The biggest disadvantage the club have to work under is having to elect directors every 12 months. Our present board have a policy which has succeeded. If you break that up next season, I think it would be fatal."

Looking to the future, *Kingstonian* wrote: "If the same 'team' exists next season, Francis tells me, he believes it will be even more important than this one. The six-week pre-season training next summer, he stressed, would be a 'polishing up period'." *Kingstonian* said that Roy outlined that "...when he began coaching, most of his material was young and some of it inexperienced. Last year, he says, they learned to absorb completely the 'elementary principles' and their experience of success against good teams this season has prepared them for the polish which he believes will come next season." Roy told him that "Mistakes that happen now do so because of inexperience ... next year they will not happen."

Roy also believed that some of the players would go on to win individual honours. He also commented on the success of the Hull pack: "I have known light packs before, but never one as successful as this. Are we going to sacrifice speed and mobility in the loose for weight in the pack? If we do that, we are only throwing an extra burden onto the backs." He also felt that the new play-the-ball rule would not lessen the Hull pack's effectiveness. He concluded by saying that "Hull have formed an attacking style in the loose, and the same methods will succeed next year."

Hull's interest in the Challenge Cup did not last beyond the first round. An 8–6 home win against Oldham in the first leg was followed by a 24–0 defeat at Watersheddings. In March, the team's form dropped for a couple of games, defeats at Batley and at home to Dewsbury. Roy was still prominent; at Batley, the *Mail* said that "Francis tried desperately to engineer a late penetration and his men frantically responded." The report added "Francis was as sinuous and subtle as ever." Against Dewsbury, "Francis ... was wily, eager and determined, urging his men to new endeavours which brought little reward and not a try."

The team turned the corner with a win at Castleford. *Kingstonian* wrote: "This tonic win will do much to restore Hull's confidence after the recent decline, but the Airlie Birds – who too often allowed Castleford to keep them down to an inferior level – are not yet back on their midwinter form. Francis, now living in Hull, intends to bring a new intensity to his coaching at The Boulevard."

The next week saw Hull complete the double over St Helens, having won at Knowsley Road earlier in the season. Roy "touched down again among a frantic pile of players to set the seal on the game."

Overall, in the league Hull finished in third place, with 26 wins and a draw from their 36 matches. It was their best league finish in peacetime since 1936, when they finished top of the table. In the Championship semi-final, they travelled to Central Park to play Wigan, and lost 13–9.

Hull were in the game until the 65th minute and were on top in a close match. Then Wigan's centre Ashcroft set up Brian Nordgren to "steak away for a wonder try" according to the *Mail*. Ryan converted to make the score 10–9 to Wigan. Near the end, Ashcroft set up Nordgren again to complete his hat-trick and make the game safe at 13–9. The *Mail* concluded that "... Hull's performance was a revelation of spirit, skill and speed, their young forwards inspiring the backs to an effort which caused many Wigan supporters to say 'The best team lost.' It was a defeat to which the word glorious can be applied without a blush, and it set the seal on a season of startling success."

It was notable that some of the younger players who had been pressing for places were now regulars. Colin Hutton, Johnny Whiteley, Mick Scott and Jim Drake were all important parts of the side. The future looked bright.

9. Hull 1952 to 1955

As with the previous campaign, Roy started Hull's pre-season training for the 1952–53 season six weeks before the first match. In the *Mail*, the sports gossip column reported that around 25 regular players and some local youngsters were at the session. The reporter said that in the previous season the team had got off to a flying start and Roy hoped to achieve the same result again. He said that "Roy spent several hours over the programme, which was designed to give the players 'a good sweat' with lots of loosening up. He also took the chance of having a 'man to man' talk with his boys."

The Hull FC Annual General Meeting took place at the end of July. The report in the *Mail* said that with success on the field and a profit of £1,636, there was little to talk about.

With a sub-head of 'Praise for Francis', the club chairman, Mr Hardaker, said that "they had finished up a little better than for a long time both from financial and League points of view." He recalled that the previous year he had told the meeting that they had decided to experiment with Roy as club coach. He continued "You all know what the experiment has proved and I am happy to say that we have entered into a reasonably permanent arrangement with Roy for a number of years." He continued: "I must say that most of our success has been due to the way he has put forward the wishes of the board with the material the board found for him. He has worked very hard and there is no doubt that it has paid reasonable dividends." Another shareholder referred to the harmony between the board and the players.

However, Hull could not maintain the consistency they had shown the previous season, and slipped to 15th in the Northern Rugby League table, with 36 points from their 36 matches. Mike Ulyatt says that "Hull were very unlucky with injuries" during the season. This certainly affected Roy, who played 20 games, scoring nine tries. He made 11 appearances at left-centre, three at right-centre, three on the left wing, two on the right and one at full-back, a new experience for him. He was out after an operation from mid-September to early November, and again from Christmas to mid-February.

Early in the season, Hull faced Leeds over two legs in the first round of the Yorkshire Cup. Hull lost the first leg at home by a point, but then won 10–2 at Headingley. The *Mail* reported that "... at last Francis got possession in the 71st minute and set off on a powerful run. Hemmed in by defenders, he looked round for support and held on with shrewd skill until Turner came racing up on his flank. Roy's pass to the right centre was faultless and Turner took the chance with both hands, eluding three men and finishing over the line with a flying leap."

However, a few days later, Roy had an emergency operation for appendicitis. The *Mail* said that "Roy is making good progress but is likely to be out of the game for several weeks." Colin Hutton led the side in Roy's absence. On 22 September, Hull lost 29–9 at home to Huddersfield in the Yorkshire Cup. Roy came out of the nursing home where he was convalescing to watch the match. Carl Turner played in Roy's place while he was out.

In early October, Roy was well enough to attend a forum with the captains of Hull KR – Bryn Knowelden; Neil Franklin of Hull City FC and Hull Cricket Club's Cliff Dickinson. In response to a question about whether the football season was too long, Roy commented that "At my age, the season is too long – and so is the pitch." More seriously, he agreed with Bryn Knowelden that the season was not too long. Neil Franklin expressed concern about the strain on players with extra games if floodlights were installed. Another question was about standards 20 years ago and those today. This led to a comparison of 'old' and 'new' styles of football. Roy said that "modern football was faster, but he did not think individual skill was so apparent, but both he and Knowelden agreed that there was now a more analytical type of football than 20 years ago."

On touch judges, both rugby league representatives thought that "the touch judge played too prominent a part and dealt with too trivial offences."

In another question, the panel were asked recall their most thrilling experience in sport. Roy said that his "most thrilling experience came every Saturday when his health allowed him to play football." All the other panel members recalled a particular match. Bryn Knowelden spoke about a Challenge Cup Final at Wembley; Cliff Dickinson, from Hull Cricket club, said their 1947 Cup Final win when he scored 74 not out; Neil Franklin recalled that in 1947 he played in an England win against Italy in Turin. Roy could have mentioned playing for Great Britain, or for Wales, or even his rugby union matches in the War for England. It is a strange answer, maybe given off the cuff, or maybe reflects the enjoyment, at the age of 33, that he still got from playing rugby league.

In early November, *Marksman* in the 'sports gossip' column reported that Roy had recovered in "quick time" from his operation and had been able to return to his coaching duties. His work with the team on tactics "has continued right up to games starting, as well as during the intervals. Despite this vigorous application of his knowledge and experience, he has itched to be back on the field."

He returned to action against Wakefield on 8 November, and did what "he could to put life into the Hull attack. A couple of weeks later, against Doncaster, there were some "old time dashes by Francis". In preparation for the home match with Leeds, he organised intensive indoor training in a frosty period.

Roy scored Hull's only try in a home derby defeat to Rovers on Christmas Day. The *Mail* said that it was "Hull's brightest spot. Francis dashed up at speed, kicked with beautiful judgement to the in-goal area and crowned the effort with a flying leap."

However, after his return to action had lasted seven games, Roy sustained a torn stomach muscle that kept him out of action until mid-February. This included missing a rare visit by Wigan to the Boulevard on 3 January 1953. The *Mail* commented that Hull were keyed up for the visit of Wigan – the first since 1941: "Roy Francis, Hull's captain-coach, spent many happy years at Wigan, and married a Wigan girl, so both he and his wife are anticipating the meeting with old friends. Both their sons, who are now regular Boulevarders, know Wigan well and are hoping that their new favourites will defeat their old ... Francis is still nursing a stomach injury sustained in the Hunslet match, but is straining every nerve to get fit for Saturday."

In fact, it took Roy some weeks to get over the injury. At the end of January, the club had to deny that he was retiring from playing. The *Mail* said that: "Roy Francis, Hull FC captain-coach, is not retiring and hopes soon to return to the game. This news was given to

70

the *Hull Daily Mail* today by the club chairman (Mr E Hardaker) and by Francis himself, and dispels rumours which have been circulating that pressure of business would force Francis to stop playing. The truth is that Francis tore a stomach muscle at Hunslet on Boxing Day and has not played since. Now he has seen a Hull specialist who has ordered a period of massage and diathermy, at the end of which Francis hopes to return to the side."

Hull drew Whitehaven in the Challenge Cup. Leading up to the first leg, in Cumberland, the *Mail* said that "Much will depend on strategy and in this respect Roy Francis, Hull's captain-coach, who is temporarily out of action with a torn muscle, can play a decisive part in pre-match training."

The day before the match, the paper said that: "Much will depend on what strategy has been worked out in pre-match training and talks, much also on their forwards who are among the best in the land and are greatly strengthened in aggressive power by the return of [Jim] Drake."

Hull lost the first leg 13–6, but recovered to win the second 14–5, going through by just two points on aggregate. The second round draw saw them travel to Central Park. The directors chose Roy to play at full-back at Batley the week before the Wigan game to ease him back into action. Ernest Hardaker told the paper: "We do not think it wise for Roy to go straight into the cup tie after a long absence and a complicated injury. Playing full-back at Batley he will be able to start off on an easy note. It may be that after 10 minutes or so he will feel able to move up into the centre."

Hull won at Batley, and previewing the match at Wigan, the paper said "... in attack, a big burden rests on Roy Francis who is named at full-back, and Bernard Conway at off-half."

However, Roy was not fit to play: "Francis, who had been named at full-back and who might have crowned his career with a great display at Wigan, where he started his football, was considered unfit to play. Robbed of their ace-tactician and potential matchwinner..." Hull lost 18–10.

On 21 March, Roy was chosen for the 'A' team against Hunslet. There was no first team game, so he was given a run-out at centre. However, the *Mail* reported that: "Roy appeared at full-back, to run himself in gently, but had plenty to do against a lively side whose last try was one of the best I have seen at the Boulevard this year. It was obvious that Roy was not in top gear, but he did some clever and courageous things, and scored a try which proved he is still able to flash away and make the most of an opportunity." The next day the *Mail* reported that Roy hoped to go into full training at once.

He returned to action the next week, against Batley on the right-wing, after "training intensively". He scored a hat-trick of tries in a 38–15 home win. The *Mail* said that "It was good to see Francis flashing back into the scoring picture"

Roy played again two days later against Hunslet, which saw Hull's first league defeat since 17 Jan. Another memorable occasion was a 13–2 win over Rovers on Good Friday in the first rugby league match played at Hull City's Boothferry Park. It was Rovers' home game, and a massive 27,670 saw the game. Raymond Fletcher outlined that "The match was also a battle of wits and tactics between the two player-coaches, Hull centre Roy Francis and Rovers stand-off Bryn Knowelden. Both were former Warrington and Great Britain players then in their veteran stage..." Fletcher included the game in his collection of Hull's *Fifty of the finest matches*. Of the 50 chosen, 16 were in the period 1953 to 1960, seven of the 14 years (in two spells) when Roy was coaching the team. That is almost a third of the selected games in a book published in 2003.

Against Halifax in April, there were "some flashing Francis touches" and Roy scored his last try of the season. How much Roy's two long periods of absence from the first team was a major reason for their decline from the previous campaign is hard to say. The team-sheets for the season do show regular changes. Apart from the inevitable injuries, teams at this time had to contend with players being on national service. If they were posted in England, they could often get weekend leave to play.

A positive sign this season was more Hull players winning individual county and international honours, showing how the players were developing under Roy's influence. The challenge Roy faced now was to continue to improve the performances of the Hull team and start to win some trophies.

1953–54

The 1953–54 campaign saw Hull recover their form in the Northern Rugby League. They finished fifth, just outside the play-off places. They won 25 of their 36 matches, but were eight points behind Workington, who finished in the crucial fourth place.

Roy only made 12 appearances this season, all at centre. Keith Bowman had been recruited from Hunslet, and was ever present on the right wing. Ivor Watts was the regular left-winger. At centre, Bill Riches, who had been born in Hull, had been signed from Batley, was the regular on the right, with Carl Turner on the left. Ten of Roy's appearances were on the left, with the other two on the right. He did score 11 tries, but had become 35 in January 1954 and maybe was concentrating more on coaching than playing.

In the pack, Jim Drake was again available after completing his two years national service. This was another problem facing clubs in the 1950s – unless they were in a reserved occupation, young players could become unavailable for two years due to national service. Some would have postings that made them available to play, others were overseas. As they were in the Armed Forces, where rugby league was not a recognised sport, they were allowed to play rugby union. This applied to both amateur and professional players. Some professionals even played representative rugby union at the top level in the Forces. It must have been very frustrating for the rugby league clubs when the Armed Forces rugby union officials wanted their players for weekend fixtures, meaning they could not play for their league teams.

Once again, Roy began the team's pre-season training in mid-July. The *Mail* outlined that: "Training started with physical jerks in the approved style with 'Sergeant Major' Francis in good voice. Then came some walking rugby and finally lively football, with some good runs. Intensive training starts on Thursday night. In October indoor training starts at Madeley Street Baths."

A couple of days before the season opened, the directors confirmed that Roy would continue to captain the side. However, he would become 35 years old in January 1954, and his future as a player must have been in doubt.

1953 Hull team. (Courtesy *Rugby League Journal*)

Roy before at match at Dewsbury in the early 1950s. (Courtesy *Rugby League Journal*)

Hull opened the season with a 23–14 win at the Boulevard over Leeds. *Kingstonian* commented that "Especially gratifying for the big crowd was the form and fitness of Francis, who got two tries and made another...". He was reported to be nursing an injury after the match, but recovered enough to play against Belle Vue. Hull won again, and *Kingstonian* said that the "... best features for Hull in an undistinguished match were the skill of Francis, who made three tries..."

However, at the beginning of September, the *Mail* reported that "Roy Francis ... has septic traces in his blood from various match scars and has been declared unfit for the time being by the club doctor." He did not play at Huddersfield, and his next appearance was against Halifax at the end of September. *Kingstonian* commented that "Francis flashed into the picture with a magnificent interception, but the ball was ruled back." But the next week, in a home defeat to Huddersfield, "Francis was crippled for most of the match ... Francis hobbling indeterminably in a middle position." He was injured for the next match at York, and was not back in full training until the week leading up to the Yorkshire Cup Final.

It was a highlight of the first half of the season in reaching the Yorkshire Cup Final. It was the club's first appearance since the 1946–47 season. To get there, they beat Bramley twice over two legs, then beat Halifax 16–4 at the Boulevard. In the semi-final, they were 3–2 ahead at Hunslet when the game was abandoned after 32 minutes. When the match was restaged the next day, Hull won 9–5.

A crowd of 22,147 saw Hull face Bradford Northern in the Final at Headingley. Roy did not play, and the *Mail* said that "Hull, without Francis, lacked the ideas to penetrate a tough defence. Bradford were 7–0 up at half-time, through a try and two goals. Colin Hutton kicked a goal in the second half, but it was not enough to prevent the trophy going to Odsal.

The result was an improvement on the previous week, a 40–8 defeat in the League at Odsal. By a quirk of the fixture list, Bradford were the visitors to the Boulevard the week after the final. The club's programme notes reflected on the contributions of Northern's player-coach Trevor Foster, and their loose-forward Ken Traill. The article concluded "Perhaps had our own player-coach (Roy Francis) been able to take the field there may have been another tale to tell ... who knows." In fact, the only Yorkshire Cup match Roy had played in was the second round win against Halifax.

The week after the Yorkshire Cup Final, the players "and their ladies" were invited to an 'informal' dinner by the directors before the club's annual dance. According to the *Mail*'s report, Ernest Hardaker said that "they were not broken-hearted at not having won the Yorkshire Cup. They considered that they had achieved something in reaching the final. I am disappointed; we are all disappointed but we have done something which has put rugby league football to the forefront in the city for the time being." He commented that it had been a long time since a rugby team leaving the city had been supported by the Lord Mayor of Hull. The report continued "Mr Roy Francis, Hull's coach, on behalf of the players and staff and ladies thanked the chairman and directors for the wonderful meal and company." The Lord mayor was also present and congratulated the players, saying that the match had "put Hull on the map".

With Roy having not played since the end of September, in early December the club had to deny that he had retired. *Kingstonian* reported that "A rumour that Roy Francis ... has retired from playing or is contemplating retirement is contradicted by Mr Ernest Hardaker ... today. 'Roy is participating in full-range training and satisfactory results are expected shortly,' said Mr Hardaker. 'He certainly is not contemplating retirement.'" The report pointed out that "Despite his spells of unfitness, he has continued to serve as Hull's coach and regularly travels with the team, as well as being 'on the bench' at home games."

Roy marked his return to action, against Featherstone at the Boulevard on 12 December with a try. *Kingstonian* commented that Roy was "...reintroduced ... at left-centre after missing 10 games. Francis, of course, did not let the side down and he scored a first half try, but he did not look thoroughly match fit and will no doubt need a little more time to run himself in." He missed the next match at Dewsbury, but returned for the Christmas Day derby at the Boulevard with spectacular results. It must have been a dismal Christmas for the red-and-white half of the city as Hull won 32–2. It was – at the time – the second biggest victory for Hull over Rovers. *The Mail's* report's headline was "Thrashing for Robins in Boulevard derby". *Kingstonian* said that Roy "... earned the crowd's acclaim for his unselfish service to Ivor Watts to whom he gave two tries when he might have gone over himself."

On Boxing Day, Hull were again at home, this time to Hunslet. Roy's contribution was four tries. However, he was injured during the game and finished the match 'hobbling' on the left wing. This did not stop him scoring his final try.

Roy did not play again until the end of March. On 8 January 1954, Ernest Hardaker told the *Mail* that "specialist opinion is to be sought on the injury to Roy Francis's leg, hurt against Hunslet on Boxing Day. Meanwhile, Francis is maintaining his active coaching routine." With 56 points being scored in the first two matches in January, Hull had scored 128 points in four games, admittedly all at the Boulevard. At the end of January, they beat Warrington 24–10, ending the league leader's run of 14 wins.

Although not available to play, Roy was able to take part in another sporting forum. He said that his 'dearest wish' was that rugby union and 'professional' rugby could combine to give some competition to football. He wanted to see England have three national games: rugby, soccer and cricket. An audience member said that he thought that there was much similarity between the two rugby codes. The report of the event in the *Mail* said that "Roy said that there was, in fact, little to choose between the games. He agreed that both could be very good and both very bad, but rugby union was certainly better now than before 1939. During the War various rugby league players were allowed to play rugby union – Mr Francis suggested that special notice should be taken of the word 'allowed'.

Among them were: Ernest Ward, Jim Lawrenson, Jim Stott, Gus Risman, Edwards, Trevor Foster, Ike Owens and himself. In these games this group brought into rugby union the planned movements and subtleties that had been developed in rugby league. Today it is possible to see, as in the Wales – All Blacks game, a lot of rugby league moves coming into evidence in the rugby union game. They were not there before 1939, but rugby union eyes at Murrayfield, Twickenham and Cardiff had watched and learned tactics of the best rugby league game and had bettered their game by it.

I cannot say that we in rugby league have benefitted from rugby union. The wish dearest to me   is that they would combine in some form and give some colourful competition to soccer. Then we would have three national games. It could be done, but not as long as there are 'blimps' in both codes.'"

In a discussion on consistency and success, Roy said that "success ran in cycles, regardless of effort. For a time, a team would click and then slump. It came to everyone over a period." Eventually, this reflected his experience at Hull FC, but it is surprising that he seemed to be accepting that teams could not be consistently successful. However, he was still a relatively inexperienced coach, and of course did not control either team selection or recruitment of players. His comments about the two rugby codes are still relevant today, although one rugby code is as far away as ever; and soccer is even more dominant.

At the beginning of February, the *Mail* said that "Roy Francis is being given specialist treatment for a groin injury [and is] to go into a Leeds nursing home for a short time. Ernest Hardaker said: 'Roy has some restricted movement in the area of the muscle and the specialist's recommendation is that he should have manipulative treatment under anaesthetic.'" He was expected to be in the home for a day or two.

Roy's team were showing that they could win in his absence. Until a 5–5 draw with Workington in the Challenge Cup, Hull won 11 consecutive games, including both legs of the Challenge Cup first round against Widnes.

Kingstonian said that after Hull's draw with Workington, "Roy Francis was disconsolate when I saw him in the dressing room after the game. 'It seemed that no answer could be found to Workington's obvious close game, but there were answers to be found." About the replay, Francis was hopeful: I think we can counter anything they can do at Workington.' 'Maybe you'll be blessed with a harder surface" I ventured. 'Please' he said 'Don't dwell on the mud. We should be able to play football on the heavy stuff as well as the fast grounds.'"

Hull travelled to Keswick the day before the replay, 16 players, Roy and club officials making the trip. Hull lost narrowly, 17–14. *Kingstonian* commented that: "They have learned many lessons from last week's disappointment and Roy Francis, their coach, had an intensive session with them at the Boulevard yesterday afternoon. Particular attention has been paid to variation of tactics and the vital importance of 100 per cent backing up."

Roy marked his return to action with three tries against Dewsbury on 27 March. In a report headed 'Brilliant Francis of old' he wrote that "After the match, tired but happy Roy Francis said after Hull's win 'I always knew that if I could find my fitness again, I could recapture my old form. I have no intention of retiring, and I feel that, given reasonable luck, I have at least another couple of seasons in me.' He added with a smile 'There's always the full-back position.' … Roy reminded me that since joining Hull he has had two operations and five serious injuries. He has long been troubled with a groin which has defied analysis, and his match fitness has been entirely unpredictable. Indeed, it was not known until just before the kick-off that he was playing against Dewsbury. At once he showed his old subtle touches and flashes of pace, as well as shrewd positioning and timing. He played his part in defence, and Taylor, the Dewsbury right-centre, had an unhappy time until he scored Dewsbury's only try three minutes from the end."

Roy played in four more games before the end of the season, scoring in the last one at Hunslet. He could reflect on a campaign that saw Hull in their first cup final since 1946. He had a young team that were gaining experience, and even if he was not retiring from playing, he could see that the players were learning to play without him.

One issue that always faced Hull was signing players from outside the city. It was not uncommon in those days for players to only have to attend training once a week if they lived a considerable distance from their club. Often, they could do fitness training at a local club. Maurice Bamford, in his autobiography, recalls joining Hull in October 1953 as a young player. He did not have a car, and was mainly playing in the 'A' team. He had to leave work at 12 midday, losing half a day's pay, to travel to Hull, do two hours training and then dash to the station for the long journey home, arriving home just after midnight. He does recall Roy advising him to concentrate on running, and not cycle, swim, or do weight training. This was before weight training had developed for rugby league players. He also says that Roy was "by far the best coach of his day." With little prospect of breaking into the first team, Bamford moved on to Dewsbury after a couple of years at Hull.

1954–55

Once again, the club's league performances were plagued by erratic performances. Roy must have been disappointed that instead of kicking on from fifth place to win a play-off spot, the team ended up 19th in the Northern Rugby League. Michael Ulyatt says that the team was "inconsistent" and that while they had some big victories, four teams did the double over them, including lowly Bramley.

Roy played more matches for Hull this season. He made 16 appearances at left-centre, and six at right-centre, scoring nine tries from his 22 games.

The highlight of the season was again the Yorkshire Cup. Hull beat Featherstone 18–4 in the first round. *Kingstonian*'s report was headlined 'Francis inspired Hull's revival'. It started: "What a vast difference Roy Francis made to Hull RFC on Saturday. It would be ridiculous to say that he was entirely responsible for their fine … win over Featherstone, but his captaincy and generalship were ever evident and he certainly brought the best out of the Airlie Birds in the second half."

Roy missed the league match at Workington; the *Mail* reported: "Hull FC … may be strengthened by the return of Roy Francis, who missed last Saturday's game at Workington. The inclusion of Francis would considerably strengthen the side, as the Hull player-coach is an inspiration in both playing and captaincy." Hull drew 7–7 at Fartown against Huddersfield. The *Mail* said that "Roy Francis reappeared at left centre and the team once again seem rejuvenated." The report added: "… a quick piece of thinking by Francis and Watts led to the latter getting the Airlie Birds on terms … Francis battered his way through three Huddersfield players and dribbled to within 20 yards of the line before accurately kicking the ball inside for the astute Cumberland winger to run on to and ground."

Hull won the replay a couple of days later 22–13. The *Mail's* preview had commented that "With Roy Francis at the helm, Hull should forge ahead into the semi-final. There, they got revenge for the previous season's defeat in the Final against Bradford. Hull won 10–5 to reach the Final. Again, the *Mail* stressed how important Roy was to the team: "With Francis in the centre to hold them together, Hull should have a decided advantage."

Roy and Hull FC players and officials leaving a station in the 1954–55 season. (Courtesy Robert Gate)

After a home win against Huddersfield in October, *Kingstonian* wrote that "Behind the Hull win, however, was to be seen the scheming and skill of Francis, who was the architect in chief of this great victory. His influence on the Hull players is remarkable and his keen footballing brain never seems to lack ideas."

On 21 October, in the lead-up to the final, Roy "had all the players out ... and really put them through their paces. The *Mail* said that "Afterwards he said that he was very pleased and thought that they were going to be in grand shape."

The final was again staged at Headingley, and a 25,949 crowd saw Hull face Halifax. Roy played at left-centre. It was his last final as a player. Sadly, it was another cup final defeat. Apparently, many Hull fans were disappointed because they felt that their team had missed chances to win the game. Hull were also unlucky with injuries. Keith Bowman went off injured in the second half, and at one point Hull were down to 10 fit players, with Johnny Whiteley and Tommy Harris both injured.

This was the first in a series of clashes between the two teams in the 1950s. Raymond Fletcher noted that "If this match did not reach the bitterness of the Yorkshire Cup Final replay a year later, it was tough enough and played with an intensity that kept the 25,949 [fans] absorbed throughout. Hull's young pack was still emerging as the force that would be such a power in the latter half of the decade and Halifax must take some of the credit for making them battle-hardened for what lay ahead. He also points out that Halifax had very experienced backs and half-backs, although Hull "...had the benefit of player-coach Roy Francis's vast experience..."

Hutton put Hull ahead with a penalty, but that lead was wiped out by a penalty from Griffiths. Hutton then lost the ball in a tackle after fielding a high kick; Ackerley scored and Griffiths converted. Another Hutton penalty saw Halifax 7–4 ahead at the break.

Daniels scored a converted try to make the score 12–4, but a try from Conway for Hull and a further penalty by Hutton made it 12–9. However, after Bowman went off injured, two converted tries made the score 22–9. Hull scored through Markham, who had moved to the wing to cover for Bowman. Hutton converted, but the score remained at 22–14.

1954–55 Yorkshire Cup Final. Roy about to be tackled by Daniels. Bowman (5) is supporting Roy.
(Courtesy Robert Gate)

Kingstonian commented that "Hull lost the Yorkshire Cup at Headingley because they had no answer to the fiery tackling and keen spotting [marking] of Halifax, who gave the lighter Airlie Birds forwards little opportunity of using their speed." *Kingstonian* also said, maybe diplomatically, that the Halifax tackling in the closing stages was "unnecessarily robust". Roy had a chance to score when he was clean through in the second half after "a brilliant short kick" but he failed to gather the ball. Hull did get some revenge when they knocked Halifax out of the Challenge Cup.

Four days after the final, *Kingstonian* reflected tha the price Hull had to pay for the Yorkshire Cup Final appearance was a high one: "Bowman will be out of the game for several weeks with a severely smashed face … Harris will probably be out also with badly torn stomach tissues and kidney trouble. Whiteley's head injury has improved." Whiteley and Bob Coverdale were unavailable for three weeks anyway as they were in France with Great Britain playing in the inaugural World Cup."

His report also carried the shock news that Roy had announced his retirement as a player: "At last night's meeting of the board of directors, Francis's retirement was discussed and noted with regret, said the chairman, Mr E Hardaker, today. 'There is, of course, no individual grievance', he said. 'It's purely his own decision and for that reason the matter has been left in abeyance.'"

Roy did, of course, continue to coach the side, and on 8 December, *Kingstonian* reported that Roy was making a comeback and would be in the Hull side to face Leeds at Headingley three days later. He said that Roy had been unable to be fully match fit because of an Achilles tendon problem, but had now had specialist treatment and was able to 'offer his services to the club' again as a player. *Kingstonian* said that this would be just the 'tonic' the players needed. He continued: "Undoubtedly the return of Francis will have a great effect on the team. He has felt their recent failures very keenly indeed. A lot may depend on how his troublesome leg reacts in this important game on how often he plays in the future."

Kingstonian's match preview said that "Francis should make a vast difference in the back division, and his direction of the game is generally impeccable. Few players can spot an opening so quickly, and if the Hull players back up well, some entertaining football is assured." Hull lost 15–5 at Headingley, with Roy scoring their try. *Kingstonian* said that "Making his comeback, Roy Francis was the pick of the Hull side. Looking much fitter and considerably lighter, he created several openings which could have turned the balance of the game if he had received the backing-up he deserved." Roy's try was made by Carl Turner, and Roy "backed up well and left the Leeds threes standing in a 20-yard dash for the line."

Roy played fairly regularly for the rest of the season, showing that his decision not to 'retire' had been correct. At Keighley in early January, the *Mail* commented that: "Three tries should have been scored by the Airlie Birds on the resumption as Francis and Drake worked openings on the wings. Each time, however, a pass was thrown wildly, delayed too long or just missed altogether." Despite a 5–0 defeat, the report said that "Francis, Markham, Finn and Hutton played great games."

At Huddersfield on the last Saturday of January, after two weeks of postponements due to snow, *Kingstonian* expected that "...the scheming of Francis in the Hull centre should prove a weighty asset in the Airlie Birds' favour..." The match report said that Hull "could not finish off the good work of Francis, Bowman or Watts..." It concluded that "Bowman and Francis starred for Hull."

The Challenge Cup now had only one match in the first round, the two-legged ties were abolished. Hull made more progress than for some years. They won 16–8 at Swinton in the first round, beat Halifax 4–0 in the second at home, but then lost 7–6 to Hunslet in the third.

In early February, the *Mail* reported that "Hull have resumed their normal, daylight training scheme, and next week will go through a specially prepared itinerary the aim of which will be to see that 13 fit men take the field at Swinton." The next day, with the Swinton match still a week away, it said that Hull had daylight training yesterday and "will continue with indoor and outdoor sessions next week to prepare for the forthcoming cup tie."

The week before the win at Swinton, Roy scored twice in a comfortable win against Batley. The Halifax match preview said Francis and Riches were in top form at centre. The day before the game, *Kingstonian* wrote that "In the centre Halifax have no one to match Francis, who is not likely to miss a bouncing ball on the try line as he did at Headingley. Francis felt that miss very deeply. It was something he was not used to but he has certainly not shown the slightest indication of repeating it since then." Hull won 4–0, mainly due to the pack's strength. In the narrow defeat to Hunslet, Roy narrowly missed touching down from a kick through. However, Hull's Wembley hopes would have to wait for another year.

On 2 April, Roy had to leave the pitch after 12 minutes due to a badly cut mouth. He came back 15 days later to score a hat-trick in a comfortable win at Oldham. However, he was injured at Featherstone a week later, and missed the last three matches.

Left: Touching down for Hull. Right: Explaining a point to three players
(Both courtesy Geoff Francis)

Straw bales were used to stop the pitch becoming frozen in cold weather. They also provided a
comfortable place for a team meeting. (Courtesy Geoff Francis)

Top: Looking to pass the ball. Bottom: Before some big matches, Roy took the team to Blackpool to prepare for the game. (Both courtesy Geoff Francis)

Hull chairman Ernest Hardaker (on left) makes a point to Roy. (Courtesy Geoff Francis)

Celebrating winning the Championship with the Lord Mayor of Hull.
(Courtesy Geoff Francis)

Explaining a point in training. (Courtesy Geoff Francis)

At the Hull Guildhall after the 1956 Championship Final. (Courtesy Geoff Francis)

10. Hull 1955 to 1958

Roy was now aged 36, and was starting his fifth season, 1955–56, as player-coach. He played in the first two fixtures. The first was lost 45–26 at Wakefield, a remarkable score for the time. Things settled down with a 13–7 win against Halifax two days later. Roy left the field with a hand injury and spent the night in Hull Royal Infirmary with a compound fracture of the index finger of his right hand. He had set up the first try.

The highlight of the first half of the season was again the Yorkshire Cup. Hull won comfortably at Batley and then more narrowly against Featherstone at the Boulevard to reach the semi-finals. There they had another home draw and beat Bradford Northern 23–16.

Once again, they faced Halifax in the Final at Headingley. This match, along with the 1954 Final, features in Raymond Fletcher's collection of *Hull's 50 Finest Matches*. He quotes the *Daily Mail's* Derek Marshall on the encounter: "For sustained suspense I have seen only one game to equal Saturday's Yorkshire Cup Final; for the savage pace and spirit in which it was fought it stands alone. Here was rugby stripped of finesse and dignity. Here was a match which excited and repelled." Fletcher was present at the game as a 15-year-old supporter. He recalled: "I was both shocked and thrilled by it all. To say the match was a typical cup-tie would be to call the First World War a skirmish. Yet it was also full of brilliant back play with Hull rallying magnificently from being 10–0 down to equalise with tries from wingers Ivor Watts and Keith Bowman."

A 23,520 crowd saw Halifax establish an early lead, being 8–0 up after 13 minutes. Griffiths then added a penalty to make the score 10–0. Watts scored from a grubber kick so the half-time score was 10–3. Fletcher says that "Following coach Roy Francis's interval pep talk the second half saw Hull's forwards take greater control." The last 25 minutes saw the main incidents that gave the match notoriety. Halifax's Henderson was sent off for laying out Johnny Whiteley. A scrum erupted and Hull's Bob Coverdale was left clutching his face. From the reformed scrum, Halifax's Jack Wilkinson received a cut that required four stitches.

Following two successful penalties from full-back John Watkinson, who was playing because Colin Hutton was injured, Bowman scored the equalising try with 10 minutes left. Watkinson missed the touchline conversion and saw a last-minute drop-goal attempt go narrowly wide.

The game was followed by an enquiry into the mayhem in the second half, but there were no specific conclusions reached. A statement by the Yorkshire Rugby League blamed both clubs, which was disputed by Hull's chairman, Ernest Hardaker.

The reply took place on 2 November at Odsal. Roy told the *Mail* that he "thought Hull had a 50-50 chance. He was afraid that the hullabaloo that was raised after the Headingley final would affect the game. 'The team who settles down quickest look like being the winners.'"

A 14,000 crowd saw Halifax win 7–0. Hull missed four penalties. Hull's – and Roy's – hunt for the Yorkshire Cup would continue.

Roy then had a run of four games in November. The *Mail* reported that "Roy Francis has been building himself up to peak fitness and his experience and trickery should enliven the threequarter line. At Castleford, Roy played with his fingers strapped up, and scored twice in a comfortable win. The next week, Hull made a rare trip to Blackpool for a league match. The *Mail*'s preview said that: "Roy Francis will again be leading the backs, and if they can be served as well as they were last Saturday, they should have another free style day." On the day, Blackpool went ahead, but Roy rallied his players to achieve a narrow win. Roy's contribution was "A glorious try by Francis, who intercepted inside his own half and outpaced the Blackpool backs in a 70-yard dash over by the posts." It was to be his last try in professional rugby league.

The next week, Barrow came to the Boulevard. The *Mail* said that "It will be interesting to see how RF fares against his old club. He was a Barrow man at the peak of his career and should know their style of play well." It was seven years since he had left Barrow. The paper said that he "can be a power for the Boulevarders."

However, the match was lost, and Roy was dropped by the directors – who still picked the team – after a 14–6 defeat at Odsal. Brian Cooper replaced him, and Roy's 19-year career as a rugby league player was over. However, from a coaching standpoint, the best was yet to come.

One change during the season was that floodlights were installed on the east stand which meant that training could take place outside on the pitch instead of indoors. The *Mail* commented after the Barrow defeat that there could be special tactical training at the Boulevard by Roy Francis and the board. They consider that real tactical training cannot be given at the indoor baths – the usual training venue during the winter. It is difficult to work out new moves within the confined area available at the baths. The club had a practice match which was stopped at various points so Francis could explain points to the players. A decision about whether the club will adopt this style of training during the dark evenings had not been made yet.

In December, Hull played seven matches, and won six of them. Their good form continued into the new year. Against Bradford Northern on New Year's Eve, they showed "... real championship form ... a team win ... hard fast entertaining football" according to *Kingstonian*. A few days later, the *Mail* said that Hull were "Steadily climbing the league table... the pack are in grand form." At York, they played a "remarkably high standard of football considering the shocking conditions..." The paper also wrote about the "greatly improved back division".

Against Keighley, "The Boulevarders fully deserved their victory, being the more accurate handlers of the greasy ball and moving into position faster than their opponents ...". However, at the end of January, at Halifax "Hull FC's top four hopes received a knock out blow at Thrum Hall when they were beaten by an almost perfect footballing machine." Halifax won 27–6.

In early February, Hull had special daylight training and tactical discussions to prepare for the Leeds Challenge Cup match. However, they lost at home to Leeds in the first round.

In the Northern Rugby League, the placings were decided on a percentage system. Belle Vue Rangers had withdrawn from the league just before the season started, and it was not possible to reorganise the fixtures. Twelve teams, all from Yorkshire, played 36 games, the rest 34.

It was a tight race to the end of the season. At York at the beginning of March, Hull's defence was airtight as they only conceded four points in a 12–4 win.

In March, the club welcomed back Keith Gittoes, who had played for Hull from 1948 to 1953. He was met at the station by Roy, who was still referred to as the club's player-coach. In fact, Gittoes only played a handful of games. The day after his arrival, Hull played 'brilliant football' to beat Leeds. The pack was completely superior to their Headingley rivals. At the end of March, Hull won the derby match despite Finn being sent off. Hancock was later sent off for Rovers.

Going into April, the *Mail* reported on the "tussle for fourth place." Hull needed to win at Barrow and then see how Barrow got on with five games left, including one against Hull. Featherstone and Wigan were also in the running.

Barrow had a Challenge Cup replay including extra time the day before they played Hull. The Boulevarders won 30-11 at Barrow. Only Featherstone could now challenge Hull for a top four place. On 17 April, the paper reported that Featherstone had been beaten by Leeds, so Hull would travel to Warrington in the play-offs semi-final.

The next day the *Mail* said that "Roy Francis, Hull's player-coach, lost no time in organising special training for the team once the club's top four position was assured and at this session the Boulevarders are seen getting down to play the ball practice in determined style." An action picture of the training session accompanied the report, which concluded "look out Warrington."

Hull had finished fourth, with a 70.83 per cent record. They were 3.19 per cent ahead of Wigan in fifth place. Warrington had finished top of the table, so Hull made the trip to Wilderspool for the semi-final. Warrington had won the Championship for the last two seasons, and the Challenge Cup in 1954.

The semi-final at Wilderspool is one of the club's greatest results, "a truly outstanding performance" according to the *Centenary Brochure*. It can also be seen as the result of five years' work by Roy in developing the Hull team. Raymond Fletcher commented that "...the match was to prove the breakthrough for a side that went on to be a major force for the next four years."

He said that "This was one of the greatest wins in Hull's long, proud history. It stunned the rest of the League. The result was unexpected enough, but the emphatic [17–0] scoreline was almost unbelievable. Warrington were the League leaders and aiming to win the Championship for the third successive season. They had not been beaten at home by a Yorkshire team for 17 years and included legendary players such as Brian Bevan, Gerry Helme and Harry Bath."

Hull played to their strength – the pack that were now more 'battel hardened' than a couple of years before. Harry Sunderland, the man who had transferred Roy from Wigan to Barrow 17 years before, was now working as a journalist. He outlined that "The secret of Hull's success was the splendid all-round work of one of the best set of forwards in the League. I have rarely seen a better performance than that given by the last three men down, Harry Markham, Bill Drake and Johnny Whiteley."

Warrington actually won the scrums 26–18. Despite this, Hull's pack dominated the game, supported by the backs. Brian Bevan scored 57 tries this season. Hull's Keith Bowman had scored 23, and Hull's right winger a mere three. Brian Darlington was only playing his third first team game.

Brian Cooper touched down after 20 minutes to put Hull ahead. Hutton converted. Hull were under tremendous pressure for the rest of the half, but went into the break having preserved their 5–0 lead. This continued in the second half. However, the turning point came with a run from second-rower Harry Markham, which ended close to the Warrington line. A Hutton penalty after 60 minutes made the score 7–0. The last 10 minutes saw Hull complete an incredible victory. First Bill Drake touched down after a pass from Mick Scott, and then Tommy Harris scored the third. Colin Hutton converted both tries. The score stunned the 20,148 fans, and earned the Hull players a £25 a man bonus. They left the field to the sound of Old Faithful being sung by their supporters.

Roy Francis explained the mobility shown by Hull's pack: "I train my forwards like backs … In fact, now and again in training, the backs pack down and the forwards line out." He was asked about the two late tries: "I don't believe in stringing out for an obvious cross-field passing movement. I tell my boys to line out in a sort of staggered formation so that when they receive the ball, they can go either way." Raymond Fletcher wryly commented that "Warrington did not know which way they went."

Roy had arranged for the players to travel to Blackpool on the Friday, and have a short training session on the Saturday morning at Blackpool's ground, so they were ready for Warrington.

Kingstonian commented: "On this performance, the Hull pack can more than play their bitter Thrum Hall rivals off their feet. It is extremely doubtful if there has ever been a better forward display than that of the Boulevarders in this game. He also quoted a Warrington fan who said "Hull were the more determined side throughout. I have never seen such a powerful, fast pack as this in 25 years of rugby league supporting."

In the other semi-final, Halifax beat St Helens 23–8. The next week, on 28 April, St Helens reversed the result in the Challenge Cup Final, winning 13–2. The Championship Final at Maine Road would be the fifth meeting between the two sides this season. Both teams had won their home league fixture, but Halifax had won the Yorkshire Cup Final replay.

No doubt the RFL officials hoped that there would be no repeat of the violent play that had marred the Yorkshire Cup Final. With two Yorkshire sides in the final, there were calls for the match to be switched to Headingley. However, the RFL stuck with Maine Road, although the attendance of 36,675 as the lowest of the 11 Championship finals played there. It was also the first Championship final to be televised. Regional broadcaster ABC paid £1,500 for the privilege, which may also have had some effect on the attendance.

Halifax were pre-match favourites, although there was very little to choose between the teams. They had had a two week break since their Challenge Cup Final defeat. The match was scheduled for 12 May. On 1 May, the *Mail* reported that there were not enough tickets for the Maine Rd Final. It was Hull's biggest match for 20 years

Four days before the big game, the *Mail* said that all Hull's players were at peak fitness. They had had a three week lay-off. There was to be special training this week, tactical discussions and work outs with player-coach Roy Francis. The team were to travel to Blackpool on Friday and loosen up at Blackpool Borough's ground on Saturday morning before travelling to Maine Road. It was exactly the same routine as for the Warrington match.

Most of players, with Roy, had gone to Wembley to watch Halifax lose to St Helens in the Challenge Cup Final.

Kingstonian also pointed out that if Hull won, it would only be the second time a fourth placed team had won the championship. The last was in 1922–23, when Hull KR pulled off this feat.

Three days before the final, it was reported that Hull had not gone ahead with a request that the Maine Road pitch be watered. According to the *Mail*, Ernest Hardaker discussed the matter with player-coach Roy Francis after the team's special training session. Roy was firmly of the opinion that a firm pitch and lively ball will be more to Hull's advantage than detriment. It will suit the Airlie-Birds' style of football and make things difficult for the Thrum-Hallers, who, however, may decide to press for the softening of the pitch themselves.

Quite a few spectators had turned up at the Boulevard to see Roy put the Hull team through their paces. General tactics and ways and means of breaking tight Halifax cover were concentrated on.

Hull's strength was in their pack. Graham Morris says that "Hull's mighty pack was generally able to dictate in a match full of incident." However, Raymond Fletcher outlined that "Hull coach Roy Francis was happy to let everybody, and particularly Halifax, believe his side would rely entirely on their formidable pack. He encouraged that belief by sending his forwards out to blast a way up the middle, but then they were to let the backs into the game. The plan worked as Hull's much maligned back division surprised the opposition with their enterprise and eager support play. Even the newly-formed half-back partnership of Carl Turner and Tommy Finn began to get the better of Halifax's inseparable Ken Dean and Stan Kielty."

Hull's first try came from Tommy Harris, set up by Bob Coverdale and Johnny Whiteley. Colin Hutton kicked the goal. He had previously missed with two penalties. Halifax had also missed a penalty. Hull kept their 5–0 lead until half-time. Just before the break, Brian Darlington was injured, and was little more than a passenger on the wing. Early in the second half, Tommy Finn scored in the corner to make the score 8–0. Hutton missed the conversion.

Then the match swung in Halifax's favour. Three unconverted tries gave them a 9–8 lead. With a couple of minutes left, Darlington, despite his injury, made a break. Halifax were caught offside, and Colin Hutton was given the chance by his captain, Mick Scott, to kick the goal from the touchline.

Hutton was successful with the kick, and said afterwards that it was the type of kick he had been practicing in training at Blackpool Borough's ground that morning. Raymond Fletcher said that it was the most memorable kick in Hull's history at that time. Halifax had no time to come back and Hull won their first Championship since 1936.

Kingstonian said that "The Boulevarders were thoroughly deserved winners of this pulsating, thrill-a-minute game, voted unanimously afterwards as the best final seen at Maine Road for many, many years." He concluded "The whole Hull team deserve praise for their efforts. They accomplished what Roy Francis asked them to do in a moving speech in the bus on the way to the ground – "Let's take back the Cup for the city of Hull. They want it very badly and deserve it.""

Hull FC 1956 team. (Courtesy Robert Gate)

Hull FC: 1956 Champions. (Courtesy *Rugby League Journal*)

Roy with the Championship Trophy in 1956. It was 20 years since Hull had last won it.
(Courtesy *Rugby League Journal*)

Back in Hull, the team was presented to the Lord Mayor & Mayoress of Hull by Roy Francis. The *Mail* said that "Holding the cup aloft, Francis was greeted with a terrific cheer. Roy Francis said the triumph was shared by many backroom people who would probably never be mentioned. He was glad the team had backed up his words of the end of last season, when he said Hull would win the league this season. He asked all to remember the other players who had, during the course of the season, played a big part in putting Hull on top, but who, through illness or changes, were not in the Manchester team."

The season was not quite finished. Roy invited St Helens, the Challenge Cup winners, to come to play a friendly at the Boulevard on 26 May. Hull won 28–20, and Roy had organised the game to raise funds for the joint testimonial of Ivor Watts and Arthur Bedford. *Kingstonian* said that "Roy Francis deserves all credit for organising it." The 13,000 crowd enjoyed a "thriller" and contributed around £1,100 to support two Hull stalwarts.

1956–57

The challenge now for Hull was to establish themselves as one of the top teams in the Northern Rugby League. The work Roy had done since 1951 was now really starting to pay dividends. Mike Ulyatt says that "An excellent team spirit ran through the whole club in 1956 [–57] and this was reflected on the field of play." Overall, Hull scored 930 points. The Northern Rugby League now had 38 matches, and Hull won 29 and drew two to finish second in the league table, six points behind Oldham.

Roy did not allow any complacency to develop. Before the final practice match, *Marksman* reported in the *Mail* that "Hull RL players might have shown some good form at the Boulevard on Saturday, but there was another old favourite who was in his most scintillating form in another sense. I refer to the club coach, Roy Francis, who from a strategic position at the top of the dressing room steps, delivered the most sizzling, hard-hitting pep talk before the practice game began, that I have heard from anyone for years. Dominating Roy knew what he wanted and it didn't take him long to make it clear that he is going to get just that.

He began by pointing out that on certain occasions last year there were one or two who played for the individual and that he didn't like at all. Play had to be for the team all the time the length and width of the field.

His policy, which he said had the full support of the board, was to have at least 18 players as first-teamers. Last season's senior successes, he pointed out, were obtained not by just 13 players, but by 23. He did not want deserving 'A'-teamers to have to wait for injuries in the first team to get their chance. They would be blooded if they merited it in suitable first team games. Francis concluded with a dire warning of the necessity for attention to training."

However, after a 26–5 defeat at Huddersfield in early September, the *Mail* said that "No doubt there has been some straight talking by coach Roy Francis this week, following Saturday's lethargic display and supporters will probably see a marked difference on Saturday." There was an immediate improvement with a 17–6 win over St Helens.

A couple of weeks later, Roy missed out on a trip to Wigan. The *Mail* reported that "Roy Francis, Hull FC's player-coach, will not see the Boulevarders in action against Wigan at Central Park this afternoon. He is assisting the 'A' team against Wakefield 'A' at the Boulevard as, due to injuries to first and second team men, no other players were available. Out of a register of 49, Hull only had 27 men available for today's two matches."

The Australians were in Great Britain on tour. Roy went to watch both teams train before the game, and wrote about the test match in the *Mail*. He also wrote for the Saturday *Sports Mail* special edition, and there were plans for him to speak at a forum with the famous footballer Stan Mortenson, who was playing for Hull City at the time. It was to be held at Roy's Beverley hotel, and the funds raised would go to the Mother Humber Fund. However, before the event could be organised, Mortensen joined Southport, returning to Lancashire where he had spent much of his career.

One controversy that Roy commented on at the end of November was the ban on the 'arm tackle' in the sport. There was uncertainty about what was an 'arm tackle'. *Marksman* wrote in the *Mail* that "any tackle in which the man with the ball is thrown to the ground by leverage of the arm must be considered foul play." Roy commented to the paper that "Until referees go into the dressing room on Saturday and explain what an arm tackle is, I am at a loss. Which tackle has been banned? Is it the short-arm, stiff arm or arm throw?".

At the end of January, the *Mail* reported that at the Hull FC annual dance, Ivor Watts and Arthur Bedford were presented with large cheques for long service. The report said: "The chairman paid tribute to all who had helped in raising the money for the two players who had given the Hull club the best possible service. He said much of the credit for the effort was due to player-coach Roy Francis."

Hull made little impact in the Cup competitions. In the Yorkshire Cup they lost 7–6 at home to Featherstone in the first round, having won at Post Office Road a couple of weeks earlier. In the Challenge Cup they beat Keighley before losing 9–3 at home to Halifax. Roy clearly took the Challenge Cup seriously. He had the Hull players in for special training and tactical discussions before the game, even though they had comfortably beaten Keighley in January.

The match with Halifax continued the fierce rivalry between the two sides. Just before the match, the *Mail* said that "[Hull] were a supreme fighting unit, fitter to a man than the Saints", after a 9–9 draw at St Helens. The paper's preview of the Halifax match said that "Hull's forwards are almost certain to more than hold their own with the Halifax set, if they follow the advice coach Roy Francis gave them yesterday. Hull worked out several intricate moves which are all designed to bring about the defeat of the Thurm Hallers. As Roy said, however, Halifax are playing a different a style of football this season, more open than they have done for a long time and they will not be easy to overcome."

The match itself saw Hull play with 12 men for most of the match. Sykes went off after a head high tackle by Jack Wilkinson. The score was 4–3 to Halifax with two minutes left, but they scored a further converted try to win 9–3.

One competition they did win was the European Championship. Hull and Halifax competed against Carcassonne and Albi. The league fixtures between the clubs counted in the competition. Hull won both games against Halifax, beat Carcassonne home and away, and had a win and a draw with Albi. The draw with Albi on 15 April was at The Boulevard. A last-minute drop goal from Mick Scott secured a 19–19 result for the home side. It was Hull's fifth game in 10 days. In these days, when most clubs did not have floodlights, fitting in extra fixtures was difficult and the competition was not run again. Roy had not been able to travel to France with the first team for their two matches in early November.

Raymond Fletcher recalls a 41–3 home win over York in March as "a near perfect exhibition of backs and forwards feeding off each other in devastating style." York was a mid-table team, but were taken apart with nine tries in the "dazzling" last hour of the game. *Kingstonian* in the *Mail* said that the display against York was "beautiful, thrilling, open football."

Two days before, Hull had ended Leeds's run of 18 victories with a 27–4 win at the Boulevard. The *Mail* said that "This Hull win was a team effort of the finest sort and speaks wonders for the work of coach Roy Francis during the week."

Hull's second place finish in the league table gave them a home match in the Championship semi-final. Many supporters were disappointed with the club's decision to play the match at Hull City's Boothferry Park. Apparently, the reason was that the pitch at the Boulevard was being reseeded. There was also disappointment at the 3pm kick off, which clashed with television coverage of the FA Cup Final. Despite this, 'only' 19,980 fans turned up to see Hull play Barrow.

Barrow were having a successful season, and the following week were due to play in the Challenge Cup Final for the second time in three years. Barrow had beaten Hull in their last meeting, but were taken apart in this game. Raymond Fletcher said that "Despite their wealth of outstanding players, Barrow were ripped apart by Hull's mighty pack well supported by an eager back division." The score was 16–0 to Hull at half-time, and the final result was 45–14. Roy had had a plan to stop Barrow's star half-back Willie Horne. In the end it was not really needed.

Going into the Championship Final, Hull were unbeaten since 16 March. Ten days before the Final, the directors showed their confidence in Roy's work with the team by giving him a new four-year contract. His contract had been due to run out in September 1957, and *Kingstonian* said that the new one was "a wise decision by the club, for Francis has undoubtedly been the man who has built the present team into one of the finest in the game." The report concluded "Francis is extremely popular with the players he has trained, and favourable comments on the peak fitness of the Hull players are often made at away grounds. That is a tribute to his keenness and skill in handling the men in his charge."

In the Final at Odsal, Hull faced Oldham, who had beaten fourth-placed Leeds in the other semi-final. There was a large crowd of 62,233 and record receipts of £12,054. Oldham were one of the top clubs in the latter half of the 1950s. The previous season Hull had won the Final by one point. This time, against Oldham, the Final was decided by the same margin, but not this time in Hull's favour. Graham Morris says that the match was "a titanic battle that, like the previous year, produced a cliff-hanger finish."

Hull had an early lead through a Hutton penalty. A try by John Etty, converted by Bernard Ganley, gave Oldham a 5–2 lead, but two more goals by Colin Hutton made the score 6–5 to Hull at the break. Five minutes into the second half, Carl Turner touched down and Hutton's goal made the score 11–5. A controversial penalty by Ganley – Sykes had been penalised for not playing the ball correctly, but had been injured in the tackle – reduced Hull's lead to four points.

94

Hull FC 1956–57 with the Championship Trophy. (Courtesy Robert Gate)

Hull FC 1957–58 team. This squad won the Championship. (Courtesy *Rugby League Journal*)

95

A try by Dennis Ayres, converted by Ganley, put Oldham ahead 12–11. With five minutes left, John Etty scored in the corner to stretch Oldham's lead to four points. Ganley missed the conversion.

However, two minutes later, Stan Cowan scored a breakaway try; 15–14 with Hutton's kick to come. Graham Morris outlines that "Hutton, as at Maine Road a year earlier, took centre stage as he attempted to win the match with a kickable looking conversion. To everyone's amazement, Hutton, who racked up a club record 166 goals for the season, missed." According to *Kingstonian*, the kick was about 12 yards from the posts and "grazed the wrong side of the upright".

After the game, referee Matt Coates said that he had not realised that Sykes had been injured when he penalised him. It was Hull's only defeat in a Northern Rugby League Championship final.

Kingstonian's report in the *Mail* said that "When Cyril Sykes was tackled vigorously and concussed, the referee penalised him for not playing the ball. The Hull man obviously had no idea what was happening and had to leave the field…". However, he did say that Oldham "…just about deserved to [win] being a shade faster all round than the Boulevarders."

1957–58

This was "another excellent season", according to Michael Ulyatt. However, before the season started, there was some controversy regarding the position of the Drake twins at the club. Both had missed a Saturday pre-season practice game. Jim had a hand injury and Bill was working in Scarborough. The club blamed "rumour-mongers" who had been "manufacturing stories about discord between the club and two of their finest forwards."

Kingstonian reported that Roy "… visited the Drake twins yesterday to make final arrangements for them to be at tonight's trials and he told me today 'Where this rumour originates from, I would not swear to, but I have a fair idea. I have seen much the same thing happen with other successful teams, such as Warrington, Wigan and Barrow, and other places I have been to. I think it is the work of a highly qualified scandal-monger, but as far as the Drake twins are concerned, take it from me there is absolutely no truth in it.'

'In fact,', continued Roy, 'Jim Drake has told me that he wishes he could get his hands on the person who started it.'"

In October, Hull signed a South African rugby union player, Mervyn 'Pin' McMillan. Coming from a country where Apartheid made white people the dominant race over the black majority, it must have been surprising for McMillian to meet Roy who would be his coach.

A departure from the Boulevard was Colin Hutton. He retired as a player at the age of 31 and moved across the city to become coach at Hull KR. He remained someone who has the respect of the supporters in both halves of this rugby-divided city. Peter Bateson became the team's regular goalkicker.

Another possible signing by Hull FC never happened. Towards the end of 1957, Billy Boston had been going through a bad spell at Wigan, and the *Mail* reported that Hull were interested in making a bid to sign him. The paper said that Roy Francis, Hull's coach, "is a great admirer of Boston's play, and under Roy's direction the Wigan flyer could undoubtedly rise to greater heights than he has so far attained." However, two days later, on 30 December, the paper reported that Boston was not interested in a move to Hull. It was a pity, if Boston had joined Hull and stayed, from 1961 Hull could have had Billy Boston on one wing and Clive Sullivan on the other.

In January, the *Mail* reported that the "... decision of the Rugby League to appoint two managers and a coach for this summer's tour of Australia and NZ has set Hull fans thinking. No pointers have been given towards the men who will be appointed to these jobs, but there are many Boulevard supporters who will be keen to see Roy Francis get the coach's job.

With plenty of experience and the right personality for the job, Roy would be an ideal choice. Clubs are being asked to nominate a coach for the tour. Finance may be the biggest drawback, for the coach will receive only £10 a week on tour, plus £100 bonus at the end."

Six days later, an article in the sports gossip section of the *Mail* by *Marksman* included some interesting observations about Roy. It asked: "Who are the top coaches in the rugby league? Jim Sullivan (St Helens), Gus Risman (Salford), Joe Egan (Wigan), Roy Francis (Hull), Dolly [Frank] Dawson (Halifax), Griff Jenkins (Oldham)? You may have other ideas, but you can take it for certain that the first coach ever to go to Australia this summer will be chosen from this list, not necessarily in order of favouritism. Roy Francis, doing as good a job as any pf the big six, is an ideal man for the job. Apart from being a top-flight coach, still capable of going on and playing with his charges, Roy is a physiotherapist, with the added asset of a tip-top business brain.

Francis, who would be delighted to make the trip, has the backing of the Hull directors who, at their meeting this week, in response to a request from Rugby League headquarters for nominations for the coach's job, decided to put forward Roy's name for consideration. Francis, keen as he is to go, gave me his well-known horse laugh today when I suggested he must be rated high on the list of candidates. 'I have too many enemies in high places', he declared.

The Hull coach, of course, has a straight-from-the shoulder approach, both in policy and speech, which is not always popular with the game's top brass. His qualifications are, nevertheless, very sound, and his strong will, always imposed firmly but fairly, would make him ideal tour coach.

Since joining Hull in 1949, Francis has worked wonders with limited resources. Unlike several of the game's top coaches, he did not join a club bristling with talented players worth thousands. When he was appointed coach, Hull were not in a good position financially and certainly not in a position to splash money around for players, such as clubs like Wigan, St Helens, Oldham and Halifax. Therefore, Francis had to start from scratch and make the best of the material available, and at that time it was mainly local talent that Hull depended on."

The article outlined Roy's achievements at Hull and concluded that his "... achievements as coach speak for gained without much strain being put on the club's coffers. Surely what Roy has done for Hull he could do for Britain."

On 17 February, it was reported that Jim Brough had been given the coaching role for the Lions tour. Roy had been shortlisted along with Frank Dawson, Alex Fiddes and Gus Risman. Roy was probably fortunate to miss out. Despite some success on the pitch, including retaining the Ashes, the tour was marred by disputes between the two managers, Tom

Mitchell and Bennett Manson. There was even a vote of 'no confidence' in Jim Brough, who got drawn into the disputes. The day after Brough's appointment was announced, Roy told the *Mail* that Brough, who had been on two Lions tours as a player, had the number one qualifications. There was plenty of time for him to get a tour coaching role as he was the youngest of the candidates considered.

Marksman had said in January that Roy had built an 'international pack' who all deserved a tour spot. In fact, only Tommy Harris and Johnny Whiteley were selected. Jim Drake missed out on a tour place due to a knee injury.

Roy intervened in January to help Harry Markham overcome a long-term injury. After Markham had tried several medical treatments, Roy took him to the specialist in Manchester that Roy himself had seen in 1949. Sadly, the doctor was unable to solve the problem and Markham retired in September 1958.

Once again, Hull were consistent in the league, but made no impression in the knock-out competitions, losing at home to Rochdale Hornets in the Challenge Cup and Hunslet in the Yorkshire Cup. Despite their failures in the cup competitions, they scored even more points than in the previous campaign, ending up with 987.

At the end of January, Hull had won eight successive league games, a run they continued until the second week of March. The preview of the match against Keighley said that the players were "tuned up to championship pitch due to rigorous training".

The issue of players on National Service was an ongoing one for rugby league and other sports clubs. On 1 February, the *Mail* reported that Brian Saville was in the Army, and would be released for cup ties if they do not clash with Army games. The report concluded that "He is now recognised as Hull's most progressive attacking back who, in the capable hands of coach Roy Francis, is facing a bright football future..."

In April, there were two more occasions when Roy's work was recognised. George Matthews signed for Hull because his father was an admirer of Roy, and George had played as an amateur in Barrow. He said that his son "could have no better tutor than Roy." At the end of the month, Mr Robinson, from the Hull FC Supporters Club, said that "Roy Francis had done a fine job in guiding the club to success."

Hull finished fourth in the Northern Rugby League table, with 56 points from their 38 games. Oldham had again finished top of the table, so in the semi-final, Hull faced a trip to the Watersheddings. Two weeks earlier, they had been beaten 43–9 at the same ground. Raymond Fletcher outlined that "Oldham had finished as League leaders for a second successive season after winning their last 11 matches and were expected to retain the Championship they had won by beating Hull in the Final a year earlier. But this was the sort of challenge fourth-placed Hull relished. Coach Roy Francis had given nothing away when Hull succumbed to Oldham in their last league match of the season, yet he selected the same team apart from Geoff Dannatt replacing Gordon Harrison on the left wing.

Hull opened the scoring with a try from Ivor Watts. Against the run of play, Oldham made it 3–3, Hull went ahead through a Bateson penalty, and then Cooper touched down. According to Raymond Fletcher, "The next try sent Hull fans wild as Oldham were turned inside out by a bewildering move." Bill Drake scored; Sykes added another which Bateson converted for an 18–3 Hull half-time lead.

Hull finally ran out winners 20–8, despite having Tommy Harris sent off with 17 minutes left. The dismissal meant that Harris missed the final through suspension. In the other semi-final, Workington Town won at St Helens. The Cumbrian side had also reached the Challenge Cup Final. They lost to Wigan at Wembley on 10 May, and then faced Hull at Odsal a week later.

A 57,699 crowd saw Hull win their second Championship title in three seasons. Despite missing the suspended Tommy Harris and both Drake brothers through injury, Hull were 5–3 up at half-time, and went on to win 20–3. To be fair, it should be said that Workington were missing winger Bill Wookey and prop Andy Key through injury, and lost second-rower Cec Thompson with torn ligaments after 25 minutes. However, Jack Bentley of the *Daily Express* said that "Even if Workington hadn't lost Cec Thompson, I'm convinced Hull still would have won. Hull had the power and drive, the pace and ideas."

Workington actually took the lead on 28 minutes, but five minutes later, Cooper touched down, and Bateson converted to put Hull 5–3 ahead. A Johnny Whiteley converted try on 51 minutes put Hull two scores ahead, and they never looked back.

Hull's pack, usually the driving force of their game, was made up of local players. Roy said after the game: "While I'm extremely sorry that the Drake twins and Tommy Harris were unable to play for various reasons, I was very, very proud of the performances of the 'A' team players Alan [Holdstock] and Peter [Whiteley]." The *Mail* commented that "The open-style, classical handling, which Roy Francis brought to the Boulevard, was too much for a bewildered Workington, whose much-vaunted defence crumbled gradually."

When the Hull team returned to the city, they were given a great welcome. The *Mail* reported that: "The cheering did not die away until coach Roy Francis, beaming with pleasure, went to the microphone to say 'Thank you very much for such a wonderful reception.' He was called back twice more, once to thank the supporters and the people behind the scenes. And again, to announce that there would be a victory ride through the city early this week. One of the biggest roars of the evening went up when he pointed to the right of the balcony and called for a cheer for the Drake twins, both out of the team through injury."

Johnny Whiteley driving at Sutton Golf Club in 1958 ...

and is the winner of the golf tournament. (Both courtesy Robert Gate)

11. Hull 1958 to 1960

Hull's league form dropped just a little in 1958–59 compared to the previous season, enough to see them finish seventh, six points behind Oldham who were fourth. In the Yorkshire Cup, Hull won comfortably at Bramley in the first round, but then lost at home to Wakefield by a point. The *Mail* had reported that "Roy Francis has worked out several alternatives to [Ken] Traill's style of play which should effectively strangle those moves before they have a chance to develop." Whatever the plan was, it did not stop Wakefield's narrow victory.

In August, Roy told the *Mail* that the club had "the strongest 'A' team in the game." The first team started the season well, but after a defeat at Halifax on 20 September, were not as consistent as in the previous campaign. By the end of the year, eight league games had been lost, which made it extremely difficult for Hull to qualify for the play-offs.

One of Roy's concerns was always the welfare of his players. Against Bramley at the end of September, Eddie Wanklyn broke his cheekbone and tried to carry on playing. Roy stopped him, and made sure that he was sent to hospital to have the injury properly treated.

In October, Hull lost at home to York. It was their first home defeat in a league match since March 1957.

One new initiative Roy took at this time was to film matches, so that he and the players could study the films and learn from them. This became 'controversial'. At the end of October, the *Mail* said "That a certain Sunday newspaper columnist who seems to delight in trying to stir up trouble in Hull Rugby League circles has turned his attention to Hull coach Roy Francis. According to this expert, Roy has been under fire from Hull fans for using his cine-camera during Boulevard matches. Of all the ridiculous ideas this caps the lot. Apart from the fact that Hull's supporters are intelligent enough to realise that R's camera work is for the club's benefit. his filming does not interfere with spectators at all. Says Roy: 'I saw you-know-who last week and I certainly did not mention anything about the Boulevard crowd criticising me.'"

A few days later, Roy told the *Mail* that "I am absolutely cheesed off with various reports in national papers with the function and purpose of the cine camera. I ma not particularly concerned with the individuals who have written these articles. But it is extremely important from the point of view of the Hull supporters and the players of the club that this should be put right.

The camera was purchased with the sole idea of bringing another medium of coaching and training in the club. It was not bought with any idea of publicity or personal glory. This is, in my opinion, the best and only way of showing players their shortcomings, their strengths and weaknesses."

He emphasised: "Wives, sweethearts and what have you do not attend these shows. It is purely for players alone, and I would hate the impression to get abroad that this is some ... 'Around the world in 80 days' gimmick. This is a genuine method to improve, I hope, not only the standard of senior football of Hull FC, but when a sufficient library of films is acquired, then also to benefit junior football and anyone who is interested in rugby league football in Hull. So, for the sake of myself and all people connected with Hull FC, it would be greatly appreciated if we could be left alone to try and develop this technique in our way."

In November, the club started indoor training. The *Mail* outlined that "... The fit men, however, tonight start the winter indoor training programme at Madeley St Baths. Coach Roy Francis is keen on this type of training to keep the edge on players who cannot train outdoors and the team themselves enjoy the change in the keep fit routine." A couple of weeks later, it was reported that Hull had 11 players injured, which may have been a factor in the team's inconsistency.

The importance of Roy's role was shown against Keighley on 3 January 1959. Hull won 35–0. It was 8–0 at half -time, and the *Mail* reported that: "Coach Roy Francis's interval talk produced a remarkable transformation on the resumption, for fast, bewildering handling, plus clever backing-up, saw Keighley's cover shattered time after time."

Roy also influenced individual players. The *Mail* commented that "Another with a bright future is [Arthur] Keegan, who under Francis's direction could become one of the game's best backs." Youngster Colin Ali said: "I am still learning with every game and with a coach like Roy Francis – who was one of the finest backs in the game- I shall be learning for some time yet."

In February, Hull announced that Pin McMillan had been released, and was expected to return to South Africa. It has been written that Roy did not want McMillan at the club because he was a white South African. It is true that McMillan was probably shocked to find out that his coach was black, and at home in South Africa would have been carrying his bags rather than directing him in training. However, the truth is that McMillan never quite made it in rugby league at Hull. He played regularly for the 'A' team, although his progress was hampered by a wrist injury that took time to heal. Also, Hull kept signing new players at centre or full-back, his best position. He had the opportunity to move to a club where he would have more chance of a first team place, but chose not to move. As with players who 'came north' from Wales, not every South African who moved to Great Britain and switched codes to rugby league in the 1950s and 1960s was a success.

The undoubted highlight of the season was reaching the Challenge Cup Final. They had last won the Cup in 1913–14, and had been runners-up five times, three in consecutive seasons before the First World War. It was also the first time Hull had played at Wembley Stadium. Their last Challenge Cup Final appearance was in 1923, when the Stadium itself opened, but the Challenge Cup Final did not move there until 1929.

To reach the Final, Hull beat Blackpool in the first round. Even though the opposition was not strong, the *Mail* said that "Throughout the week, the Boulevard players have undergone special training, which wound up today with a tactical discussion, during which coach Roy Francis, and the players, worked out the moves and manner of play which Hull are hoping will shatter Blackpool's defence."

Hull then drew 4–4 with Wakefield at the Boulevard. They won the replay at Belle Vue 16–10 and then beat Hull KR 23–9 in the third round. A 24,000 crowd squeezed into the Boulevard to see Hull lead 5–4 at half-time before winning comfortably in the second half. Before the local derby clash, the Mail reported that the Hull players were due to appear at the Continental Theatre three days before the game, "but trainer Roy Francis, on consideration, stated today that he thought it inadvisable for the players to go out tonight in view of Saturday's important game. The visit has therefore been postponed...".

102

Hull FC 1958–59. (Courtesy *Rugby League Journal*)

Defeat at Oldham, followed by another loss in Lancashire at St Helens, effectively ended Hull's Championship play-off hopes.

In the semi-final, Hull met Featherstone Rovers at Odsal. A 52,500 crowd saw them win 15–5. Raymond Fletcher recalled that: "The match turned out to be a triumph for coach Roy Francis's tactical planning, which he had outlined to the press before the game. His plan was simply to win plenty of possession, blot out any threat from the Featherstone half-backs at source and let Hull's forwards do the rest. He had told [20-year-old George] Matthews and his scrum-half partner Frank Broadhurst to follow the Rovers pair everywhere – 'even if they left the field'."

Writing in the *Mail* after the game, Roy said that "The way I saw it, Featherstone tanned the St Helens pack out of sight and, quite naturally, fancied they could do the same to us. We respected their confidence and their performance against Saints, and it was decided, when they had the ball, to make their pack come down the middle and we should put them to the test. When we had the ball, we decided to use it over approximately 6,500 square yards of Odsal. The first part worked, and the Featherstone pack ended up leg-weary and beaten. The second part worked only on occasions, but sufficiently to register the points."

In the other semi-final, Wigan beat Leigh 5–0 at Swinton. Sadly, for the 20,000 Hull fans who travelled to Wembley, as part of a 79,811 crowd, it turned out to be a horrible anti-climax.

103

In mid-April, there was a letter in the *Mail* saying that Roy should lead out the Hull team at Wembley. This did not happen; the long-serving chairman Ernest Hardaker had that honour. Despite all the pressures of the Wembley final, Roy arranged a benefit match on 30 May for Mick Scott, Carl Turner and Harry Markham. Wigan came to the Boulevard for the match, but there was more serious business first.

The *Mail* reported that Hull were staying at home for pre–Cup Final training: "Coach Roy Francis will conduct the usual weekly training sessions tomorrow night and Thursday before getting down to his pre-match tightening up work at the weekend. This begins on Sunday when the Wembley team play a full-scale match against 'The Rest' – behind closed doors. Hull will train again on Monday, Tuesday and Wednesday before travelling to London on Thursday." Wigan were going to Blackpool for training. Roy went to Central Park on 2 May to see Wigan lose to Hunslet in the Championship play-offs.

The Hull players and officials, after visiting Wembley on the Friday morning, spent the afternoon travelling around London in their coach visiting various well known tourist sites. This shows how rare a visit to London was for the people involved, but surely a light training session would have been better for the players than being stuck in a coach all afternoon. They did have a pre-match training session at Hendon Football Club.

On 9 May at Wembley, it was expected that Wigan's backs would be stronger than Hull's – they included Great Britain stars Billy Boston, Eric Ashton and Mick Sullivan, with South African Fred Griffiths at full-back. However, Hull's famous pack was beaten by the Wigan six on the day. Was it nerves? Most of the side had played in major matches for Hull, including Championship finals. Raymond Fletcher commented that "Even Hull coach Roy Francis admitted that although he did not believe in such things as nerves effecting experienced players he could think of no other reason for his team's inept performance."

According to David Bond, there had been speculation before the Wembley Final that Halifax were interested in recruiting Roy as their coach. This had first arisen at the end of April. He writes: "But speculation mounted again before the Wembley defeat by Wigan. Their preparations on the day were disrupted by rumours that Francis has been offered the job to coach Halifax, who had recently failed to land Jim Sullivan for the role, so he had to break off to deny them. The Francis link had been debunked a fortnight earlier, but then it was revived and he was supposedly ready to meet Halifax officials in Leeds." Did this have an effect on the Hull players, who were very loyal to Roy?

Had Hull scored first, it might have settled the team down. However, Wigan scored a converted try after eight minutes, and although Keegan got two points back with a penalty, Wigan effectively won the game with three tries in 13 minutes. The half-time score was 20–4. Hull improved in the second half, with Finn scoring a try and Keegan kicking another four goals, but 30–13 was the final score. Wigan's tally was the highest ever in a Wembley Challenge Cup Final, although sadly for Hull, that record only lasted one season.

Roy was publicly critical of the team's performance after the game. He said that "It is the worst game Hull have played in the last seven years and the players agree with that statement."

The national papers were also universally critical or disappointed with Hull's performance. Gus Risman said that "Wembley inexperience made Hull a team full of fumblers." Lewis Jones commented that "Who could have thought any player could have run into that normally resolute Hull pack and emerged on the other side in one piece?" Other writers felt that Hull were nervous and that "their usual killer spirit was missing."

The Wembley match was also subject to discussion at the club's AGM in July. The *Mail* reported that in answer to questions, Ernest Hardaker said that staying in a west end hotel "could not be blamed" and that there was no other accommodation available. That seems unlikely, given the number of hotels in and around London, and it is notable that in 1960, Hull stayed well away from the centre of London.

Remarkably, given the Wembley result, 10,000 fans turned out to see Wigan win the benefit match Roy had arranged for 30 May. The result was 36–32 to the Lancastrians, and the three players involved split £1050 between them.

1959–60

The stability Roy had built at Hull was shown when Tommy Harris and Bryan Cooper shared a 10-year benefit. The next season Johnny Whiteley and Bill Drake did the same.

Overall, this was a season of 'so near, yet so far'. Hull were runners-up in the Challenge Cup and Yorkshire Cup, and – through finishing third – qualified for the Championship play-offs, where they were beaten by Wakefield.

As well as discussing the Wembley defeat, the club AGM in July also discussed the approach by Halifax to Roy. Former club secretary Wilf Ward said that it had been "an extremely good publicity stunt" according to the report of the meeting in the *Mail*. Ernest Hardaker did confirm that Halifax had made an approach. The report said that "Halifax were told that the negotiations were subject, finally, to whether Hull would release Francis, but it was only natural that Francis should be interested. Asked whether there was any clause in the coach's contract to prevent this kind of thing, Mr Hardaker replied: 'Looking at it from a purely business point of view, what good would he have been as a servant to the club if the club had said they would not release him.'"

Roy applied his usual energy to pre-season training. He decided that the players should train three nights a week from mid-July for two months. The *Mail* said that Roy had confirmed that 'there was a great deal of enthusiasm amongst the players.'

Towards the end of July, Hull announced that they had removed Colin Hutton from their players register. This meant that he could play for Hull KR, where he had been coaching since November 1957. He was aged 33, so a playing return was possible, but he seems to have concentrated on coaching.

On 6 August, *Marksman* in the *Mail* commented that "... Roy Francis, with more time to devote to coaching now that he has given up his Beverley hotel, is tackling his task with great enthusiasm and is so fit that he can play and keep up a commentary in a parade ground voice at the same time. 'Well tacked that man. Now give the lad his head back!' was the stentorian shout that greeted me as I looked in at the Boulevard this week. Roy, despite his 40 years, is still a master of the interception and appears as fast on the burst as he was in his hey-day."

Roy checking an injury at training. (Courtesy Robert Gate)

Roy emphasising a point to the players. (Courtesy Robert Gate)

A week before the league campaign started, the *Mail* reported that "all the regular playing staff" from the previous season were available. The list of 43 registered players included 'RL Francis', but there were no plans for Roy to resume his 'player-coach' role.

There was one change on the coaching set-up. In October, Ivor Watts became Roy's assistant. He was out of action following a cartilage operation, but it was thought that when he was fit, he could play for the 'A' team to develop the club's younger players. He did not play for the first team again this season.

Hull started the campaign with a defeat at Hunslet. However, Halifax and Bramley were beaten in the next two games, and the team started playing more consistently.

On 31 October, Hull had faced Featherstone in the Yorkshire Cup Final at Headingley. Hull had not won the Yorkshire Cup for 36 years. To reach the final, Hull had beaten Bradford Northern at Odsal 23–10, won at Bramley in the second round and beaten Halifax 18–9 at The Boulevard in the semi-final. Featherstone were ahead 13–7 at half-time, but Hull won the second half 7–2 to lose by a point. It was their fourth Yorkshire Cup Final defeat under Roy's direction, and he never did manage to bring the trophy back to the Boulevard. This result was particularly frustrating as Hull had won 19–8 at Featherstone three weeks before the final. This was the third final that Roy had been involved in that had been decided by a single point. There would be one more, later in his coaching career.

There was a letter in the *Mail* 10 days after the final criticising Roy's tactics in the final, and saying that he needed to work out some new moves. Featherstone finished fifth in the league table, three points behind Hull, so the Yorkshire Cup final defeat was hardly an act of giant-killing. Interestingly, in Ron Bailey's book on Featherstone's 50 finest matches, he writes that Rovers had learned from their two previous losses to Hull and: "... it was obvious from the first minute, as Fox booted the ball down into Hull territory, that they were not going to be drawn into close-quarter football with their opposing forwards." To be fair to Hull, Peter Bateson came close to winning the game with a drop-goal in the final minutes.

A week later, Roy missed the first team's visit to Batley to watch the 'A' team. The *Mail* said that he "will have realised that there is good material there, and with coaching to take off the rough edges, some of them could be serious contenders for first team places,"

Roy wasn't the only family member to feature in the *Mail's* sports pages. On 24 November, their rugby union reports included coverage of Ian Francis, Roy's younger son, scoring the match-winning try for Marist College Old Boys. He "gathered a low pass to beat the entire defence in a 60 yards run to place between the sticks." Ian played club rugby union for some years, mainly for Ionians, but never switched to rugby league.

In January, Hull signed two Tongan players from Doncaster, Namumi Halafihi and Sam Faletau. Roy went to talk to John Henderson, a former York prop, who had retired due to travel difficulties. Roy found out that Henderson worked in Halifax, would not move to Hull unless he got a good offer. The next day, Roy reported to the Hull board that Henderson has good digs and a job with Halifax council. He would need a similar set-up to join Hull. In fact, the move fell through because York wanted a fee for him. While Hull still had a strong squad, this was maybe a warning sign for the future.

In the *Mail*, there was a letter saying that Hull City should have a team of rugby league players, and named a team. The writer added that Roy should be the trainer. Also, there was a comment in the paper: "How long before another Francis pulls on a black and white shirt?" Presumably this was a refence to Ian, but it never happened.

At the beginning of February, the *Mail* reported that Brian Hambling was to retire after a £2500 transfer fee for him had been set by Hull The paper said: "He [Ernest Hardaker] was rather surprised that Hambling had not discussed any grievances with coach Roy Francis. 'Usually, players have a word with Roy first to see what can be done,'" commented Mr Hardaker.

Hull continued to play well in the league. Their narrow win at Bramley on 26 March, with Halafihi scoring their only try, was their 12th consecutive win. However, Roy told the *Mail* that "It's the worst game we have played for a long time." For the rest of the season, Hull only dropped points in a draw against Huddersfield and a defeat at St Helens.

Hull once again qualified for the Championship play-offs. They finished third in the table, with 57 points from their 38 games, one clear of Wigan and three clear of Featherstone who were fifth. In the semi-final, they travelled to Belle Vue to face Wakefield, and lost 24–4. Jim Drake had been injured against Huddersfield the week before, and missed the match. Peter Bateson was severely concussed during the game by a challenge from Wakefield's Derek Turner. Some Hull players were carrying injuries, and Roy had given a report on the club's injured players a few days before the game when he was involved in a sports quiz. Wakefield went on to play Wigan in the final, and lost 27–3 before a gigantic 83,190 crowd at Odsal.

In the Challenge Cup, Hull again reached the Final. Before a narrow 2–0 win at York in the first round, Roy had organised daylight training for the players, to concentrate on tactics. After the game, the report in the *Mail* said that "Francis was pleased with the fact that Hull had surmounted the first hurdle. "The first round is always the most difficult", he said. He felt that Hull could have exploited the short kick to greater advantage, as York had been lying well up on top of the Boulevarders – including [York] full-back Willie Hargreaves."

This was followed by a 30-point win at Keighley. In the third round, Wigan came to the Boulevard, and Hull took revenge for both the previous season's Final and a 24–2 defeat at Central Park earlier in the season. Hull won 12–8. Again, Roy had held special daylight training sessions for the match. Afterwards, the *Mail* outlined that "Hull's coach Roy Francis was pleased that the team had beaten Wigan ... but he was far from satisfied with the performance. 'We won, but we played 50 per cent below our normal standard', he said. 'The backs didn't link up as I'd hoped and the forwards looked out of touch. We could have played a lot better, and we are going to have to sharpen up from now on. We are in the position when every match facing us is as important as a semi-final. It's going to be hard concentrating on the top four and the Cup, but I'm looking forward to it.' Commenting on the Oldham draw [in the semi-final], Roy said 'We have plenty of games before that. We'll deal with that match when we come to it.'"

In the semi-final, Hull scraped through 12–9 against Oldham at Swinton. Roy had, as usual, organised additional daylight training for the match. Four days before the game, the Mail reported that there would be a "Strenuous workout this afternoon under the supervision of coach Roy Francis." More training sessions would be held on the Wednesday and Thursday, but they would take things easy on the Friday, when there would be "tactical talks to which Francis attaches the greatest importance."

Roy adjusting Tommy Harris's scrum cap in the 1960 Challenge Cup Final. (Courtesy Geoff Francis)

In Dave Barlow (*Kingstonian*)'s semi-final preview, he said that "… if Harris wins the strike, Hull will be able to develop the moves taught them by coach Roy Francis during the past few years and emphasised again during this week's strenuous training stint."

After the match, Barlow wrote that "Hull's second successive visit to Wembley is a tribute to club coach Roy Francis, who has achieved remarkable results since taking over the reins 10 years ago." It was announced by the club that for the Final, the players would stay outside London along with two directors. The other directors would stay in London. They stayed at a hotel in Twyford, and then moved to the Mount Royal in Marble Arch after the game. At Wembley, Hull would face Wakefield Trinity, a week after their 24–4 Championship semi-final defeat.

Hull's injury problems were made worse when full-back Peter Bateson was ruled out after being concussed by Derek Turner. Also missing were the Drake twins, Peter Whiteley and Cyril Sykes. Jack Kershaw, who came in at full-back, had to have a pain-killing injection before the match. For Hull, 22-year-old Mike Smith made his first team debut in the Challenge Cup Final. Three days before the game, there were 20 players under consideration for a Wembley place.

Johnny Whiteley told the *Mail:* "Last Saturday's pack were pushed together. We have, under Roy Francis's direction, ironed out a lot of faults in this week's training...". However, the day before the Final, Dave Barlow said that "In view of Hull's many problems I consider Hull's chances of victory very remote."

On the day of the match, Roy said that "The team has been selected on the basis of fitness." Three hours before kick-off, he commented: "All I'm asking for are two things – firstly the breaks to which we are entitled after so much bad luck and, secondly, determination. This year's Wembley will not be the formality that has been suggested."

Hull had further injury problems during the game. After Wakefield had taken an early lead, Hull fought back and the half-time score was 7–5. However, in the second half, the injuries caught up with Hull and Trinity scored five tries in the last 20 minutes, to win 38–5. Tommy Harris won the Lance Todd Trophy for his heroic performance in the onslaught. The margin of defeat may have been bigger than in 1959, but this time the Hull players were given a hero's reception after the game. An unwanted 'honour' was that Hull were the fist club to lose two successive Wembley Challenge Cup Finals.

Tommy Harris said after the game: "I feel sorry for coach Roy Francis who has put in a lot of hard work with this game in mind. It has been an obsession for him for a year, and it must be disappointing for him to see us fail on a second visit through sheer bad luck and injuries."

A couple of days after the Challenge Cup Final, Roy was still busy, trying to arrange an end of season benefit match for Tommy Harris and Bryan Cooper. The *Mail* said that Roy "always takes a keen interest in the welfare of his players" and was trying to arrange the match for 28 May.

His efforts were successful, and 10,000 fans saw a Humberside XIII play an All-Stars team. The All-Stars won 72–57, in what the *Mail* called a 'rugby league frolic'; but it helped the two beneficiaries. The *Mail* said that "This game was a tribute to the efforts of Hull coach Roy Francis, who organised it almost entirely, and the benefit fund has been considerably increased as a result."

The players and club officials attended a celebration evening organised by the Supporters Club. Their president, Tom Robinson, said the players had shown courage in the Wembley defeat, playing with a 'much-weakened' side. The *Mail* reported: "He told the players and officials that their record during the past seven years had been second to none, and much of the credit for this was due to the astute coaching of Roy Francis."

12. Hull 1960 to 1963

The first season of a new decade, 1960–61, was not particularly successful for Hull. Roy's team lacked the consistency of previous seasons. An early warning sign was a 30–9 home defeat against Wigan in the third game of the season. The *Mail* said that "The days when Hull's pack automatically mastered the opposition, no matter how good, are gone." They finished in 11th place in the Northern Rugby League with 41 points from their 36 games. They were a point clear of Hull KR, but 13 away from St Helens who finished in fourth place.

Hull made little impact in the Yorkshire Cup, losing 18–15 at Keighley in the first round. Keighley finished 14 places below Hull in the NRL, so that result was very disappointing.

In the autumn, the World Cup was played in Great Britain. Roy went to watch the trial match, Great Britain versus Rest of the League at St Helens on 12 September. Tommy Harris and Johnny Whiteley were both in the Great Britain side. Roy's assessment of the game in an article for the *Mail* was that "General opinion ... last night was that as a guide to picking Great Britain's team it was uninstructive and generally useless. Now, I would like to go along with this – after all, it's nice to be on the same side as the experts – but, try as I may, I cannot see how this match failed in its purpose if, as we are told, the purpose of this match was to pick men for the World Cup squad who are on form." Roy went on to analyse the players contending for different positions.

The normal league matches continued during the World Cup, but Hull had no game on 8 October, so Roy went to the Great Britain versus Australia match at Odsal. The competition was run on a league basis, so this match was effectively the final. Roy thought that it was a poor game, with "punch-ups galore" and "small doses of class and large dollops of clash". He did say that it was poor viewing for the television audience, but pointed out, that with the World Cup at stake "no one expects a Great Britain versus Australia match to be like a tea party – especially with the World Cup at stake."

In December, it was reported that there had been speculation about Roy's future in rugby league. The *Mail* pointed out that his contract with Hull would expire at the end of the season. The report said that Roy was "not thinking of turning his back on the game he has graced for over 20 years, as has been hinted in some quarters."

Part of the reason for the speculation about Roy's future was that he had sat the British Boxing Board of Control's exam to hold a boxing trainer's and second's licence. Roy had been waiting for official confirmation before making the matter public, but the information had 'leaked'. Dave Richards, the secretary of the Central Area Council of the Board of Control had recommended Roy as a "fit and proper person to hold a trainer's and second's licence."

The report also said that Johnny Halafihi, a contender for the British Empire cruiserweight title, had already been training under Roy's direction at Roy's gym in Beverley. Roy had assured Ernest Hardaker that he was not abandoning rugby league. He wanted 'another string to his bow'. Roy told the *Mail* that he wanted to stay in rugby league for as long as he could. The report also pointed out that there had been connection between some Northern Union men and wrestling, but this was believed to be the first time a rugby league trainer-coach had got a boxing trainer's and second's licence.

The team again had a good run in the Challenge Cup. In the first round they beat Oldham 4–2 at The Boulevard. For Hull, Peter Bateson kicked two goals from four kicks, while Ganley for Oldham missed four out of five.

Their reward for that victory was a home tie with Hull KR. Interviewed by Mike Ackroyd in the *Mail* on the eve of the game, in an article headed 'Hull camp has air of quiet confidence', Roy would not predict the result, and outlined that "One of the nice things about a cup tie, and in particular a Hull v Rovers tie, is that some official prophet is going to be wrong. Wilf Spaven [Hull KR Chairman], Ernest Hardaker, Colin Hutton or myself. Come opening time tomorrow night, two of the four are going to be crying in their best bitter. Not being over fond of watered-down beer, I hope it is Wilf and Colin. Having had three successive Yorkshire finals, and three successive Championship [finals], a third trip to town would be just great – not to mention a record.

While I am all for brotherly love, share and share alike, and new faces at Wembley, the faces of Hull Kingston Rovers are the ones I do not want to see at Wembley this year."

Hull won comfortably 16–3. Hull were 2–0 up at the break in front of a 14,333 crowd. However, in the second half they scored two tries, both set up by Tommy Harris, and Peter Bateson kicked another four goals to see them home comfortably.

Three days before the big local derby, Roy and Colin Hutton were both on the panel for a local sports forum. Roy opposed the idea of a Ministry of Sport, saying there were "enough boys trying to do jobs." Another topic discussed was the relationship between Rugby League and Rugby Union. Roy and Colin Hutton agreed with the Hull and East Riding club spokesman that at a players' level there was a "friendly atmosphere" between the two codes. They also agreed that the differences came "from the top" and that a more friendly approach would be good for both codes. However, they also agreed that the two codes were "poles apart". Roy felt that they "would never come together."

The third round produced another home tie, and another close game. Featherstone were beaten 10–9. However, the *Mail's* report said that Hull "barely deserved to win against Featherstone." A last minute try for Hull by Terry Hollindrake was disputed, and Featherstone felt that he had been in touch before he scored.

Before the semi-final against St Helens at Odsal, there was some controversy after Tom van Vollenhoven, Saints' star South African winger, said that Hull should not play again at Wembley because of their two heavy Challenge Cup final defeats.

In any case, there was not going to be a third consecutive Wembley appearance. Hull lost 26–9 in front of 42,074 fans. At half-time the score was 5–4 to St Helens. Van Vollenhoven scored just before half-time, a "brilliant solo effort" according to Mike Ackroyd in the *Mail*. Ackroyd did say that "St Helens twice stepped in to score tries against the run of play". He said that Hull's forwards had dominated play in the first half, but Hull lacked the cutting edge that van Vollenhoven and Mick Sullivan gave St Helens. In the end, the Saints won comfortably. They went on to beat Wigan at Wembley.

After the semi-final, the issues of renewing Roy's contract was discussed by the board. Negotiations had started before the semi-final, and Roy staying with the club was linked to longer term plans for the club's development, and the need to recruit younger players who Roy could develop. Interestingly, the report in the *Mail* was headlined "... big plans, but there will be no spending spree." Maybe Roy should have taken note of those words – there was recruitment in his last period at Hull, but the team did not challenge for honours again.

At the end of April, Roy was in hospital for a few days for tests. Mike Ackroyd reported that "It is understood, however, that there is nothing seriously wrong with him and that his trouble may stem from over-strain." Ackroyd said that Roy told him that "I will soon be back and rarin' to go."

Once again, Roy organised a benefit match at the end of the season, this time for Johnny Whiteley and Jim Drake. The match was planned to be on Saturday 27 May, but had to be brought forward to 22 May because there was a clash with the County Championship play-off.

Once again, the fixture was a points festival. The Other Nationalities XIII beat A Great Britain XIII 63–36. Roy was managing the Other Nationalities team. Sadly, being a midweek game reduced the crowd to around 5,000. It was the last time Roy organised such a match at Hull.

1961–62

Michael Ulyatt says that Hull were in a 'transitional period' at this time. Tommy Harris left to become player-coach at York, and Jim Drake moved across the city to join Hull KR in November. Four other players were also on the transfer list, although Brian Saville was the only one who had made an impact at first team level.

Two new – and very contrasting – wingers were signed. Clive Sullivan was recruited from the Army, and went on to become a legend of both teams in the city, along with being the first black captain of both Great Britain and any British team in a major sport. Former Springbok Wilf Rosenberg was signed by Hull from Leeds. He was studying to be become a dentist, and when he completed his studies soon retired from rugby league because he could not risk damaging his hands while playing.

A sign of Hull's decline came in early October, when Featherstone won at the Boulevard for the first time since 1933. Later in October, Hull had to postpone two matches because of an outbreak of Polio in the city. Initially, all major sport in the city was cancelled, and the following week, their match at Hunslet was postponed. The team returned to action in November.

Wilf Rosenberg had been a major success at Leeds, but after recovering from a broken jaw, had not been able to secure a regular first team place, and had only played once for Leeds this season. He had first spoken to Oldham before meeting officials from Hull., Other clubs were interested, but he moved to the Boulevard for a £5,750 transfer fee, having originally been listed for £8,000, £2,000 more than the signing on fee he received from Leeds.

While Hull were recruiting Rosenberg, there were rumours of a fall-out with Johnny Whiteley. These were dismissed by both Ernest Hardaker and Roy. The *Mail* reported that "Coach Roy Francis also ridiculed this suggestion. 'My difficulty is to stop him training', said Roy … Francis said the rumour may have arisen from the fact that Whiteley did not take part in Madeley Street baths training … 'Johnny was incapable of training indoors last week', said Francis. 'With his fractured finger, he would have been unable to undertake a strenuous programme of exercises on the floor, so quite sensibly elected to do some road work around Hessle. There has been a spate of silly rumours during our lean spell and such silly things as the Whiteley story do untold damage."

Clive Sullivan was a serving soldier when he signed for Hull. He was a 'regular', not a two-year national service recruit. He had played an unsuccessful trial with Bradford's 'A' team. Fortunately for rugby league in the city of Hull, one of the touch-judges that day was Jim Harker who got the bus back to the station with Sullivan. Harker was from Hull and contacted Hull FC director Alf Smith about the young winger's potential. On 9 December, Hull fans saw Wilf Rosenberg make his debut on the right wing, and a 'mystery winger', Clive Sullivan, on the left. Sullivan scored a hat-trick and Rosenberg touched down twice in a 29–9 win. Mike Ackroyd's report, maybe inevitably, compared Sullivan to Billy Boston, but stressed that the whole team seemed revitalised in this victory. Ackroyd said that after two "straightforward" tries, Sullivan's third was "a great individual effort which covered over half the length of the field." This by a player who, according to Joe Latus in his biography of Sullivan, had been told by Bradford officials to go away and learn how to play rugby.

The Hull directors realised Sullivan's potential, and after the game told him to return to his hotel and not to speak to anyone until they arrived to complete the paperwork. There was concern that a contingent from Halifax were also interested in the player. However, when they arrived at the hotel, Sullivan was not there! After a frantic search around the city's pubs, they found out that Roy had also realised the importance of looking after Sullivan and had taken him to his home in Beverley. He signed for Hull the next day.

Roy said to the *Mail* that Sullivan, despite his lack of 'big-time' rugby union experience, "has a natural aptitude for the game. He has speed, a useful swerve, and was a splendid handler of the ball.". The report continued: "Roy was sure he would make the grade. Clive had the breaks against Bramley, but it was the way he finished off the movements which showed his potential, said the Hull coach. Francis described the new signing as a shy, unassuming boy, passionately fond of sport. Sullivan has recorded good times over 100 yards since he joined the Army, and has also boxed for his unit."

The article also talked about other black rugby league players who came from the Tiger Bay area of Cardiff. It also claimed that Hull had been interested in the player for six months, although this contradicts with the account in Latus's biography.

Clive often stayed with Roy and his family while in Hull. The club did not try to 'buy him out' of his three-year Army contract. The specialist military training he had received would have made this expensive. At times this limited his availability, particularly for midweek matches. In March 1962, he had 20 months still to serve in the Army. His brother Brian also later signed for Hull.

At the end of 1961, Frank Broadhurst left the club to live in Lancashire. Never always sure of a first-team place, he had lodged with Roy in Beverley for much of his time with Hull.

Early in the new year, Tommy Harris got the coach's job at York, and retired as a player. The *Mail* said that the "... departure of Harris means that one more link with the famed Boulevard pack of recent seasons is broken. Commenting on his fellow Welshman's appointment, Roy Francis said 'I think there is every chance he will make a successful coach.

Left: Johnny Whiteley and Roy. (Courtesy Robert Gate)

Bottom left: Ernest Hardaker, Hull FC Chairman. (Courtesy *Rugby League Journal*)

Bottom right: Roy with Clive Sullivan. (Courtesy Robert Gate)

He had an outstanding international career, having played rugby league in every country where it is played. If he views coaching with the same intensity of purpose that he has applied to his career, then there is no doubt it will be successful." Harris was aged 34. Around the same times, prop forward Trevor Whitehead was signed from Leeds.

One of Tommy Harris's first acts at York was to arrange a trial for Roy's older son, Geoff. Geoff had trained regularly with the players at Hull, so Harris knew of his pace and potential. The match against Bramley was his first full rugby league match, although he had had trials for Leeds. Geoff had been playing rugby union for Riding Nomads, and had also been the East Yorkshire athletics champion at 100 and 220 yards. Later in the season, Geoff was expected to play for York against Hull, but an injured shoulder meant he missed both matches against Roy's team. Geoff played for York in 1962–63, but then was offered a promotion at work which meant moving to London, so he retired from rugby league.

At the end of January, the *Mail* reported on Roy's boxing training with Johnny Halafihi. The boxer was going to join manager Jim Wicks's group, which also included Henry Cooper. Roy had been in London at a catering exhibition, and joined Halafihi at the famous Thomas A' Beckett gym where he signed for Wicks.

In February, Roy decided not to apply for the trainer-baggage man role with the British Lions who were touring Australia and New Zealand that summer. Apart from the limits of the role, he would have had to miss pre-season training with Hull and it would probably have been financially not worthwhile for Roy to have to be away from his catering businesses.

Despite the new recruits, Hull were still struggling. On 24 March, they were 'nilled' for the first time in almost three years. A week later, they lost 16–8 at Bramley, their eighth defeat in 10 games. The report in the *Mail* said that they needed a goalkicker, but Peter Bateson had been in the 'A' team. In April, there were two letters in the *Mail* from Hull supporters saying that Roy should pick the team. Both letters pointed out that Roy had first-hand knowledge of the players' fitness and capabilities. There never seemed to be much chance of that happening, and maybe this was a factor in Roy's eventual departure from the Boulevard.

Another change was that for the first time in many years, Hull finished below Hull KR in the Northern Rugby League. Rovers climbed the table to eighth; Hull sunk to 16th, just below halfway in a 30-team league. Hull finished with 18 wins and a draw from their 36 matches. After much debate in the sport, the league split into a First and Second Division for the 1962–63 season. By finishing in 16th place, Hull just scraped into the new top flight.

There was little joy in the Cups. In the Challenge Cup, Hull lost 32–16 at Oldham in the first round. They had made a little more progress in the Yorkshire Cup, beating Huddersfield 9–8 at the Boulevard before going down 13–7 to Wakefield Trinity in the second round.

1962–63

This season was dominated by the worst winter since the 1947–48 season. From Boxing Day to early March, only a handful of games were played, and the season continued well into May. Only a minority of clubs had floodlights at this stage in the sport's development, meaning that the backlog of fixtures in April and May was even worse than usual.

As well the League and the Challenge Cup, the RFL introduced the Eastern and Western Divisional Championship. The aim was to give the Second Division clubs visits from their First Division neighbours. In the Eastern Division, Hull finished in 11th place in a 16-team competition, with two wins from eight matches. To add to the fans' frustration, Hull KR finished in second place, and beat Huddersfield in the Final 13–10. It was the first silverware won by either of the city's teams since Hull's 1958 Championship win.

Hull's hopes for the season were not helped when Johnny Whiteley sustained an Achilles tendon injury, and missed the whole campaign. Clive Sullivan was also out of action for six weeks in the autumn, and also missed some matches through Army commitments.

In the First Division, Hull finished three points clear of the relegation zone, in 14th place. Bramley with 18 points finished bottom of the table and along with Oldham on 19 were relegated. Hull finished with 22 points, from 10 wins and two draws from their 30 fixtures. Hull played seven matches in April and the same number in May, finishing on the 27th. Mike Ackroyd said in the *Mail* that "Early in the First Division campaign, Hull FC coach Roy Francis predicted that the team would 'come good' and his forecast now seems to be accurate." Ackroyd wrote this after Hull beat Leeds 17–9 early in May. However, they finished the season with five consecutive defeats.

In the Challenge Cup, Hull succumbed in the first round, 7–0 at home to Wigan. They fared a little better in the Yorkshire Cup, beating Huddersfield 12–3 at The Boulevard before losing 18–7 at Hunslet.

In September, another member of the Francis family was covered in the *Mail's* sports pages. Roy's younger son, Ian, scored two tries on his debut for the Ionians rugby union club.

In October, the *Mail* reported that Roy was selling his *Haveasnack* café in Beverley and was "having a rest" at his new home in Cottingham before returning to the licensing trade. In early May, it was reported that Roy was to become the licensee of *The Whistler* pub in Dewsbury. It was around 50 yards from Crown Flatt, the home of Dewsbury RLFC. It was the fourth pub that Roy had managed, and he was returning to the area where he had enjoyed a lot of success with Dewsbury RLFC during the War.

Ernest Hardaker said in the *Mail* that it was "a personal matter for Roy" and that "It will not make any difference to his coaching, for he will be about only 1¼ hous drive away." That is an optimistic estimate – today, using the M62, the time is estimated at one hour nine minutes. Maybe Roy was thinking that his future lay away from Hull, and with one of the club's nearer to his new home. The report in the *Mail* did say that he was "rugby league's longest serving coach", but maybe he was thinking about seeking a new challenge.

1963–64

Hull managed just one win in the first 10 matches of the new season, at Widnes in the league. The first league match of the season was a 31–7 loss at the Boulevard against Leeds. The directors had an emergency meeting after the game, which Ernest Hardaker described in the *Mail* as "a deplorable exhibition." The directors announced five changes to the team to play Widnes a couple of days later. Hardaker also said that "We are not standing for this.

We had a good performance against Rovers and then comes this poor show against Leeds. There is definitely something adrift somewhere and we are determined to find out what it is all about. The fitness and ability are there but, for some reason or other, we are not getting the cohesion ... We may be wrong to suggest that something is diabolically amiss. Any team can lose a match, but it seemed to be done in such an indifferent manner."

They went out of the Yorkshire Cup 25–9 at Huddersfield. The decline of the past two seasons continued. The team lost 12 consecutive league matches, although a couple were narrow one- or two-point defeats. On 7 September, Hull supporter Barbara Coburn said in a letter published in the *Mail* that was critical of the club's transfers and lack of signings: "A last word to Roy Francis. Someone once said 'A good coach is a coach who can turn a losing team into a winning outfit.' I know you haven't the players on the books you would like, Roy, but you wouldn't be human if, in your little touchline shelter, your thoughts hark back to those great days of not so long ago. One cheerful thought, Roy, you are being paid to watch. It costs me 3s [15p] a week."

The board were looking for new players. However, at the end of October, in a shock move, Roy left the club that had been his base since 1950. Leeds had advertised for a new coach, and it was announced that Roy had asked Hull to be released from his contract on 30 October 1963 so he could become coach at Leeds. Hull's chairman Ernest Hardaker consulted the club's board before reluctantly agreeing to Roy's request. His contract had another two years to run.

Mike Ackroyd said in the *Mail* that it was "the end of an era for the Boulevard club." His report says that "Francis asked the board to release him so that he could take up a too-good-to-refuse offer from Leeds that was made to him confidentially on Monday evening although he had not applied for the post." Given that Leeds had been recruiting a new coach for a month, and had advertised openly for applicants, it seems unlikely that they would have offered it to Roy without an interview.

Hardaker said that the board had reluctantly "agreed to release him forthwith. Hardaker also said in the *Mail* that their joint efforts "...cannot come to an end without me thinking back to the happy days that have been the make-up of his association with the club." Although the last two seasons had seen a decline in results, Roy had, for a period, made Hull one of the game's leading clubs. Maybe the team had grown old together, and Hull would have been relegated in 1964 if it had not been agreed to return the sport to one division.

The *Mail* reported that "Francis said he was sorry to be leaving Hull because it was difficult to make a break with people one had known for 14 years ... he thought it [the Leeds offer] would give him greater opportunities." He also had a special message for the supporters in the Threepenny Stand who he thanked for their "magnificent support over the years."

Roy could look back on: three Championship finals, including two wins; a Championship semi-final; two Challenge Cup finals and one semi-final; and four Yorkshire Cup finals.

Many of the Hull players had also won individual honours at international and county level. Johnny Whiteley took over as player-coach. Roy did one more coaching session with Hull, then on the Saturday sat in the stand watching his new team defeat his old one 30–7.

New challenges awaited Roy at Leeds. His relationship with Hull would resume in the future.

Renee and Roy behind the bar at the Lamwath pub ... (Courtesy Geoff Francis)

and with sons Ian and Geoff. (Courtesy Geoff Francis)

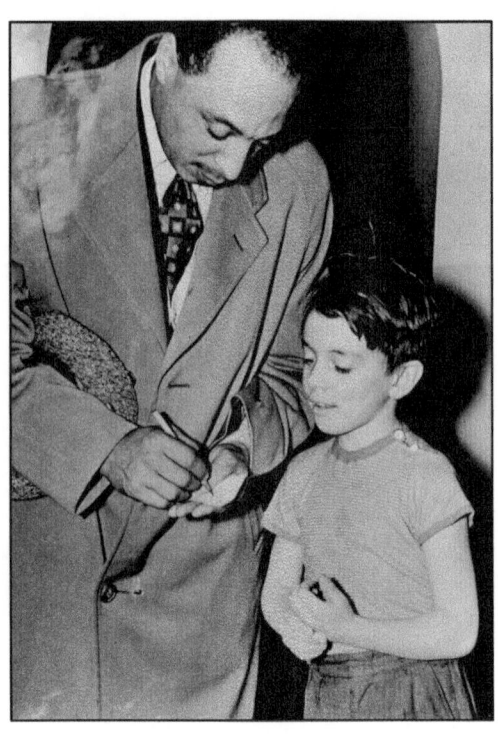

Left: Renee and Roy enjoying a dance. Roy is wearing a Wales Rugby League blazer.
Above: Making a young fan happy by signing his autograph book. (Both courtesy Geoff Francis).

Above and right: On holiday in Majorca in 1962. (Both courtesy Geoff Francis)

13. Leeds 1963 to 1966

In moving to Headingley, Roy faced the challenge of bringing more consistency to one of the sport's great clubs. Leeds had finally won their first Championship in 1961, but then had slipped to seventh place the following season. In the new First Division, they had also finished seventh, with 32 points from their 30 games.

Leeds started the 1963–64 campaign poorly, with only two wins in the first nine matches, although one of these was at the Boulevard. In the Yorkshire Cup they beat Castleford at Headingley, but then lost at Featherstone. In the Eastern Division, Leeds won at Doncaster, but then lost the return match at Headingley 22–11, with the visitors inspired by Eric Horsman, who had been transferred from Leeds to Doncaster the previous season.

Away to Hull Kingston Rovers in the first game of the season, Leeds were "well beaten by the end" according to the *Yorkshire Post*. At home to Keighley, Alfred Drewry said they were "hapless" as they gave up a 10–0 lead to lose 14–10. At Wigan, in another defeat, the post said that there was a "lack of penetration and punch among the Leeds forwards and backs." At home to Hunslet, Leeds were "well beaten", and the *Post* commented that Hunslet could have won by more than five points.

In early October, Leeds went three hours without scoring a try. The directors did recognise the need for new players. In September, Alan Lockwood was signed from Hull KR, and Mick Clark was recruited from Salford.

Roy's old Army friend, Trevor Foster, had been appointed as Leeds coach on 4 December 1961, taking over from Dai Prosser. Trevor had full responsibility for coaching, training and selecting the team.

However, in early October, Leeds announced that second team coach Jack Evans would be leaving the club because he was moving to South Wales to take up a new job. The *Yorkshire Evening News* (The *News*), reported that the club would be advertising for a coach for either the first or second team, and that Trevor Foster had agreed to coach the second team if a new appointment was made at first team level. A couple of days later, the club said that they would consider a player-coach for either position.

After the position was advertised, Great Britain international and Wakefield captain, Derek Turner, told Arthur Haddock in the *News* that he was 'very interested' in the post. Haddock outlined that a player-coach role at a senior club was not uncommon. Eric Ashton was doing it at Wigan, Jim Challinor had joined Barrow on this basis; Frank Dyson was player-coach at Oldham and Fred Ward held the post at Hunslet.

The Leeds board then changed their minds about Trevor Foster continuing to work with the first team, and on 15 October, Arthur Clues, the Australian former Leeds and Hunslet forward, took the position on a temporary basis. Leeds chairman Noel Stockdale said that this would give the board a 'breathing space' to make a new appointment.

There was more speculation that Derek Turner was the front-runner. However, there was speculation that he was in the running for a Great Britain place after a poor display against the Australians in the first test at Wembley. Could someone be a player-coach at one of the sport's leading clubs and play for Great Britain? In the event he was not selected for either of the two final test matches.

The *News* said on 26 October that he would be paid £15 a week during the season for the coaching role, and £20 for a win or £10 for a defeat as a player. A 50 percent winning record could give him £30 a week, "one of the game's plums" according to the report. Leeds had reportedly interviewed three people, including Turner. Wakefield made it clear that if Leeds wanted Turner to play, they would have to pay a transfer fee for him.

However, on 28 October, the *News* reported that Turner had decided to stay at Wakefield, and that there were four other candidates under consideration for the £700 a year job. The next day, Haddock wrote that Roy Francis was being linked with the post, and the next day it was confirmed that Roy had left Hull to join Leeds with a three-year contract. Roy said his priority in his new post was to find out "why the Leeds team had slumped so badly." Roy commented that "It is no intention of mine to arrive on the scene wielding a big stick, rather to use a poker and stir the ashes to see what I can find. After this has been done, I can get to work on a job which I am frankly relishing and which I think will be very enjoyable." The report said that Roy was known in the game "as a 'no nonsense' man. He is a highly engaging character, but also a disciplinarian." Noel Stockdale said that Roy's "first job was to get the best out of existing personnel. The club would then act on his team building recommendations."

Roy seemed to have control of team selection, although the football committee did seem to intervene on occasions. Transfers were under their control, although Roy seemed to have a major say in players to be retained and released.

Simon Foster, Trevor Foster's son, recalls: "When Roy replaced Trevor at Headingley in 1963 as the first team coach there was no animosity whatsoever, they had great respect for one another. Trevor understood that his transitional role with Leeds had been one of settling things down after an unsteady period at the club and importantly to nurture the talented young players to ensure they fulfilled their potential. The likes of Mike Shoebottom, Barry Seabourne and Alan Smith were gradually brought into the first team under Trevor's watchful eye and proved soon to become stars of Roy' coaching methods and success at Leeds.

Trevor became heavily involved at the time with the Bradford Northern reformation and was happy to step down to coach the 'A' team at Leeds under Roy`s direction and continued to work with the younger players. Interestingly, I often attended first team and some second team matches at Headingley as a nipper with my dad in the 1960s. I well remember Roy in the early days of his tenure invited all the players' wives, partners and children to matches and on to the after-match refreshments and social. There was a real family atmosphere of togetherness." Simon also points out that Don Revie had become manager at Leeds United in 1961, and also encouraged a family atmosphere for the players at Leeds United.

On his way home from his final training session with Hull, Roy was involved in a nasty car accident which saw his Zodiac wrecked. He had been given a St Christopher medallion by the Hull players as a leaving gift, and it did its job. Wilf Rosenberg, Terry Hollindrake, Peter McVeigh and Jack Kershaw were in the car with Roy. Fortunately, no one was hurt. Rosenberg told the *News*: "Another car cut across, forced Roy onto a verge and then, after spinning round twice, we hit some roadworks. When we got out of the car, it was unbelievable."

On 2 November, Roy watched Leeds beat Hull 30–7. The Football Committee selected some younger players for that game, including Barry Seabourne, Ray Batten and Jack Thomas. Three new forwards were signed in November, including Bill Drake from Hull. Another recruit from Hull was Dick Gemmell, with Roy travelling to Hull to persuade the player and his wife that a move to Leeds was the best option for them. In a protracted transfer, Leeds managed to resist a last-minute bid by Wakefield Trinity for the player. Clearly Roy recognised the potential of the younger players at the club, but needed some experience to bolster the side in the short term. Gemmell made his debut in January against Hull KR, and broke his hand, leaving him on the sidelines until 28 March.

After a 30–6 home loss to Widnes on 16 November, Alfred Drewry commented in the *Yorkshire Post* (the *Post*) that Leeds were heading for the Second Division. The team's first win under Roy's control was against Castleford on 14 December, although Alfred Drewry said that the visitors were the better side. At the turn of the year, in the league Leeds had won just four out of 17 matches. Their display at Wakefield was described in the *Post* as one of their worst at Belle Vue since the War.

Things improved in January and February, with four successive wins in the league. On 8 February, Leeds's run in the Challenge Cup ended at Salford with a 10–6 defeat. However, the following week they won at St Helens for the first time in 17 seasons despite, or maybe because of, Roy's decision to allow his players to go to the Rugby League Queen's dance at Headingley the evening before the match. According to Phil Caplan's biography of Mick Shoebottom, Robin Dewhurst and Mick, with their partners, took first and second places in a *Twist* competition. The *Twist* was a popular dance of the time.

However, the last nine league matches saw just two wins, but these were enough to see Leeds finish in 13th place, with 20 points, 10 clear of Keighley who finished 15th in what would have been the top relegation place had promotion and relegation continued. As it was, the sport returned to one division for the 1964–65 season. Hull would have been relegated had two divisions continued.

In March, Roy had been disappointed that the club failed to sign Mervyn Hicks. The player had agreed to visit Leeds to look at houses as part of a transfer, but instead signed for St Helens. At the end of March, an Eastern Division match, admittedly of little importance, attracted a 'crowd' of just 2,806 to Headingley.

At the end of the season, Lewis Jones left Headingley for a player-coach role in Australia. His last match was on 31 March when Leeds beat Halifax. Interviewed by Phil Caplan, Ken Eyre says that Roy told him that he had to sign experienced players initially. However, the departure of Jones meant that the young players had to take more responsibility, and not just look to the Welsh legend for a lead. Roy recognised the potential in the 'A' team, but could only bring the youngsters in gradually. They were coached by Trevor Foster, the friendship between the two meaning that they both were comfortable with Trevor continuing to develop the club's younger players in the second team.

In February, it was reported that Roy was planning an off-season trip to Australia. This was also around the time the transfer ban between the two countries started to be relaxed.

This was not the reason for Roy's trip. He described it as a 'semi-working holiday;', and had been invited by Australian tour captain Arthur Summons and joint tour manager Arthur Sparks. Leeds agreed that Roy could make the trip, where he intended to study and film coaching methods in Australia. He would also look out for any younger players who may have potential for Leeds. It is interesting to wonder if Roy was also using the trip to find out more about a possible move to coach in Australia.

1964–65

The new season saw two important innovations. The Championship was to be decided by play-offs involving the top 16 clubs, rather than the four when the sport last had one division. Also, substitutes were allowed for injured players. Although they would not have been aware of it, had two divisions continued, with the team who finished top of the table becoming the Champions, this would very much have been in Leeds's favour in Roy's time at the club.

Roy's influence saw the club start to turn the corner. Ken Dalby outlined that "Bare as the Headingley sideboard was at the end of the season, 'Operation Recovery' basically went according to plan, with the younger players gaining invaluable experience, and the overall record a vast improvement on that of the previous season. Regrettably, winning matches was to prove far easier than winning back spectator support, and Headingley's empty terraces reflected the general decline in rugby league attendances."

There were less than 5,500 people at Headingley for the first league match, against Warrington. The *Yorkshire Evening Post* (the *Evening Post*) had letters critical of the club, but not of Roy. One said "I am very pleased that I have not got the lot of Roy Francis, the coach. It looks like being a long lean season at Headingley." Only 6,710 supporters were at the Leeds versus Hunslet local derby on 4 September. In 1960, the same match attracted 15,491. To be fair, this was not just a Leeds problem, the game itself was seeing attendances decline overall.

It was the football committee who still had the final say on transfers. They agreed a deal with York to sign Albert Firth. Roy and Joe Warham went to sign him, but Firth was not at home. They waited until 11pm, and then left, arranging for Frith to ring Roy when he got home. Roy signed Firth at 12.45am, after the player had phoned Roy, who returned to Frith's Wakefield home to sign him.

At the Leeds club AGM, the *Evening Post* reported that: "Roy Francis, went on Mr Sharman, was now providing leadership off the field and newly-appointed captain Dick Gemmell the leadership on it." The report also said that it was the club's policy to look to youth, "which took time and hard work." Another recruit followed that week, when Ron Morgan was signed from Swinton.

One highlight was reaching the Yorkshire Cup Final. Leeds beat Hunslet and Keighley at Headingley before beat ing Halifax 20–7 at Thrum Hall in the semi-final. "Purpose, teamwork, individual brilliance, faultless tackling, determination under pressure" was what Leslie Temlett said about Leeds against Halifax. "A great win, in which the influence of coach Roy Francis was apparent in the Leeds work. Much of their 'togetherness' was reminiscent of the great Hull team which he moulded and took to so many finals."

In the final at Odsal, Leeds were beaten 18–2 by Wakefield. Roy had organised a special daylight training session before the match. Ken Dalby said in his history of Leeds: "... we lacked sufficient all-round experience and maturity to straddle the peaks of consistent success. Confirmation came in the Yorkshire Cup Final at Fartown where Wakefield Trinity moved the ball around with dazzling speed and assurance..." However, as with Hull when the team had started to be successful, the County Cup Final was valuable experience for the younger players, and a sign of the start of a revival at Headingley. However, a letter in the *Evening Post* said that "After the shocking display ... at Fartown it is about time the Headingley officials got down to some hard training in tackling and backing up. Leeds also need two young big prop forwards – a must– a good loose forward. Mr Francis – show them how to tackle, how to take a pass on the burst, how to give a reverse on the move..."

More recruits followed. Australian winger Bill Landers was signed. The *Evening Post* had a photo of Roy coming to tackle him in training. In October, a young Syd Hynes had been signed from the Leeds NALGO rugby union club. On 26 November, the *Evening Post* said that Olympic sprinter Alf Meakin could play against Featherstone. He had a work out under chief coach Roy Francis. Leeds Football Cttee favoured saying "We'll play him" when they tackled team selection. Meakin did play, but was then chosen for the 'A' team the following week. Possibly this was one occasion when Roy was over-ruled – the Football Committee probably hoped that Meakin's appearance would draw in some extra fans. The player was not retained by Leeds, but did have a professional career with Blackpool.

Just before Christmas, declining crowds, despite the team's improvement, saw the Leeds directors ask the players to take a £2 cut in winning money. The *Evening Post* reported Noel Stockdale as saying: "We went into the figures, and put the position to our coach, Roy Francis – that the players were taking more than the lot at the moment. Francis was told that the club would honour their contact with the players, but that if the players would be prepared to knock £2 off winning pay, we would be grateful, and it was left to him to put the matter to the team. We asked them to think it over for a week. Last Thursday, the captain, Dick Gemmell, told us that the team understood, and that it was ok with them."

Soon after this, Jack Myerscough became Leeds chairman. It was reported that he had a long discussion with Roy, and confirmed that building on young promising players was the way forward. The club were not interested in other teams' 'cast-offs'.

In the Challenge Cup, Leeds beat Liverpool comfortably 19–6. As always, Roy organised two extra training sessions, and a team meal to discuss tactics for the match. Then Leeds beat Bramley narrowly, again after extra training. Both wins were at Headingley. Leeds went down 7–5 at Hunslet in the third round. They missed three penalties. Regular kicker Robin Dewhurst was out injured.

In the league, Leeds climbed to 10th place in the table, with 20 wins from their 34 matches. This was despite a poor run towards the end of the season with only one win in their last six games. Their league position gave them a play-off match at Halifax, who had finished seventh. Leeds went down 28–11 at Thrum Hall. Halifax went on to win the Championship, despite finishing 11 points behind St Helens in the table. Some of the younger players had established themselves in the first team. The scrum-half spot was held either by

Barry Seabourne or Ray Batten. Mick Shoebottom was the regular stand-off. Some of the younger players also featured in the pack.

Part of the learning process for the Leeds youngsters was shown by Alan Hardisty's recollection, in his biography, of playing against Mick Shoebottom. Hardisty recalled that Roy would tell Mick to stick to him, which Mick would do for the first 20 minutes, and then decide that Hardisty wasn't interested and play his normal game. The next thing he knew was Hardisty touching down under the sticks. Apparently, Roy would "go spare" with Mick at half-time, but it was all part of the learning process for the very talented Leeds protégé. With the new arrivals and younger players, Leeds were in a stronger position to challenge for honours than they had been when Roy arrived at the club.

1965–66

Leeds continued to improve both in the league and cup competitions. At the start of the season, *Airedale* said in the *Rugby Leaguer* that Leeds since 1962 were "a tale of much promise but moderate fulfilment." Several significant signings were made during the season. At the start of the campaign, scrum-half Ken Rollin – who had been out of the game for a year – and Ken Owens, an Australian who had played for Hull were both recruited. John Atkinson had been signed from Roundhay Rugby Union club in May, but was really one for the future, and only made his first team debut in March 1966.

Signing Rollin meant that Barry Seabourne only played occasional first team matches. Ray Batten played some games in the pack, but lost his place when Harry Poole joined the club and played at loose-forward.

Australian full-back Ken Thornett was signed on a short-term basis to play for three months in the autumn. The agreement for Thornett to return to the club from Paramatta originally expired on 31 December, but was then extended to the first week of February. However, his commitments in Australia meant that he did not play his first match for Leeds until 9 October.

In October, loose forward Harry Poole was recruited from Hull KR. The *Evening Post* reported that "Roy Francis, the Leeds coach, said he was confident Poole would be a valuable capture. 'I have waited for the right player, when waiting has not been easy, but it has been worthwhile. This man can do the job." In December, *Airedale* wrote that there was a "new found strength and purpose that have helped bring about such a marked improvement in Leeds' status since mid-October."

In February, with Thornett having gone home, and Robin Dewhurst injured, Leeds signed Bev Risman from Leigh, and Roy played him at full-back rather than centre or stand-off where he had played for Leigh. Phil Caplan says that "Another selection masterstroke by Roy Francis was his choice of who to replace Thornett and cure the goalkicking dilemma for good measure, an inspired signing bringing Bev Risman across the Pennines from Leigh."

Risman recalls in his autobiography how different the training that Roy organised at Leeds was from anything he had experienced before, with an emphasis on fitness and speed. He initially struggled to keep up with the other players, despite working as a Physical Education teacher and believing that he was fairly fit.

Risman's recollections are particularly interesting. He says that "Our coach was Roy Francis, who played in the same era as my dad [Gus Risman]. He was a revolutionary thinker about the game, the master of player psychology and a fanatical fitness guru, a visionary far ahead of his time." He says that the players put spikes on as they went onto the cricket field for a fitness run. He was "not prepared for what was to come as Roy took over. His philosophy revolved around quality and the development of speed and the whole session was built around improving the players as athletes with exercises to increase flexibility and pace. Over 50 years ago he was using the training methods prevalent nowadays and there is no doubt that it made a fundamental difference to our performance." Risman concludes that the training regime made "an enormous difference to my game" and his general level of fitness improved.

Another player developing his career at Leeds was Syd Hynes. *Airedale* commented how Roy had kept faith with the youngster when he was being criticised and he was now showing his full potential. He went on to play over 350 games for Leeds.

In the league, Leeds finished in sixth place, with 24 wins from their 34 matches. There was a notable step up from the previous campaign. On 20 August, Leeds beat Doncaster 26–9, and Arthur Haddock commented that "The side as a whole certainly looked an improvement on last season". At the end of August, Leeds played Hunslet, and then faced Bramley in the Yorkshire Cup. John Bapty pointed out in the *Evening Post* that in the two games Leeds scored 77 points and conceded 11, and scored 15 "attractive" tries while only conceding one. However, the team's occasional inconsistency was shown when Leeds lost in the league at Bramley. Similarly, against Leigh at the end of October, Leeds won 22–2 at Headingley, "in a most promising fashion" according to Arthur Haddock, but then lost the return match six weeks later.

After the defeat at Leigh. Leeds were unchanged in their next match, against Oldham at Headingley: Arthur Haddock reported: "The 'no changes' decision of Leeds coach Roy Francis will probably surprise some of the club's fans who saw the defeat at Leigh. They felt that second-rower Neumann should be brought back. He is in the 'A' team with Chamberlain and Sykes at Dewsbury. Francis, it would appear has in mind how this same line-up played well in beating Oldham 10–2 at Watersheddings." However, Oldham won 13–10, and John Bapty commented that "The old failings were displayed in full – faulty handling, inability to retain possession and a lack of the movements produced by the Oldham men who were so ready to back up. The Leeds forwards will have to get on their toes again – and stay there."

In the Yorkshire Cup, after Leeds beat Bramley, they lost to Huddersfield at Fartown. Leeds also entered the BBC2 Floodlit Trophy, despite not actually having floodlights, which were installed the following season. Leeds drew at Castleford and lost at St Helens in the qualifying matches, and so did not reach the semi-finals.

In the Challenge Cup, Leeds had their best run since 1956–57, when they won the Cup. York and Hull were both beaten comfortably at Headingley. Arthur Haddock pointed out that when Leeds were drawn against Hull "... for Headingley coach Roy Francis it is a moment of reflection. He has to plan the downfall of the club he helped to take to Wembley twice – in 1959 and 1960." Of course, Leeds had faced Hull in league matches since Roy had moved to Leeds. Roy organised special training before the match, with 18 players involved. Leeds went into the game on a run of nine successive wins, including a 9–6 win against Hull. In the cup tie, Leeds won more easily, 22–12.

The third round draw took Leeds to Wilderspool, where they drew 2–2 with Warrington. The report in the *Evening Post* said that "Leeds have never tackled better in earning the replay."

That game, nine days later, had to be fitted into an already over-full schedule of matches. Arthur Haddock wrote in the *Evening Post* that "After their fourth game in six days at Wakefield on Monday the Leeds rugby league team are going to a west coast hide-away to rest before the third round cup replay with Warrington on Friday. They will 'take it easy' from Tuesday morning to Friday morning. Roy Francis, the Headingley coach, said today: 'I'm not saying where we are going. We are keeping it quiet because the whole idea is to have a few peaceful days with no distractions.'" Not surprisingly, the west coast hide-away turned out to be Blackpool, where Roy had often taken his Hull team before a big game. The players trained at the Blackpool rugby league team's Borough Park, had use of the football club's treatment rooms and played golf in Stanley Park.

Leeds won 8–0, but eight days later lost 7–2 to Wigan at Fartown in the semi-final. For the semi-final, Leeds did some extra training, but did not leave the city. The *Evening Post* reported: "But expecting the playing area to be heavy, no matter what the improvements in the weather, the Leeds players have had their workouts on the muddy training pitch and the old bowling green at Headingley, 'These are approximate to the conditions we anticipate at Fartown' says coach Roy Francis. Francis is confident of a Leeds win. "We are going to Wembley he said today. 'All we ask is thousands of spectators displaying blue and amber colours to go to Fartown and cheer us on our way. I want to see the biggest Leeds following for years at Huddersfield.'"

Leeds put Wigan under a lot of pressure in the match, but could not score the vital try that could have tied the scores. Mick Shoebottom was missing, still recovering from an injury against Warrington. Arthur Haddock felt that Leeds did not vary their tactics sufficiently to break down the Wigan defence. A couple of high kicks had Wigan in trouble, but he felt that this tactic was not applied early enough.

Roy told Arthur Haddock after the game: "We still have the championship to chase and must have a good chance. We tried very hard to get to Wembley and were not disgraced at Fartown. I thought we were the better team in the first half but we could have shown more inventiveness in the second half." Leeds played nine matches in April, losing four in the league, their worst run of the season, and twice had to play matches on consecutive days.

St Helens again topped the table, but Leeds were only nine points behind them. In the Championship play-offs, Leeds beat Huddersfield at Headingley before losing 22–5 to Wigan at Central Park. The score was 9–5 when one of the Leeds players had the ball knocked out of his hands and Wigan broke away to score. The *Evening Post* report said that "Leeds need strengthening for next season if the club is to go that bit further." That is true, but the team had improved each season under Roy's tenure. The challenge facing him and his team now was to win trophies. Ken Dalby said that "An end of term report … could justifiably have read: 'Making very good progress. Given reasonable luck and consistent effort, Leeds now have the potential to attain the highest honours in the immediate future.'"

14. Leeds 1966 to 1968

In the 1966–67 campaign, the work that Roy and the club had put in, in terms of training and building the team over the past couple of seasons now paid off. Leeds finished top of the table for the first time since the 1960–61 campaign and won the League Leaders trophy. They also won the Yorkshire League title. Leeds won 29 of their 34 league games. They opened the season with 11 wins before losing at St Helens on 28 October. It was Leeds's best ever start to a season. They only lost one more game, a narrow defeat at Oldham, before Christmas. Playing their third game in four days, they lost away to Hull KR on 27 December, but then only lost two more games, at Castleford and Wakefield. Leeds finished four points clear of runners-up Hull KR. In the *Post*, Alfred Drewry pointed out that the rugby league fixtures at Christmas and other holidays had "a faint suggestion of sadism" with Leeds facing three hard matches in four days.

One early season recruit for Leeds was Ken Eyre from Hunslet. The *Evening Post* reported that "Headingley chairman Mr Jack Myerscough said: "I am having a talk with our coach, Roy Francis, to decide whether we should put in a bid for Eyre." The next day they signed Eyre for £3750.

However, Roy felt that Eyre was overweight when he signed for Leeds, and Arthur Haddock reported that "Roly-poly Eyre weighed 16 stones three pounds when he joined Leeds. Roy wanted him to reduce his weight by just over a stone in three weeks. Haddock said that "Roy Francis is giving him special training and has put the international prop on a diet. Eyre has been told – no beer, no sugar, no bread, no potatoes, no pastries. He can have lean meat, fish, cheese, eggs and fresh vegetables. Roy told Haddock "Ken should be fighting fit in two or three weeks." He was considering playing him in the first half of the forthcoming match against Wigan. Roy had also put 'A' team forward, 19-year-old Philip Sunderland on a diet and reduced his weight by nearly two stone. Haddock said that the young player's mother said: "What does Mr Francis say we can have to eat today" before preparing his meals.

Leeds beat Wigan 38–25, although according to Arthur Haddock, "perfectionist" Roy was unhappy with their performance, saying that the team had disobeyed his instructions in the last 15 minutes, when they conceded 15 points.

At the end of September, the Leeds club AGM heard that a surplus of £374 had been made for the period ending 31 May 1966. This reflected the improvement in the team's performances.

In the Yorkshire Cup, Leeds surprisingly lost at home to Bramley in the first round. In the BBC2 Floodlit Trophy, having launched their new floodlights in September, Leeds drew with Castleford at Headingley, and lost at Swinton. The draw with Castleford had been played under the new 'four tackle' rule. This resulted in an open game. However, it was another challenge that coaches faced in the autumn because it was a major change to the rules. Roy was initially cautious, not wanting to use the new rule for a key match at St Helens. On 28 October he told Arthur Haddock: "I favour it [the new rule] because it will make players use their brains more, but I am not keen to play it at the moment.

Alfred Drewry, reporting on Leeds's comfortable win against Oldham at Headingley in early November, felt that the new rule made for a "sparkling game crammed with skill and surprise and character." He felt it would have a positive effect on attendances.

After three months of experiment and debate, the new rule was agreed at a meeting of the clubs in December. The same meeting agreed that matches could be held on Sundays if both clubs agreed. Both decisions were important for the future of the game.

Interestingly, though, an analysis by the *Post* of results overall compared to those played under the new rule, showed that Leeds performed better in the 'overall' results. However, Leeds had only played eight games under the new rule, and their success later in the season shows that Roy and his team adapted well to the new challenge.

In January, Roy had the unusual situation of one of his players being in court charged with assaulting a spectator. The incident involved Dick Gemmell after the Hull versus Leeds game on 31 December. The stipendiary magistrate (equivalent to a District Judge today) who heard the case found Gemmell guilty, but realised there had been considerable provocation, and gave the player an absolute discharge, although he did have to pay costs of £10/10/0. Roy does not seem to have been involved in the case and is not mentioned in the newspaper report.

In the Challenge Cup, Leeds beat Blackpool 15–3. They then faced a trip to Oldham. Leeds had not won a Challenge Cup match in Lancashire for 20 years, but beat a "mediocre" Oldham side 13–4. Alfred Drewry reported in the *Post* that Leeds had been 6–2 up at half-time, playing into a strong wind and at times driving rain.

A few days after the Oldham game, Jack Myerscough declared that Leeds were aiming to win the Challenge Cup and the Championship. This was a very difficult target, because both competitions concluded at the end of the season, with play-off matches to be fitted in before the Challenge Cup Final. Particularly when many clubs still did not have floodlights, teams also had a backlog of fixtures to complete in April.

In the second week of March, Arthur Haddock said that "Leeds are poised to start 'collecting silver' as Headingley coach Roy Francis puts it." He said that Leeds should win the League Leaders trophy and the Yorkshire League. Then they would face the challenge of knock-out matches.

To prepare for their match against Swinton, Roy took the team to Harrogate. Leeds were joint favourites with Castleford for the Challenge Cup. Arthur Haddock said that "Brine baths, a stroll and a meal at a quiet country 'pub' are part of a programme this week designed to get the team into a relaxed mood... the schedule for the next few days is aimed at lifting the tension, and will be rounded off with a tactical talk by coach Roy Francis on Thursday."

The day before the game, Roy told Arthur Haddock: "I am relying on the side which did me proud against Wigan, Oldham and St Helens." On their prospects for a win, he said: "What's the point in making inane remarks when this team has done the talking for itself?" Haddock commented that "Top-scoring Leeds have got where they are with fast, open football from a mobile pack and sound backs who always get a fair share of the ball from hooker Lockwood."

Leeds beat Swinton 17–15 to reach the semi-finals for the second consecutive season. Arthur Haddock said in the *Evening Post* that "...skilful youngsters, Seabourne and Batten, had much to do with this deserved win…" and credited Leeds for not being drawn into physical confrontation and head-high tackles by Swinton.

A week after the Swinton game, a 16,561 crowd saw Leeds beat Hunslet at Headingley. The team's success on the pitch was being reflected in the attendance figures.

The following week, Leeds faced Featherstone in the Challenge Cup semi-final, having played three games over Easter leading up to the match. Roy would not predict the outcome, just saying "I just hope that by 4.30 tomorrow 25,000 Leeds folk can book their transport to Wembley."

However, it was not to be. Leeds lost 16–8 at Fartown. A return to Wembley would have to wait for another year. Arthur Haddock wrote that "Featherstone hunted and harried Leeds, threw them off balance, and when they had the wind after half-time kicked frequently to keep play at the Leeds end." He concluded that Leeds did not produce the cohesion they had so often this season. Featherstone went on to win the Cup, beating Barrow 17–12 in the Final.

On 13 April, it was reported by Arthur Haddock that Roy was to stay at Leeds for the 1967–68 season. His contract, which ran out in June, would be renewed.

In the Championship play-offs, Leeds beat Widnes 27–18, with several reserves in the team. However, they then lost at home to Castleford 13–9. Trevor Watson wrote in the *Evening Post* that Leeds were "crippled by injuries, which have put a complete pack out of action." Leeds had been 7–0 ahead after 30 minutes, but an error gave Castleford a try. An interception try put Castleford ahead, and they never lost their lead.

However, this season should be recognised as the start of a four-year run of consistent success for the club, "an era of unprecedented success" as Ken Dalby put it. As at Hull, it had taken Roy three seasons to build a team that could play and win consistently.

Phil Caplan, in his biography of Mick Shoebottom, says that Alan Smith recognised Roy's ability to develop the younger players like himself by using experienced players to work with them. Ken Eyre told Caplan that "Roy had this ability to spot and turn potential into exceptional footballers…" Barry Seabourne said to Caplan that one of Roy's strengths was to get everyone working for each other. He recalls meeting in the players bar after the games at Headingley along with the players' families.

1967–68

At Hull, Roy had won the Championship twice, but had seen his team lose twice at Wembley in the Challenge Cup. There were two of the sport's traditional trophies he had not won as a coach – the Challenge Cup and a county cup. The Challenge Cup was fulfilled this season with Leeds's 11–10 win over Wakefield Trinity at Wembley. There has been so much written and debated about the 1968 "Watersplash" Challenge Cup Final to not cover that ground again here. No one would have wished to – or been able to predict or plan for – Wakefield's Don Fox missing a last minute conversion that could have taken the cup to Belle Vue. The pitch had been flooded by a huge storm, and was made worse by further rain during the match. But with Wembley packed and a huge television audience watching the referee thought he could not postpone the game. The playing of the match, and the referee's

131

decisions during the game are still debated to this day. Bev Risman says in his autobiography that after the game "The only one who seemed unhappy by what had happened was Roy Francis, who felt his team had been denied the chance to show what it was truly capable of."

Simon Foster recalls: "In 1968 I was sat with my dad [Trevor Foster] in the stands at Wembley watching the Leeds versus Wakefield Trinity Challenge Cup Final. Trevor remarked a couple of times that despite the terrible wet weather the Leeds team looked incredibly fit and fast on the slippery surface, Roy he said was a genius at improving fitness levels and enhancing the speed of execution in various plays. He said the small technical things Roy had introduced made the difference. He said Roy was a deep thinker about the game."

Before the match, Leslie Temlett wrote in the *Rugby Leaguer:* "As Roy Francis, their coach, put it to me: "It would be the icing on the cake." Although they have had a wonderful season, Francis, as usual, could not be drawn into a forecast. If Leeds do win, it will be the realisation of a dream. Twice, before, when he was Hull's coach, he has taken a team to Wembley. On each occasion, in 1959, and again the following year, his men lost... No wonder Roy has his fingers crossed for this visit, but there is a confidence that Leeds can 'do it', there is also a realisation of the task which lies ahead." Leeds captain Mick Clark said: "We have confidence in Roy Francis who has led us to this great final and who also has first-hand knowledge of Wembley."

Trevor Watson reported in the *Evening Post* how Roy was "sticking rigidly to the schedule he mapped out a fortnight ago to ensure peak fitness for the side for Saturday's Rugby League Cup Final." Three training sessions were planned before the players headed south on Thursday 9 May. They were staying at the Crystal Palace National Sports Centre. The players did get a trip into central London, and saw singer Tom Jones at the London Palladium.

Roy was concerned because his players had not played for two weeks. He said that "It should be a classic Wembley, but I think we will have the edge." A tough training session the day before the final ensured that the players were ready for their big day.

There were many messages of support for Leeds before the game. One, which was sent to Roy, was from the father of an 11-year-old Leeds fan who had Chicken Pox and could not travel to Wembley. Roy sent the boy a telegram saying that he should get well and that the players would do their best for him.

To reach the Final, Leeds had beaten Liverpool City, then Bramley and then won at Oldham. They did not concede a point in the second and third round matches. Leeds beat Liverpool 23–12, but Bill Bowes reported in the *Evening Post* that the margin would have been larger had Shoebottom and Atkinson taken two chances to ground the ball.

Before the match against Bramley, Roy's main concern was the fitness of Mick Clark. He told the *Evening Post:* "Mick has not trained so far this week because of his thigh injury. I stopped him as a precaution, and we'll have to see how he is tonight." Clark did play, and Roy fielded an unchanged team from the one that had beaten Halifax 35–0 the week before. Against Bramley, Leeds also kept a clean sheet, and ran up 29 points to progress comfortably to the third round. Arthur Haddock said it was a one-sided match, in which Leeds got revenge for Bramley's shock win at Headingley in November.

Roy checking out Wembley before the final. (Courtesy Geoff Francis)

Leeds celebrate winning the Challenge Cup in 1968.
(Andrew Varley Picture Agency)

For the match at Oldham in the third round, Leeds sold 5,000 tickets for the tie. Roy organised extra training, and took the players out for a meal a couple of nights before the game. Despite missing Bill Ramsey, and losing Mick Clark to an injury after 35 minutes, the Leeds pack outplayed the Oldham forwards and provided the platform for a 13–0 win.

Before the semi-final against Wigan, Leslie Temlett said that "Coach Roy Francis, very pleased at how his lads fared at Oldham, is even more so at the possibility of going into the final at the expense of his old club (his first club) Wigan. Roy is a perfectionist, so it will not surprise those who know him when I say that while full of praise for the lads at Watersheddings, he thinks they should have won more easily. He is so hopeful that this season he will take Leeds to Wembley, as he twice took Hull, and that this time he will return as coach of a Rugby League Cup winning side. Underneath this perfectionism of Roy, however, there lies a tremendous pride, a belief in his team. Having voiced his brief regret that Leeds failed to get two tries he thinks they should have got, he revealed "They are a great bunch." He added his special word of praise for Mick Joyce, who so covered himself in glory with the opportunist try he scored after coming on as a substitute for his injured skipper, Mick Clark. "It was", said Francis, "a typical bit of quick thinking and action by a very good player."

Before the match, Roy took 26 players to watch Wigan play a midweek game at Salford. The *Evening Post* reported that "Roy Francis said he wanted all his first team players and each understudy to take a good look at the opposition."

Wigan had beaten Leeds five times in 10 years in the Challenge Cup. However, that counted for nothing as Leeds won comfortably. hey beat Wigan 25–4 at Swinton, in front of a 30,058 crowd. Ken Dalby said that "At long last Wigan had been given a double dose of their own unpalatable medicine. Moreover, the Loiners had done it their way: a la Francis!" Leslie Temlett commented that "The attitude of the team and that of coach Roy Francis is "We know we've a tough job on. We know how Wigan rise to the occasion in cup football. We still think we shall come out on top." There was no extra training but "I am willing to bet, however, that schemes based on what Francis and his men saw at Salford would be tried out and perfected." In the *Evening Post,* Arthur Haddock said that "... the plain fact is that Leeds were slicker and smarter all round, and their superiority was bound to tell. Wigan were fortunate that their opponents gained only four second half heels; but for that it could have been a 'cricket score'."

In a discussion with the *Rugby Leaguer's* Ian Proctor in 1988, Roy said that this victory over Wigan was his 'most memorable moment in the game.' Roy told Proctor that: "Our last try crystallised everything I'd striven for – perfection on a football field. Barry Seabourne scored the fifth Leeds try that day, with five of his colleagues in support and not a Wigan man in sight as he touched down. We had totally overwhelmed a (good) Wigan side which had held a hoodoo over us for years."

A couple of days after the semi-final, a letter from a Mr S. Pepper in the paper said "Credit must be handed to manager-coach Roy Francis. An amazing transformation has come over the Headingley scene since his arrival – and how magnificently the players have responded. Even reserves such as Joyce, Hick, Brown and Ratcliffe have slotted into the picture."

Left: Newspaper advert for the 1968 Challenge Cup semi-final against Wigan, which Roy said was one of the best displays by his Leeds team.

Renee and Roy with the Challenge Cup. (Courtesy Geoff Francis)

In the league, Leeds were again a model of consistency, winning 28 of their 34 matches. They finished top of the table, seven points clear of runners-up Wakefield. Leeds lost five games before Christmas, including three at Headingley. In early September, Leeds had lost 13–12 at Batley, and the *Evening Post* reported that "At Headingley there will be an 'inquest' regarding the shock defeat at Batley – and coach Roy Francis will not mince his words. He will tell his players that inconsistency is inexcusable and generally 'lay into' them regarding their lethargic display."

However, on Boxing Day they beat Wakefield at Headingley, and then went on a 14-game winning run. In January, Leslie Temlett wrote in the *Rugby Leaguer* that Leeds were "on top of the world, if not quite the league table. A few weeks back, Roy Francis, the Leeds coach, told me he considered there were only two further 'hard' matches for his team to play - the visits to Workington and St Helens. Leeds narrowly lost at Workington ... due at St Helens tomorrow."

In Phil Caplan's biography of Mick Shoebottom, Syd Hynes recalls that the team had stayed in Keswick the night before the Workington game, and "been out on the drink", thinking they were invincible. He says that "Roy Francis went absolutely berserk, but it was just the wake-up call we needed." A month later, Leeds became the first team to score six tries in a match against Hull KR for three years. Roy was reported to be pleased with the performance, but still noted things that needed improving."

Their next defeat was in the last league game of the season, at Belle Vue, when the top of the table spot and the League Leaders trophy were already won. They also won the Yorkshire League.

However, there was again disappointment in the Championship. Widnes were beaten at Headingley, but in the second round, Wigan won 11–7 to get revenge for their Challenge Cup semi-final defeat.

In the Yorkshire Cup, Leeds won at Batley, and beat Hunslet at home before losing 31–6 at The Boulevard in the semi-final. This was probably Leeds's worst result of the season, although Hull were playing well. Arthur Haddock said that Leeds "had many weaknesses but the vital one was up front where their forwards were no match for the home six."

The BBC2 Floodlit Trophy was now played on a knock-out basis. Leeds beat Halifax after a replay, but then lost 12–9 at Castleford.

One new innovation during the season was the use of gumshields. In January, Arthur Haddock wrote that Leeds and Castleford were considering this for their players. Roy said that Harry Poole and John Whiteley had both used them on occasions. Haddock asked Roy if their use was an indication of more head-high tackles. Roy did not agree, and said tha "What I find is that players today are more conscious about their looks than they used to be. They are vainer than the old-type rugby league man." This was the 1960s after all!

In Phil Caplan's biography of Mick Shoebottom, John Atkinson says that Roy concentrated on the players' fitness, and relied on their ability, but did not provide a particular game plan. He outlines that "Our only instructions were to play when the opportunity arose and react to situations as they came up." He also says that Roy adapted to the four-tackle rule quicker than anyone else, and that the six-tackles that came in later would have suited that Leeds team even more.

Leeds 1968 Yorkshire Cup winners. (Andrew Varley Picture Agency)

1968–69

In the close season, Roy went to Australia to work as a 'coaching consultant' with North Sydney. This period is covered in the next chapter, but was the first step in his departure from Headingley.

Leeds started the season with a defeat at Leigh, but then won their next four games. One trophy that Roy had never won as a coach was a county cup. The county cup competitions, played in the few months of the season, were hard fought, often with local rivalries at stake. Leeds also did not have a good record in the competition since the end of the Second World War. They had been in four Yorkshire Cup finals, all against Wakefield Trinity, and only won one, in 1958. Roy had a similar record – four defeats while with Hull in the 1950s and one with Leeds in 1964–65. The first round draw took Leeds to the Boulevard. After a poor first half, dominated by Hull's pack, Leeds turned the game round, and with five goals and a try from Risman, and four drop-goals by Barry Seabourne, won 30–9.

Ten days later, Leeds went to Featherstone in the second round and won 18–10. Arthur Haddock commented that "... it begins to look as though Leeds are going to put the Yorkshire Cup alongside the [Challenge] Cup." Leeds won despite Crosby being sent off near the end of the game for 'remarks to the referee'.

The semi-final draw saw Leeds away from Headingley for the third time, with a trip to Thrum Hall. Ken Dalby said that there "survival was always the name of the game, no quarter was asked or given, with the result hanging in the balance until Hynes engineered the vital

137

links for Alan Smith and Ratcliffe to power their way over in the closing minutes." Leeds won through 12–5. In the final, they faced Castleford at Belle Vue.

Leeds were 10–8 ahead at half-time, and stretched their lead to 15–8. Castleford pulled back a try, but a try by Hick, converted by Risman, and a penalty from Risman saw the Cup go to Headingley with a 22–11 win. Ken Dalby said that after a hard-fought match, "... the men in blue and amber roused themselves to put the result beyond all possible doubt in a rip-roaring finish...".

On 11 September, Trevor Watson reported in the *Evening Post* that it had been reported in Australia that North Sydney wanted to recruit Roy as their new coach. Jack Myerscough told Watson that "There has been no communication whatever from North Sydney to Leeds asking us to release Roy. Neither has there been any application from Roy asking us to consider curtailing his contract." Roy was also mystified by the report. He said "I would not do anything to upset the Leeds club, they will be informed of any moves that are made." The report in Australia said that Roy would work full-time as a manager, and would have responsibilities including supporting injured players, signing new players and advising the committee on transfers, and coaching in schools."

A week later, on 18 September, the *Evening Post* reported that Roy had submitted a written request to be released from his contract to allow him to join North Sydney. His contract ran until 31 May 1970. Jack Myerscough said that the matter would be considered by the board at its next meeting.

At the end of September, in the *Rugby Leaguer*, Leslie Temlett reported that there was speculation about whether Roy Francis will be released from his contract with Leeds to coach a Sydney club. There was also speculation that Lou Neumann would return from Australia. Temlett said that the general feeling among Leeds followers is that Roy will be allowed to end his contract. He added that Roy "has done a great deal for Leeds in recent years, and who, with the club has realised his ambition of coaching a winning Wembley final team"

However, next to the article was a photo of Roy with Renee. She was holding a large toy koala bear that he had brought back for her from Australia. The article with the photo quoted Roy as saying: "Subject to the contract being signed, and of course my release by Leeds, I have decided to accept the offer made to me by the North Sydney club, but it took me a long time thinking it over. I will miss the lads at Leeds and everything connected with Headingley. It's a great club." The contract was worth £12,000 over three years.

John Atkinson told Phil Caplan that before Roy's departure was confirmed, some Australians came to watch a Leeds training session. He says that Roy used the session to impress the Australians, with Atkinson saying the players "...went through every bit of our repertoire...". Atkinson adds that the players, especially the younger ones, were "absolutely devastated" at Roy's departure, and says "... he was a conman; he used to lull you into doing things; we cottoned on very quickly but for us he was everything we wanted. He encouraged the backs in particular to play the rugby we wanted to play."

Ten days after the Yorkshire Cup Final, the Leeds board agreed to release Roy from his contract. His last game in charge of the team was a 39–8 win at York on 9 November. He stayed on the Leeds pay-roll until the end of November. He watched the game against Hull at Headingley from the stand. Jack Myerscough said that the timing of Roy's departure had been mutually agreed.

In 1988, Roy told Ian Proctor that he regretted leaving Leeds: "All I wanted from the Leeds board was a sign they wanted to retain my services, not necessarily greater financial reward, but a sense of feeling appreciated, but it never came. They appeared to have resigned themselves to allowing me to go. After all the hard work spent in building Leeds into a force, the last thing I wanted was to leave. The fruits of much hard labour were there to be enjoyed." These comments from Roy are vey interesting, but one does wonder if he made them in hindsight, now aware of how his career developed in Australia.

Roy started work with North Sydney in February 1969. Jack Nelson covered the coaching position. However, sadly he suddenly collapsed and died on Christmas Day. He was only 42 years old. Joe Warham took over the coaching role for the rest of the season.

In October, just before the Yorkshire Cup Final, Roy said in the *Rugby Leaguer* that the club needed to keep players at Leeds to cover injuries, as well as bringing through young players: "I think that the position of Leeds, while it is an extremely happy one, and one hard-worked for and meritously gained, is also one that to be carefully nurtured at the present time." He added that "Reserve strength in depth is the thing to work on."

Leeds finished top of the table again, with 29 wins and two draws from 34 matches. This time they fought their way through the play-offs to beat Castleford in the final, and bring the Championship to Headingley. While Roy had left by this time, it was the team he had built, and can be seen as the culmination of his work in this spell at Leeds. Leeds also won the League Leaders trophy in 1969–70, but lost the Championship Final to St Helens.

Before Roy and Renee left for Sydney, a presentation was made to Roy by the Leeds Supporters Club, in recognition of his achievements for the club. Reflecting on Roy's time at Leeds, Ken Dalby said that "Extremely vital, too, was the contribution of coach Roy Francis, who developed and established the style of play which took Leeds from that valley of near-despair to peaks of matchless glory, with trophies merely the by-product of rugby as superb as any ever witnessed at Headingley ... or elsewhere."

Leeds won the Mackeson trophy during Roy's time at Headingley. (Courtesy Geoff Francis)

15. North Sydney

In moving to North Sydney, albeit in stages, Roy was joining one of the foundation clubs of Australian rugby league. However, their last Premiership win had been in 1922, and their last Grand Final in 1943. Rugby league in Australia was based around two competitions, one based in Brisbane and one in Sydney.

In moving to Australia, Roy was going to a country which for much of the twentieth century had seen itself as the representative of the 'British' i.e., white race, in the South Seas. Although these policies had been gradually relaxed in the 1950s and 1960s, it was not until 1973 that racial discrimination was officially removed from criteria to emigrate to the country. Also, the country's indigenous Aborigine population had been treated very badly and only got full voting rights throughout the country in 1965.

Having been drifting in the lower reaches of the league for some years, the North Sydney management, particularly club president Harry McKinnon, wanted to employ a full-time manager-coach. This would be funded by income granted by the North Sydney Leagues Club.

They invited Roy to come as a 'consultant coach' for six weeks in the English league's close season in 1968. He was recommended to the club by a sports journalist, and by now had an impressive record with Hull and then Leeds.

What North Sydney maybe did not take into account was that it had taken Roy two or three seasons of work to gradually transform the fortunes of both clubs. Would he be given this time by Norths?

The other issue for this short visit in 1968 was that Norths already had a coach. Colin Greenwood was a white former South African rugby union player who had switched to rugby league in 1961, having achieved Springbok honours in South Africa. He won a Challenge Cup medal with Wakefield Trinity in 1963 before joining Norths in 1964. He was in his first season as player-coach.

News of Roy's pending arrival was not well received by the North Sydney players. On 4 June, the *Sydney Morning Herald* reported that Greenwood intended to leave the club because of their appointment of Roy. He did however, manage to dissuade the players from going on strike. The paper reported that "Greenwood's move follows news that the club committee intends engaging outstanding English coach Roy Francis to life the bottom-of-the-ladder side out of the doldrums ... Greenwood is terribly disappointed at the club's move and last night said that to withdraw as coach was the 'only honourable way out'." He said that he would continue as captain-coach until Roy arrived.

Five days later, Greenwood said that the match against Western Suburbs would be his last with the club. The *Herald* reported him as saying "I have made up my mind and will not play again after the West match."

So, what was Roy inheriting?

Andrew Moore, in his history of the club, says that Greenwood "had moved swiftly to overturn the more lackadaisical methods of his immediate predecessors. Special pre-season training sessions for backs and forwards had been introduced to enhance stamina and strength. These were followed by iced fruit juices rather than beer. He had moved to standardise 'moves' within the club so that player substitutions would not be unnecessarily disruptive. Detailed statistics were maintained about tackles, moves and penalty counts."

However, Moore also says that "Francis also found that Sydney football lacked the professional approach of British rugby league. This, of course, was before the tide of British-Australian rugby league supremacy turned. To Roy Francis, professionalism meant ensuring rigorous, gut-wrenching physical fitness. At that time, Norths' training schedules had more commonly entailed a few laps round the oval followed by a number of schooners of reviving ale. Indeed, as captain-coach, Billy Wilson had reputedly insisted that players drink beer in generous quantities after training sessions to help team morale and 'bonding'." Wilson had preceded Greenwood as coach.

Maybe in tribute to Greenwood, who had been with the club since 1964, Norths had their best game of the season, going down 18–13. Greenwood scored the team's first try after two minutes.

Roy arrived in Sydney on 16 June. The *Herald* reported that he had met the players and was having a training run with them in the evening before having "an important talk" with the players. He said that "I want to find out what they think is going wrong with their play, both individually and as a team". The report did say that he did not "believe he will work miracles in his six weeks with the club." It was reported that Roy "ran the players solidly for 80 minutes" at training, and that "instilling confidence in the players was his main objective." Harry McKinnon, maybe optimistically, said that Roy had already won the players over. On the eve of Roy's first match in charge, the *Herald* commented that "under the driving leadership of Francis the Norths players have worked as they have never worked before this week and on fitness alone will be a much better proposition."

In Roy's first game in charge, Norths secured their second win of the season, 18–11 against Cronulla. However, they had beaten the same team by a slightly bigger margin in their first win. Roy told the *Herald* that "apparently it was an improvement, but there is still room for a lot more. The main thing is that the boys took the two points and that will make them feel better and more confident."

Roy went to watch North's next opponents, Manly, the day after the Cronulla game. The *Herald* reported that "Manly's strengths and weaknesses were carefully noted by the astute Mr Francis and last night he had his team working for over 90 minutes to try and make use of the weak points." The paper also noted that Colin Greenwood was for sale for $2,000.

Manly won 12–11, but the report noted that Norths' defence had improved and they had more 'all-round resolution'. Norths scored the game's only try – the rest of the points came from penalties or drop-goals. Previewing Norths' next match at home to Penrith, the *Herald* said that the team "had a new lease of life" and that "North's players have at last realised they are competent footballers and are going into matches now with a lot more confidence." However, despite leading 7–6 at half-time, Norths lost 16–7 to Penrith. Roy said afterwards that the game had been lost in the first half, and there was "too much individualism". Also, according to the report, the game turned when Norths' hooker went off injured.

Another defeat followed, at home to Canterbury, and then Norths secured their third win of the season, 15–13 at Newtown, who were also struggling. Then came a shock win, 22–2, against Parramatta at the North Sydney Oval. The *Herald* commented that it was "one of the biggest rugby league upsets in years." The report added that "North's dressing room was a joyful scene for the club has been in the doldrums for the past few years." Roy told the reporter that "It's like winning the Cup Final." He also said that "The forwards will never fail Norths again." Norths scored four tries to nil, and missed several good chances.

Sadly, Norths could not maintain their good form for the rest of the season. Roy went home to fulfil his commitments to Leeds, and the last four league games were lost. Norths did come within three points away to South Sydney, but the other defeats were all by at least 10 points. The team finished in 11th place in the table, with four wins from their 22 matches.

On 19 August, Alan Clarkson reported that Norths had offered Roy a contract "that could be worth more than $40,000 over three years as manager-coach. He would receive $30,000 for three years, and a $3,000 bonus if Norths reached a grand final. The club would also buy out the remainder of his contract with Leeds, pay his and Renee's air fares to and from Australia and help with his accommodation costs in Sydney. The offer would make him the highest paid person in rugby league, although it is not clear if this meant in Australia or world-wide.

Today (2022), the $30,000 Roy was guaranteed would be worth $390,000, or £211,000. Of course, with the sport going full-time at the top-level, and the growth in commercial and television income, comparisons are difficult to make, but it was still a very substantial offer in a sport where both players and coaches were part-time.

Clarkson said that Roy was "one of the most astute football 'brains' in the code [and] greatly impressed North Sydney officials during his short term as coach..."

The next day, Rod Humphries used his column in the *Herald* to examine the offer to Roy. He agreed that Roy was "one of the most astute and experienced coaches in the game today", but said that the offer to Roy was "staggering". He said that if the deal went ahead, Roy would want new players for the team. He commented that "Francis is wise enough to know he wouldn't make a grand final with some of the present bunch." He said that the club had calculated that if they reached one semi-final, the increase in trade at the Leagues club would cover the cost of the outlay on Roy. He said that the club could have secured former Australian international Harry Bath as coach for less than half of what they offered Roy. He added that Colin Greenwood was only paid $1,000 for the season, and had unsuccessfully pressed club officials to invest in new players. He concluded by pointing out that the top coaches in Sydney earned around $2,000 a year, and that Norths were "pinning a lot of faith in Francis. For the sake of its bewildered followers, I hope the club is doing the right thing."

The following week, Humphries included in his column a defence of North's plans from club president Harry McKinnon. He said that Mr McKinnon and the club committee "... thought it was advisable to pay a full-time manager-coach now rather than have a full-time secretary. It felt the coach was the most important man in the club – with the ability to lift his team and the consequent gate taking and licensed club profits. Francis was also a fully qualified physiotherapist and his experience with football injuries would prove invaluable. Last, but not least, during the week Francis would act as a liaison officer with North Sydney area schools and help with junior football..."

Two weeks later, on 12 September, it was reported that Roy had accepted the North Sydney offer. However, this was denied in England, and it took a few weeks before the Leeds board agreed to release Roy from his contract.

In November, it was announced that Norths had signed Leo Toohey, a stand-off from Canterbury Bankstown. The *Herald* reported that Roy had been keen to secure Toohey after seeing him play against Norths.

When he returned to Leeds after his short stay, he spoke to Leslie Temlett for the *Rugby Leaguer*. His reflections are very interesting. Temlett wrote: "48 hours after his return to England from his successful summer coaching spell with North Sydney club, Roy Francis, the Leeds coach, told me: 'I think the Australian approach to the game lacks the professional one we have in this country. But if ever they get the professional approach, they will be an even greater force to be reckoned with.' Sparing a few minutes from his first coaching spell of the season with the Leeds players, Roy spoke about what he found on his visit Down Under. 'The Australian players are tremendously fit and keen but I do not think they let the ball do enough work. I do not think the game in Australia has come to grips with the four-tackle rule so completely as we have. It is not developed and exploited as it could be.'

Roy, who has come home with memories of a very happy time – 'I was tremendously well treated' he says – was struck by the great interest of Australians in members of past British Rugby League touring teams. They have an exceptional interest in tourists they have seen, and are always glad to hear of what has happened to men like Dicky Williams and Ernest Ward. It may or may not be true that Australians are drifting apart politically from this country, but from the point of view of sport the bonds remain as strong as ever.'

A number of young Australian players impressed Francis. Among those whom he praised are three stand-off halves – John Peard (Eastern Suburbs) a former rugby union player, Phil Hawthorne (St George) and Bobby Fulton (Manly Warringah) who was Australia's stand-off in this year's World Cup.

He had similar words of praise for scrum-half Bobby Laing (North Sydney) and his club-mate Eric Pitt, a second rower who he described as 'as big as Des Foreman and as fast – if anything faster'. Pitt was a Thursday Islander.

During his coaching in Sydney – coaching which saw Norths climb three places from the bottom of the Premier League table, win three of their last six matches and lose to leaders Manly by only one point – Roy renewed acquaintance with many rugby league players he had known in the British game who were now associated with the game in Australia. In the side he coached were George Ambrum, who played wing with Bradford Northern, and Dave Wood who was with St Helens.

He met Mervyn Hicks, formerly of Doncaster, Warrington and St Helens, Dave Bolton the former Wigan star, Lou Neumann, the South African who had played for Leeds, Harry Bath, the Australian forward who skippered Warrington, Harry Hammond, the ex-Dewsbury prop, Rex Mossop, the Australian who was with Leigh, Fred Pickup the Leeds centre and Lewis Jones. What Norths thought of Roy and his coaching (he is not to be drawn about whether he may have another visit next close season) is shown by the fact that three separate presentations were made to him before his farewell."

1969

Roy and Renee arrived in Sydney in early February. They had come by ship on the Canberra, but had not been allowed to disembark when the ship called in at Cape Town due to South Africa's apartheid laws. He met the players and warned them that they were in for "a hard year". He said that he expected a lot from them, and it was up to them to respond. He concluded that there was "no easy road for a football team." The training had been taken by Bob Sullivan, but Roy said that he would run the next session.

Two days later, Clarkson reported that Roy "left some tired and aching limbs behind him after he presided over his first training session for the club ... Francis ran the team for 75 hard and fast minutes. He told the players last Tuesday night his reign was going to be tough and he certainly gave the players a good sample of what is to come." The league matches started at the end of March, so Roy had seven weeks to get the players fit and develop the team.

Roy had tried to get Colin Greenwood to stay with Norths as a player, but Greenwood, unsurprisingly, was not interested. Two weeks after Roy's arrival, Greenwood was transferred to Canterbury-Bankstown for a $2,000 fee. Greenwood had a dispute with the club, which came close to going to court before it was resolved. Andrew Moore outlines that "In February 1969 Greenwood wrote a generous letter to Roy Francis explaining his court action against the North Sydney club 'in no way involves you as a person or questions your ability as a coach ... look after the boys, they are a fine bunch of lads."

One of the issues Roy faced was to build the team's confidence and establish some consistency. In the pre-season Willis Cup, "Francis 'magic' inspires North" was the headline for their 28–18 win against Parramatta at the Cumberland Oval. Norths scored six tries to Parramatta's two. Roy spoke to the press after the game, but only after he had given all his players towels soaked in iced water to help them recuperate. He said that the result "augurs well for the future, but with this sport it's one game at a time. That one's over and now we have our next game to worry about. The thing that pleased me was that the boys were looking to play football. Today's win will give them the incentive to win more, to be better and to train harder." The Norths officials were delighted with the result.

However, in the next round Norths lost 18–8 to St George in a poor, error-strewn match. Roy was disappointed with the display, and said: "No team worth its salt goes from up there to right down there in a week." Roy said that he would talk to the players at training on the following Tuesday.

Roy conducted the next training session behind closed doors, with even club officials barred from attending. He ran a "rugged" session for 90 minutes after finishing talking to the players about their display against St George.

Things improved in a pre-season encounter with Balmain. Norths won 22–12, and Roy said: "That was more pleasing" and that he had two weeks before the Premiership matches started. Norths fought back from being 8–0 down early on to lead at half-time and won comfortably in the end.

Norths first league fixture was away to Cronulla, who had finished one place above them in the table in 1968. It was the sort of match they needed to win if they were to climb the

145

table. Despite Graham Williams and Noel Cavanagh being missing through injury, Norths won comfortably 25–10. They won their next two games, before losing at home to Manly and at Canterbury. That established the pattern for the season, some good results, including wins against Manly and Canterbury in the return fixtures, followed by runs of two or three defeats.

For their home fixture with Easts, Norths had to switch the match to the Sydney Cricket Ground, which was used to stage a big match each week. This was an honour for the club, which Roy recognised, although he said he preferred the usual home and away fixtures he was used to in England.

Easts' captain-coach was (in apartheid terms) 'coloured' South African Louis Neumann, who had played for Roy at Leeds. Easts' hooker, Peter Moscatt, had also played for Roy at Leeds. Roy, who welcomed new recruit English half-back Graham Williams, said that "If we win, we'll probably be a step nearer to acceptance by the football public."

Williams, who had played for Swinton at home, was the star as Norths won 32–23. Williams scored a try and set up two more. Roy said that he would "be better and certainly a lot, lot sharper" about his new recruit who was playing his first match for six months. In his newspaper column, former Australian referee Col Pearce praised Williams for his display, and said "Full marks to coach Roy Francis for what proved a master stroke."

Roy's reputation was even reaching the other code. Randwick rugby union coach Jack Hovey told the *Herald* that "I'm no Roy Francis, I can't work miracles."

Norths led 6–4 against Manly but poor defence saw them concede four tries in the last 30 minutes to lost 26–8. Their cause was not helped by missing seven goal-kicks. Roy said that "We'll just have to go back to the drawing board for the basics. We'll start again."

An issue that faced Australian rugby league at this time was dirty play. Col Pearce gave credit to Roy for his stand on the issue: "At the start of the season Roy Francis declared that North Sydney would not be playing any dirty football this year and called for drastic penalties against players who did. Francis has lived up to his promise. Why can't other clubs follow suit."

After a poor display away to St George, which Rod Humphries said reminded him of Norths' displays in the past, Roy said that "You have your ups and downs" before taking the first team squad on a training trip to Newcastle for a week.

Humphries predicted that Souths would beat Norths by at least 10 points in their next match "unless Roy Francis has taught his players how to tackle." In fact, Norths won 21–12, but followed that win with two home defeats. Roy then dropped Graham Williams, who he felt had been giving away too many penalties. Norths got a 12–12 draw away to Easts, and then won three consecutive games.

At this stage, Norths had the possibility of reaching the play-offs, which were contested by the top-four clubs. Alan Clarkson said that the team were "in turn the despair and the delight of their followers", and that proved to be the case. Against Manly, Norths won 17–7 at the Sydney Cricket Ground. Roy said that "We thought Manly would try and play it up the middle so we planned to take them on there. We killed them in the middle and we took it from there." Clarkson noted the "transformation" in the Norths team since Roy had been in charge.

However, a run of just one win in the last seven matches saw them finish in seventh place, with 10 wins and a draw from their 22 matches. It was a considerable improvement on the 1968 campaign, but maybe not enough given the investment the club had made.

Their improvement was reflected at the turnstiles. The biggest home crowd was 19,401 against Balmain, and their average home gate was 10,001, up from 5,881 in 1968. Looking back on the season, Col Pearce said that "Roy Francis's effort in almost getting Norths into the semi-finals was another indication of importance of skill in tactics."

As well as coaching North Sydney, Roy acted as a 'go-between' for British players hoping to move to Australia. The *Herald* reported that he was helping St Helens half-back Tommy Bishop find a club, and that the transfer fee could be paid in instalments. This does seem a strange arrangement, but presumably the North Sydney officials accepted this activity, or maybe were powerless to stop it.

1970

If Roy was to justify the investment Norths had made in him, it was important that the team became more consistent, and at least reached the play-offs. Instead, the team went backwards, finishing in ninth place with just 15 competition points from seven wins and a draw. They never really recovered from starting the league season with five consecutive defeats. Their longest unbeaten run was three matches, but this came in the last three games of the season, when any hope of the play-offs had gone.

The season started in February with speculation that Norths would sign Alan Burwell from Hull KR. The player arrived in Sydney, with Roy acting as his 'advisor', according to a report in the *Herald*. In fact, he joined Canterbury-Bankstown.

One change that Roy did make was to appoint Ken Irvine as North Sydney captain. He was arguably the club's greatest player, but had resigned as captain in 1967, saying that the job could not be done effectively by a winger. Loose forward John McDonell was made vice-captain.

These two players were at the centre of an incident in Norths' first league match, away to Canterbury-Bankstown. They were both sent off just before half-time when "Irvine appeared to be kneed and kicked by a Canterbury forward after he had dived on a loose ball close to his own try line" according to the report in the *Herald*. An all-in melee followed; McDonell was sent off by the referee after a report from the touch-judge. The Canterbury forward who started the trouble was not spoken to by the referee. Before Canterbury could take the penalty, the referee spoke to Norths' John Payne for 'chatting'. Irvine, presumably as captain, joined them and was sent off.

Three Norths players tried to walk off the field with Irvine in protest, but Norths officials, including Roy, stopped them. The *Herald* reported that "Norths officials later claimed that the players were coming off the field because they thought it was half-time. The tragedy of the whole affair is that it probably could have been avoided had either the referee or the linesman spotted the original trouble-maker and dealt with him." Canterbury led 6–2 at half-time, but only won 16–14 after Ron Costello touched down for Canterbury in the last minute.

147

McDonell was given a two-match ban, and Irvine was suspended for one game. The next day, The New South Wales Rugby League announced that there would be an inquiry into the threatened walk-off. The following week, Irvine and centre Denis Cubis were charged with misconduct. No blame was attached to the North Sydney club.

In the middle of all this, Roy was invited to speak to a meeting of the NSW Referees Association. He said that he felt that Australia should adopt the English system of appointing referees to fixtures for six weeks at a time. He believed that the Australian system, where a referee did not know from week to week what fixture they would be doing, or at what grade, did not enable them to build up confidence. He also said that an exchange programme between referees in the two countries would be a good idea.

On 10 April, in the *Herald*, Rod Humphries examined the financial position of the game. There was an issue about tax and the 'leagues clubs' (social clubs) which many of the rugby league club relied on for income. He said that in 1969, North Sydney's gate receipts were $20,819. The cost of employing Roy was $17,504. This included his salary of $6,426; $6,992 to purchase his contract from Leeds and $2,303 in air fares. He also pointed out that the club had signed 10 new players, including Jim Mills for a $17,000 transfer fee.   While the financial management of the club was not Roy's responsibility, this did increase the pressure on him to deliver results. Humphries concluded that the difference between gate receipts and what the players were paid was putting the game in danger.

Norths lost the first two home matches of the season as part of their run of five defeats. Against Balmain, they were 17–7 up but conceded 31 points in the last 43 minutes. The *Herald* said the result was a "disappointment" for both Roy and the club's fans. Roy's cause was not helped when Ken Irvine was given a two-match ban for the 'walk-off incident. Roy was questioned by the general committee who were deciding on the case.

For the home match with St George, Roy gave fellow Welshman Jim Mills his debut, and made other changes to the team. However, the team lost 40–29. The *Herald's* headline was 'Form of Norths disgusts coach' and the report said that Roy found the performance "humiliating". It said "Indicating his olive skin, Francis said 'To be born with this is to be born with humiliation.' Then referring to the game: "But I was not born with this humiliation."

At a press conference after the game, Roy said that the players showed 'indifference' to their 'dignity'. He felt that they had let down the people who pay at the gate. However, the report said that he was "adamant that he will see out his contract which is due to conclude at the end of next season. And he said he still had faith in believing that he could win a premiership – maybe this year, if not next year. 'It's all right speaking from the top but I'm speaking from the bottom of the bucket. My team won 18 on the trot at Leeds and I think the material is here to win a premiership' he said."

The following Saturday, Rod Humphries said in his 'Looks at League' column that Harry McKinnon had refused to speak to him after the game and threatened to punch him. He said that Roy, on the other hand, was "tactful and friendly".

He said that Roy was "determined to have a premiership before he leaves for home..." but felt that Norths had signed too many new players, "instead of buying a few men in key

Left: Roy and Jim Mills playing snooker at the North Sydney Leagues Club.

Below left: Jim Mills playing for North Sydney against Wests in 1971. (Both courtesy Jim Mills)

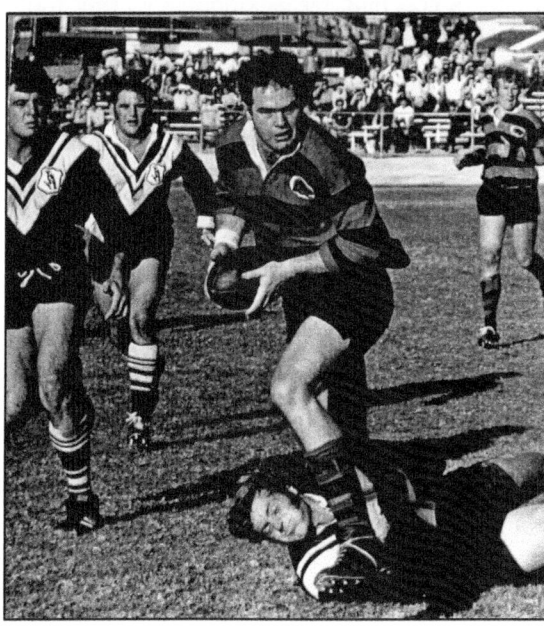

positions." He recognised the importance and quality of Roy's coaching. He makes a fair point about the number of new players.

Roy needed time to develop the team, something he had been given at Hull and Leeds, but was not in the 22-game season in Sydney.

The fifth defeat in a row came at Manly, where Roy was disappointed, and said that his team "had it in the bag", but "... let Manly back into the game".

Things did improve for Roy. The following week Cronulla were beaten, and the team finished the season with three wins and a draw in the last five games. However, the damage had been done in the first five weeks of the campaign. A final record of seven wins and a draw was not what North Sydney had hoped for, given their investment in new players.

In July, Roy did find time to use his physiotherapy skills on Great Britain tourist Terry Price, who had a bad back. However, other players were not as appreciative of Roy. Andrew Moore says in *The Mighty Bears!* that "Ken Irvine was one of those who never warmed to

149

this particular Welsh wizard. Francis was sharply critical of Irvine's lack of leg power at the start of the 1969 season. The winger regarded the coach as being obsessed with training and was cheeky bordering on the insubordinate." Moore says that Roy "did not brook criticism", even from the club's most famous player. The club's management supported Roy, and Irvine left to join Manly-Warringah in February 1971. He had been Norths' top try scorer in the 1970 season.

At the club's AGM in September, club president Harry McKinnon told the meeting that expenditure would have to be curbed in the 1971 season. The report in the Herald says that details of the expenditure on Roy were "shrouded" in the club's annual report. McKinnon said that the 1970 season had been "dismal". However, he added "Whether we like Roy Francis or not, he is here for another 12 months. I would suggest that we get behind hm and support him." The report said that "Commenting on Francis's coaching Mr McKinnon said that there was no doubt that he knew how to coach and train players."

1971

For the new season, Norths signed Merv Hicks, who Roy had previously tried to sign for Leeds. There had been a dispute over a possible transfer of Hicks to Norths in 1970, which ended up in a court case with his club, Canterbury Bankstown. However, this time the transfer was agreed between the clubs. Harry McKinnon said that "Roy Francis, our coach, has always been keen on Hicks, and naturally we're pleased to have him."

The 1971 campaign did not start well for Norths. The first floodlit match at their ground saw them lose 22–9 to St George. Norths were affected by injuries, and Roy used the game to try out different combinations. However, 10 days later came the surprising news that Roy and Renee had decided to leave Australia 'for business reasons'. Roy had decided to return to his former role as a publican, and had been offered the licence of *The Buckles Inn* on the York-Tadcaster Road.

The club announced that Merv Hicks, who had been in Australia since 1966, would be captain-coach for the new season. Roy told the meeting that he had seen the other teams training and believed that Norths could finish in the top four. He was going to help Hicks until he returned home in a few weeks. Sadly, things did not work out for Hicks. He was only aged 27 when given the post, although choosing the team went back to the selection committee system. Norths only won five games in 1971, and drew one. Two of those wins were in the last two games of the season. They finished in 11th place in the 12 team competition.

Rod Humphries said in the *Herald* that "Francis, one of the most controversial coaches ever in Sydney, was relieved of the remainder of his contract, which was due to terminate at the end of this season." Humphries also wrote that Roy had had "virtually no success with Norths." Roy explained that he needed to leave before the season started to avoid having to leave in the middle of the campaign, which would be bad psychologically for the players. He said that he could not wait for the end of the season because of work that needed to be done on the pub. He also wanted to sell his two current catering businesses.

Roy said that this was the first contract in rugby league that he had not finished, although it should be pointed out that he left both Hull and Leeds – with agreement – before his contracts had expired. Humphries's report says that "He [Francis] said that it was upsetting that he had a wealth of talent but 'after having bought it, I can't utilise it.'"

The report says that "Harry McKinnon said Francis had left in happy circumstances. 'I liken Roy to possibly a great artist, who possibly never achieved much in his time, but when he passed on, his work became famous ... Roy didn't achieve much as far as points on the board were concerned, but he taught us a lot about football."

Andrew Moore says that Noel Cavanagh, who played at North Sydney during Roy's time there, said that Roy was "an intelligent, erudite teacher who patiently instilled expertise and morale into a body of men despondent over continued humiliation."

Jim Mills recalls in his biography that Roy was "a coach in the Vince Karalius mould, very forward thinking. He brought a lot of things into the game that the Australians are using today. Jack Gibson, the great Australian coach, would ring Roy every week and talk about the teams in the league and tactics. When Roy put the phone down, he would say to me 'he's picking my brains', with a smile on his face. Roy had a hard time in Australia with the press and it became too hard to do the job, so in the end he went home, but I'm sure he left a legacy." Frank Stanton also had regular discussions with Roy.

Andrew Moore says that Graham Williams recalls that Gibson benefitted from Roy's knowledge and ideas. He says that Roy "... bequeathed a substantial, if largely unrecognised legacy to the culture of Sydney rugby league. He may have been the first Sydney coach to plot intricate game plans and player profiles. Combined with an emphasis on player self-esteem and sports psychology, he was in these aspects years ahead of his time."

Moore also highlights the support Roy gave to his players, often working long hours to treat injuries and – with Renee – looking after the players' children so the players' wives could attend club activities. He does believe that Roy developed the team's attacking play, but was weak on defence. This is strange because in England Roy's teams had always been strong defensively. Moore concludes that Roy "... was a warm-hearted, generous man; his unstinting fatherly concern sustained Graham Williams through a dark period of Williams's life after his wife died in a tragic accident."

Roy said that he had started negotiations to take over the pub when he returned to England at the end of the 1970 season. There was no other reason why he was leaving Norths.

In April, Humphries reported that Roy had wanted to sign the Welsh Great Britain international Colin Dixon, and Manly forward Mick Simmons for Norths, and "... it is believed arguments over their purchase had a great deal to do with Francis leaving the club." Dixon had a long career in British rugby league, but never played for an Australian club.

In May, Roy and Renee returned home, and he confirmed in a press interview that "I haven't been approached by any English League club wanting my services and I've decided to become a publican." Roy outlined his views on Australian rugby league: "One of the things I learned is that one is very much appreciative of England and its concepts of fair play and its organisation only after you've left it. I found League in Australia flourishing, virile but not quite achieving the efficiency that we have in England. As far as the press is concerned, the press in Sydney but not in Brisbane – I rather like Brisbane – does tend to be very vicious and I found rather anti-Pommie". Asked why, he continued: "This I cannot explain nor understand. The impression I got was that the attitude of the ordinary Australian you talk to, in the street is 'why are you here?'

If you explained as I did that it was a challenge, something I wanted to do, a new facet of sport that I wanted to experience, you were inevitably faced with the categorical statement 'you are only out here for the money and not for the country'. I said to more than one person 'I'm not out here to take the sand from Manly beach back. I'm here to do a job.'"

Roy then outlined the difficulties some of the British players he had signed had experienced. He had to move Graham Williams to stand-off because he was penalised so often at scrum-half. Eventually that was resolved through meeting the referees. However, in a North Sydney match, the referee told his players to "Get back onside you Pommies" although Roy's team only had three or four British players."

What Roy does not talk about in this interview is the racism that he experienced in Australia. However, this is well covered by Andrew Moore, who points out that Harry McKinnon was outraged by the press hostility to Roy. Moore says that some of this was "old-fashioned 'Pommie bashing'" but adds "Yet Roy Francis compounded this 'sin'. He was black, and this is where the issue becomes murky."

Moore says that there was an "undercurrent of racism that dogged ... [his] ... time at North Sydney. Part of the media campaign was tinged with racial hostility." He recalls that Roy walked out of a television interview with Ron Casey, believing that "Casey was discriminating against him and making references to his colour." Jim Mills also recalls that sections of the press were racist towards Roy.

Moore quotes an interview with Mike Gibson that Roy gave in April 1971, just before leaving Sydney. Roy said: "Racialism, discrimination, whatever you like to call it, is so very difficult to tabulate ... so very difficult. You see it as subtle differences in the feeling of someone towards you, subtle changes, remarks, acceptance one moment, non-acceptance the next. Its rather like 'flu you know. You know you've got it but you don't quite know where it is. I would prefer to say this about racialism. Racialism is the pain. It is a very personal thing and I would prefer to say that I would like to keep it that way."

However, Moore also says that Roy had in his papers a Sydney newspaper cutting from March 1971. He says that the article concluded: "... and when all your critics are through dealing with you Mr Francis, Sydney will be only too willing to forget you. Unfortunate, but true. You are coloured you see Mr Francis and even if you were a reincarnation of Dally Messenger you would not have made it in the small world that is Sydney rugby league."

Roy had visited Australia twice, in 1964 and 1968, before accepting the contract with North Sydney. He must have been aware of the racist attitudes in sections of Australian society. It was a great opportunity – the chance to work full-time in the sport, and to face the challenge of applying his ideas in a different rugby league setting. The press hostility and racism they faced undoubtedly did have an effect on Roy and Renee and I believe were a major factor in them returning home.

Roy said that he had not been approached by any English clubs when he left Australia, and that was true. However, he was not yet finished with rugby league. New opportunities came after he returned home.

16. Back to Hull

When Roy and Renee returned from Australia, they were busy sorting out their catering businesses and establishing themselves as landlords of the *Buckles Inn*. In May 1971, Roy's name had been mentioned in the *Wigan Post* as a possible contender for the Warrington coaching job, but nothing came of this. However, for the 1972–73 season, Roy returned to Hull as football manager, or "team supremo" as the *Mail* put it in their report of the club's AGM.

Since Roy had left the club in 1963, their only major success was reaching the Yorkshire Cup Final in 1967, when they lost to Hull KR by a point at Headingley. Their best league position was eighth in 1970–71, but in 1971–72 they dropped to 19th out of 30 teams. The coach was former player Ivor Watts, who had been appointed in 1970 and played with Roy in the 1950s, and Johnny Whiteley, who returned to the club after a short spell on the other side of the city with Hull KR.

One player who remained from Roy's time at the club was Clive Sullivan, who was now an established international and went on to captain Great Britain in winning the World Cup in France in the first part of the season.

One sad note just before the season began was the death of former club chairman Ernest Hardaker. He died following a road accident. He was aged 73, and had been chairman of the club until the late 1960s.

The club AGM just before the start of the season was told that the club had made a profit of £3,699 in 1971–72. However, receipts from the rugby league matches were down – the profit came from income paid by the Hull Vikings speedway team who were based at the Boulevard. The report in the *Mail* said that Roy's return had given the club new optimism. Sadly, however, things did not work out as planned.

Roy had implemented a programme of pre-season training three times a week, as always putting a lot of stress on fitness. In the *Mail*, Richard Tingle reported that "Under the leadership of Francis and his two coaches Ivor Watts and Johnny Whiteley, Hull players have been put through a tough pre-season programme which has already made a tremendous difference to the side."

However, the *Rugby Leaguer's* Tony Fairhurst correctly cautioned the club's supporters about being over-optimistic, and said that it would take time for Roy to turn things around. He did say that "Francis has demanded a near super-human effort as they have striven for peak fitness and those extra yards in mobility."

There was some debate in the letters column on the *Mail's* sports pages about Roy's return. One writer said that Roy made his name through the 'greatness of Hull's pack' in the 1950s. In reply, another correspondent pointed out that Roy had built the pack that had been the basis of Hull's success in the 1950s and that Roy had won two Championships for the club.

The team started poorly, with just one draw in their first seven matches. The situation was probably not helped by Roy being given a month's leave of absence a few days before the season started. Tony Fairhurst reported that this came after his "extensive and rigorous pre-season preparations." Roy needed the time off to "sort out business problems". His wife Renee had had the sole responsibility of running *The Buckles Inn*. Roy told the *Mail:* "This does not mean that I shall not come to the Boulevard, but I cannot guarantee I will be there for all training sessions and on match days."

Hull did beat Rovers 43–8 in the pre-season Hardaker Cup. Roy commented that "After six weeks training this was what I expected, but, after another month, I think we will be more capable of surprising quite a few teams."

The season started poorly for Hull, with six defeats in the first seven games. The only positive result was a draw at Wakefield in the BBC2 Floodlit Trophy. After the opening day defeat at Warrington, Roy told Richard Tingle: "Obviously errors cost us the match, but we have only just started our rebuilding programme. We must bring onto the field what we have been doing in training. At times, Warrington showed us just what I am looking for, but, after all, they were one of the top teams at the back end of last season..."

Defeat at Warrington was not a great surprise. A home defeat to Huddersfield was, albeit through a last-minute try. Roy felt that the defence was the problem. He outlined that Hull had scored 41 points in two games, with Clive Sullivan getting five tries. He continued: "In two games we have conceded 57 points and our defence is by no means up to standard. Our cover and recovery from play-the-ball is well under par and this must be altered fast."

The day after the Huddersfield match, the club AGM saw chairman Charles Watson lose his seat on the board. He had been one of the key people in Roy's return to Hull. He told the meeting: "I was responsible for bringing Francis back and now everyone can see the difference in the players' fitness. Roy is the greatest coach in England."

Hull's next defeat was at home to Leeds in the Yorkshire Cup. Before the game, Roy said that the defence needed to improve, but also that "We have a lack of strength in depth which only leads to complacency among the players." He said that the club must not 'penny pinch'.

Roy was a bit more satisfied with the team's performance against his old club. He outlined in the *Mail:* "We could have won this game as well. Leeds were by no means unbeatable, but let's face it, we had not the equipment to do it." The report also said that Roy and Renee were planning a holiday in Jamaica, and that Ivor Watts and Johnny Whiteley were to manage the team in his absence.

Before the BBC2 Floodlit Trophy match at Wakefield, Roy said that he was looking for new players for the club and would present proposals to the board. One player they hoped to sign was Leeds half-back Tony Wainwright. A deal had been agreed, but then Wainwright changed his mind and joined Oldham. Roy told Richard Tingle: "I am upset to say the least about the whole affair. In fact, I am fuming."

Roy did use his contacts in Australia to help the club. A couple of former Hull players, Duncan Jackson and Frank Adams, helped identify potential recruits. *The Leaguer* reported in September that two British players, Mervyn Hicks and Graham Williams could be coming to the Boulevard. Both did arrive, but Hicks had a limited impact, playing only six games. Williams made 17 first team appearances. The report said that Roy believed the first team squad needed strengthening.

In October, the *Leaguer* said that Roy hoped to recruit a couple more players from Australia. However, the club did hope to re-sign John Maloney, who had been playing for

York. Roy managed to complete this deal, and said that "his goalkicking abilities will be a great asset to the club..."

In late September and October, the team did improve. With a run of five wins in seven games. The *Leaguer* said that Roy thought that the crowds would improve if the team played attractive winning rugby. On 15 October, a crowd of 350 watched Hull's 'A' team win 45–5 against Halifax. The unusually high attendance was to see six players from 'Down Under'. *The Leaguer* commented that "... Roy Francis has suggested that it will be a few weeks before the Australians are properly acclimatised and ready for first-team football, there is little doubt that they will soon be challenging for places."

One recruit who did make a sizeable contribution was Len Dittmar, who had represented Queensland and played for the Brisbane Brothers club. Roy said that "Len is a right big 'un and I think he could well go places." Dittmar scored on his debut, a welcome 29–13 win at the Boulevard against Halifax.

On 28 October, Hull lost 23–17 at Headingley. Tony Fairhurst commented that this result "was an indication of what has yet to be done at the Boulevard as team boss Roy Francis continues his rebuilding programme." Hull were missing Clive Sullivan – in the World Cup – and Graham Williams who was injured. The report said that Roy "... has now attracted to the Boulevard in only two months, nearly a full team! Eight ... from Australia..." Fairhurst also mentioned John Maloney and Arthur Gibbons, two British recruits. He also said that international class forward Mike Harrison was still recovering from injury. He said that Roy was still "trying to find the best combination from the talent he now has available."

However, more worryingly for Hull supporters, Fairhurst said that there were rumours that Roy may have to leave his post because of his business commitments. The following week, this was confirmed. Roy was leaving the club to concentrate on running *The Buckles Inn,* although he said that he was hoping to return to the club in January or February. Ivor Watts and Johnny Whiteley would manage the team in his absence. A further blow was that Mervyn Hicks also was leaving to return to Australia.

The *Mail* reported on 31 October that Roy was leaving the club "for some time", but that he hoped to be able to return in January or February 1973. He told the paper: "It is a great disappointment for me, but a decision that I could not leave any longer. It was of vital importance for the team's sake, as well as my own, that I made the decision right away. While I could continue to do a job, I could not give all the time necessary to do the job my way and achieve the aims which I set myself and the club."

Richard Tingle commented that "Francis has injected a new life and spirit into the club which was just beginning to bring its rewards." He added that "Francis is the type of person who must give a 100 per cent to whatever job he tackles and anything less than that does not meet up to his standards."

At the end of December, Tony Fairhurst wrote that the team was struggling, and the early season optimism, based on Roy's return had gone. Only 1,900 fans had attended the home match with Warrington, although it was 10 days before Christmas, always a poor time for attendances. Only 4,200 attended the Boxing Day derby with Hull KR, although maybe this says more about the state of rugby league overall than just problems at the two Humberside clubs.

155

At the beginning of February, it became clear that Roy would not be returning due to health problems. Richard Tingle said that Roy had given up his position after an accumulation of problems, which had begun at the start of the season. He had gone with Renee for a break in Blackpool, but had been taken ill and been rushed to hospital for an operation on an abscess. He also had ongoing knee problems.

There had been rumours that Bradford Northern had been interested in Roy as their new coach, but he denied any interest in moving to Odsal. Hull finished in 25th place in the Northern Rugby League, and with the league returning to two divisions, would start the 1973–74 campaign in the Second Division.

Clearly Hull needed a longer period of rebuilding than Roy as able to implement. In reality, he was only in charge for four months, which included a one month 'leave of absence' although he was clearly still involved. He tried a 'quick fix' of bringing in Australian players, but only seven league games were won after the end of October. It took Hull until the 1976–77 season to win promotion to the First Division.

It would be almost 18 months before Roy returned to the game. There is an old saying "never go back". Roy had defied this once, and would do so again by joining Leeds as their coach for the 1974–75 campaign.

Roy during his return to Hull in 1972. (Courtesy Geoff Francis)

17. Back to Leeds

In the spring of 1974, Roy had been out of rugby league since January 1973, when he left Hull. Eric Ashton had been Leeds coach from June 1973, but after a year in the post resigned because of the travelling involved from his Lancashire base. Before him, Derek Turner had been the Leeds coach.

Since 1969, based largely on the players that Roy had developed in his time at the club, Leeds had been very successful. They had won the Championship twice, the Yorkshire League twice, the Yorkshire Cup three times, the BBC2 Floodlit Trophy and the John Player Trophy once each and been runners up in the Challenge Cup twice. They had twice won the League Leaders Trophy, in 1969–70 and 1971–72. The other three seasons in the league they had finished third. However, in 1973–74, they had only won the Yorkshire Cup. However, unlike Hull in the 1950s, or Leeds in 1963, Roy was not inheriting a struggling side.

At the beginning of August, Arthur Haddock reported in the *Evening Post* that Leeds were interested in signing Mike Harrison from Hull, and Roy told Haddock that there were also three Welsh "notable" rugby union players under consideration. However, in the Leaguer, Keith Grehan said that Leeds – at the beginning of September – already had 49 players registered, and would have to release or part-exchange players to bring in new talent The maximum number of players who could be registered was 50. He also commented on the efficient Leeds scouting system, which covered Yorkshire, Wales and Scotland.

Mike Harrison did move to Headingley, replacing David Jeanes who was inactive due to work commitments. Roy said that in the *Evening Post* that "I had to get my front row right. That is where you build from in rugby league".

Before the start of the season, Roy was interviewed by Trevor Watson for the *Evening Post*. Watson said that "The air of optimism hanging over Leeds ... stems from the fact that Roy Francis is back in his old job as principal of the Headingley College of Classical Rugby League Education." He made the point that some players from Roy's previous time at the club had moved on, but that others had matured and developed.

Roy had full control of team affairs, and was holding in pre-season three sessions a week for the first month of training. Roy explained to Watson: This gets rid of the flab and builds strength, stamina and wind for the season. Peak physical fitness also brings the right mental attitude. You establish discipline, and perhaps more important, establish a knowledge of each other – coach and player. The pattern of behaviour is set, and from that point, while retaining the fitness peak, you can concentrate on the football and tactics." Roy said that he wanted his Leeds team to play "fast, open rugby". He recognised the importance of defence, but wanted variety in attack. He said that there was "a lot of work to do" and that success would not come overnight.

He also stressed the importance of having strength in depth – not just one good stand-off, but three. Roy reflected on his time in Australia, saying that he thought the English club game was stronger than the Australian teams. He recalled how he returned to Headingley with his Hull team in 1972, and had been applauded. He said it was "a wonderful moment." He said that he wanted Leeds to do well, and his players recognised and acknowledged in the City. He was pleased to be back with the players from his first spell at the club – "my lads" – but pointed out that discipline was essential for success. He concluded that rugby league had been good to him, and had given him the chance to leave South Wales but said that "I worked hard to take it".

The next week, the paper's columnist, Phil John, attended a Leeds training session. Maybe not surprisingly, he found it exhausting and well beyond his level of fitness. He concluded that Roy had "whipped the Headingley lads into frightening fitness. They literally took my breath away and they will definitely not fail for lack of peak physical condition."

The season started with a win at Bramley. The Yorkshire Cup started very early in the season, and after Leeds won at Keighley in the first round, they lost at Second Division Hull 12–8 in the second. The match report said that Leeds seemed to lack confidence, even when a man up after three players were sent off. One of them was Leeds half-back Keith Hepworth, who had a broken nose and two black eyes! Defeats at Wigan and St Helens early on also indicated that Leeds did not seem to travel well, especially to Lancashire.

One new initiative that Roy was involved in was the Association of Professional Coaches in rugby league. He was chairman of the new organisation, with Eric Ashton as vice-chairman, Graham Starkey as Secretary and Les Bettinson, Peter Fox and Alan Kellett also on the committee. Along with the referees, they met with representatives of the RFL for a pre-season meeting. Roy told the *Leaguer:* "We are part of an overall move within the game to put rugby league back on its feet ... I believe that this is the best thing that has happened to the game in years."

Interviewed for this book, Graham Starkey recalls the coaches having a couple of 'get-togethers' but not much more. Certainly the Association did not seem to last. Starkey does recall, as a young Rochdale fan, being very impressed with Roy when he saw him play for Barrow against the Hornets after the War. He also remembers having a long discussion with Roy about coaching after Leeds had played Wigan, where Starkey was coaching at the time.

In mid-September, Roy presented the Headingley board with a list of nine possible recruits for the first team squad. The list included some Welsh and Scottish rugby union players. However, at the AGM, Alfred Sharman, the chairman of Leeds CF & A Company, said that some clubs had "ridiculous ideas" about transfer fees. He also said that Leeds were in a period of transition. By mid-October, Leeds had only won one of five away games, and had lost at Rochdale.

One player who was signed from Welsh rugby union was Gordon Pritchard. However, he was one for the future. In November. Roy told the *Evening Post*: "He has the ability to be what Leeds have always seemed to have – a good class back, but we are going to give him a chance to fit into the scheme of things."

The first half of the season was dominated by various cup competitions. In the BBC2 Floodlit Trophy, Leeds were unlucky to be drawn away to St Helens, and went down 30–6. In the John Player No.6 Trophy, Leeds beat New Hunslet at Headingley, and then won at Keighley. On 1 December, Leeds had won at Odsal in the league, and Trevor Watson said that they "handed out a sharp all-round lesson to gain a convincing 17–10 win...". However, a week later, in the John Player quarter-finals, they lost 17–7 to Bradford Northern.

In mid-December, Leeds were fourth in the league table, with eight wins and four defeats. After Boxing Day, they were second. Roy had the chance to watch the club's 'A' team beat Wakefield Trinity, and told Phil John that his long-term prediction was that half-a-dozen of the players would be on the 1978 Lions tour to Australia and New Zealand.

In January, Leeds signed half-back Mel Mason from Featherstone. He made his debut in an 11–10 home win against St Helens, some revenge for the two heavy defeats earlier in the season at Knowsley Road. Arthur Haddock's report said that "determination and team spirit" had seen Leeds through.

One change for coaches that was introduced, and welcomed by Roy, was that at Wembley, the coach would walk out behind the club chairman onto the pitch before the match. Roy told the Leaguer on 18 December: "It's something I've been campaigning for for 15 years. Why the coach has to creep round the greyhound track when the team comes out beats me. Roy was keen to be one of the first two coaches to benefit from the change, but said that there were another 29 coaches with the same aspiration.

In the Challenge Cup, Leeds faced a tough match away to Second Division Whitehaven. Keith Hepworth had had difficulties attending training because of work commitments, and was named on the bench, along with Phil Cookson. Leeds went into the tie with a record of 10 defeats in their last 14 away matches. However, according to Trevor Watson's report, frosty nights had made the pitch more firm than usual, which suited Leeds. They took an early lead, and according to Watson, "showed a fair amount of skill and welcome determination" to win 16–7.

The draw for the second round took them to Lancashire – Salford's The Willows. Ken Dalby's summary of the season talks about "debilitating 'trans-Penninitis'", but on this occasion Leeds won deservedly 17–12. Trevor Watson said that Leeds "...turned in their best all-round performance since beating St Helens at Headingley around 17 months ago and their best away display for far longer."

Two weeks later, the quarter-finals saw Leeds entertain Bradford Northern at Headingley. Leeds got revenge for their John Player defeat and won 22–6. Arthur Haddock's report said that "The Leeds pack firmly met, well held and finally destroyed the challenge of the Bradford forwards." He said that Leeds's performance justified their rating as favourites for the Cup. The win meant Leeds were in the semi-finals for the sixth time in 11 years.

A few days after the match, Arthur Haddock wrote a profile of Leeds's young prop Steve Pitchford. He said that the player had "set about reducing his poundage by cutting out potatoes and having a 'sensible diet'." This was probably advice from Roy, who the article said had given Pitchford "words of wisdom".

In the semi-final, Leeds had to travel to Wigan to face Warrington, the holders. Their manager, Alex Murphy, was also the England manager. Murphy said that he had only seen Steve Pitchford and Mike Harrison play once, so Roy said in the *Evening Post* that "Mick and Steve have a great opportunity and the way they are playing I think they'll take it."

On the semi-final, he commented that "We have broken even with Warrington this season ... but we missed a stream of early chances at Wilderspool. By their league position Warrington can't be as good as Alex keeps saying. We are coming good at the right time and they will probably try and stop us playing. Either way I think we have the pace and power to win."

However, on the day it was Warrington who would be heading to Wembley. There was controversy over the referee not hearing the half-time hooter and allowing Warrington to score when the game should have been concluded for the half-time break. However, a John Bevan try near the end of the match settled it, making the score 11–4. Arthur Haddock said that Leeds could have "no quibbles" over the result. He said that their fans wondered why Keith Hepworth was only introduced in the 72nd minute. He also said that Warrington's cover defence "was superb".

Six days after the semi-final, Leeds faced neighbours Bramley at Headingley. The visitors were in a fight against relegation, but Trevor Watson reported that Roy said they could expect no mercy from Leeds. Roy added: "I told the lads at training 'Look, we have lost out in one competition – fair enough a major one –but now we have to start thinking about another and that's the Premiership, whatever form it takes.' We must redeem our own confidence. After a good run when we had murdered some packs, we just did not put it together against Warrington. Now we have to start again. If you lose this professional bite, you have had it. Any Bramley player with the ball tonight had better watch out. We want to win and win well."

Leeds did win comfortably, and won three of their next six games to finish their league season in third place on 39 points. They were three behind runners-up Wigan but a massive 14 points behind champions St Helens. The report of their last league match, a 21–0 defeat at Widnes, pointed out that they had lost all six league matches in Lancashire.

The Premiership was a new competition. It replaced the old Championship play-offs now that the game had two divisions. The top 12 First Division teams were joined by the top four from the Second Division.

Leeds started with a convincing 27–8 win at Featherstone, who had finished a place behind them in the league on points difference. Headingley was staging a cricket match on 30 April, so Leeds had to play Castleford in the next round two days after the Featherstone match. Leeds won comfortably, 28–8, with Arthur Haddock declaring that they were favourites to win the competition. How they were rated ahead of St Helens, who had only lost three league games all season is not clear.

However, Leeds did back Haddock's prediction with an 18–8 semi-final win over Hull KR. Trevor Watson said it was a "magnificent" match. In the final, 13 days later, Leeds would face St Helens at Wigan, returning to the ground where they had lost in the Challenge Cup semi-final.

Roy organised an extra training session in the week leading up to the final. With Mike Harrison out injured, Roy gave a final slot to Roy Dickinson, although this was no great surprise as he had played in every match since the beginning of April. Interviewed by Arthur Haddock, Roy looked to the future and enthused about the number of good youngsters at the club. He said that "The back-up of young talent is greater than it was in 1968, and I shall be surprised if, in the next five years, it will be necessary to spend £10,000. What has to be done is protect this young talent."

Left: Jack Myerscough, who was one of the key figures on the board at Leeds during both Roy's spells at Headingley. (Courtesy Peter Lush)

Two days before the match, Roy also emphasised how confident he was about his young forwards, wondering "just how long those St Helens men can last the pace against them." He also pointed out that David Ward had played in all the Premiership games at hooker. He did stress that "We have got to get straight into them – that means not hanging around waiting for things to happen, we have got to make them happen. Our football recently has improved, but it can be better, and this final seems just the right occasion."

Roy's confidence in his players was borne out. The *Evening Post's* headline was "Top show by Super Leeds". Leeds won 26–11, with Arthur Haddock saying: "With a victory as handsome as they have achieved for a long time, over opponents of proven ability, Leeds finished the official rugby league season in style with the new Premiership Trophy." Haddock commented on the "sustained driving in of the pack" as the basis for the win. Leeds were 16–0 up at half-time. St Helens scored early in the second half, but a try from Alan Smith put the result not in doubt. Ken Dalby concluded that "The Leeds team, no less than their supporters, would long remember this first ever Premiership final. St Helens would find it hard to forget their heaviest defeat for six years."

In the *Leaguer*, Roy said that "Only threequarters of the work is done. Today we did well. The Challenge Cup semi-final was one game that went wrong, but this team can go from strength to strength because it has youth on its side." He also said that it took two years to build a side, but this time he was expected to do it in one.

After such a great victory, it must have been a shock for Leeds supporters to read in the papers five days later than Roy would be leaving Headingley. Jack Myerscough issued a statement saying that the club would not be retaining his services. Roy's contract had been only for one year. Arthur Haddock pointed out that the new coach would be the fourth person to hold the post in four years. He reported that Roy had made the following statement: "I have not met the board at all over my contract. I sent them a letter around April 17 in which I tried to clarify the position. In it I said 'My contract ends on May 31 and knowing the board's preference for forward planning, I would assume my services are not required for the coming season. I can assure you that every effort will be made towards winning the Premiership.'

This was in no way a letter of resignation. I was trying to clarify things so I could arrange my holidays and make plans for the club's summer school for youngsters."

Roy added that he now planned "... to have a good holiday with my wife. I haven't any plans for next season." Leeds did say that Jack Myerscough had met with Roy and his wife after the Syd Hynes testimonial match to tell Roy that his contract was not being renewed. He had been unable to contact Roy the next day to run over the statement the club were issuing with him, and that was eventually done by his secretary.

Arthur Haddock said that Leeds had "ended the campaign well with fine performances that clinched the new Premiership Trophy, but in between it had been a disappointing season, with many defeats in Lancashire."

Haddock is being a little unfair. The club chairman had said that Leeds were "in transition." The team had reached the Challenge Cup semi-final, finished third in the league and won the Premiership. They had also reached the quarter-final of the John Player No.6 trophy, and in the BBC2 Floodlit Trophy had lost at St Helens. The worst cup result was the defeat at Hull in the Yorkshire Cup.

In Roy's place, Syd Hynes was appointed, initially as player-coach, then as coach. He stayed with the club until 1981. When Roy died in 1989, Hynes told the *Evening Post's* Trevor Watson: "Roy was a tremendous man to play under. I took over from him as coach after learning such a lot from him. One of his great strengths was his willingness to give young players a chance. I joined the club as a youngster and was lucky enough to be part of a very good team which Roy developed. We were proud to prove his judgement right. It was under his influence that Leeds really produced a tremendous style of open football and he always believed in this policy."

Interestingly, although they had success in the cup competitions, Leeds did not win the Championship again until the Super League era. They never achieved the consistency they had shown in Roy's first period at Headingley. Maybe if the Leeds directors had been a little more patient...

18. Bradford Northern

After leaving Leeds, Roy was out of the sport at the start of the 1975–76 season. However, at the end of September, a vacancy arose at Bradford Northern. The club had won the John Player No.6 Trophy in 1974–75, and finished seventh in the First Division, just six points behind Leeds. However, an inconsistent start to the new season culminated in a 32–12 home defeat to Wakefield Trinity in their defence of the John Player Trophy. They had lost 22–2 at home to Leeds in the Yorkshire Cup. According to Nigel Williams in his history of the club, club coach Ian Brooke was blamed by a section of the crowd for the disappointing performance, and "he needed a police escort to get him safely to the dressing rooms." After the defeat to Wakefield, Williams says that "The crowd showed another violent and abusive outburst towards him after the match and made it quite clear that they did not want him in charge any longer." Brooke had had enough of the situation and resigned after the Wakefield game.

Jack Scroby and Alan Kellett were also in the running for the post, but on 2 October, Northern offered Roy the job. There were "protracted negotiations" with Roy, according to club chairman Harry Womersley.

In taking the post at Northern, Roy was joining a club that had experienced some very positive and negative times in its history. Two Challenge Cup wins in the post-Second World War period were followed by a period of decline in the 1950s, culminating in their withdrawal from the Northern Rugby League in December 1963. They were the first club since the Second World War to withdraw from the league mid-season.

A new club was formed and rejoined the NRL in the summer of 1964. They continued to play at Odsal, which while being one of the sport's great historic venues, had the disadvantage of having no cover for fans on the terraces on cold winter afternoons, and the ongoing costs of maintaining the stadium. In the early 1950s, the club was one of the first to install floodlights, but had been unable to maintain them, and were now one of a minority of clubs without this facility. This meant if there was a backlog of fixtures, they would be played in April rather than spread throughout the second half of the season. This was a disadvantage for the club.

Roy was the club's 10th coach in 11 years, according to Brian Smith in the *Bradford Telegraph & Argus (T&A)*. Smith said that "Francis is known throughout the game for his elaborate planning and attention to detail in dealing both with the opposition and his own players." Smith says that when Roy spoke to the players, he had on display "huge sheets of paper" with the 'headlines' of his approach: "respect, loyalty, devotion, dedication, determination and pride."

In the *Leaguer*, Ken Bryan said that the appointment had gone down well with the fans. He continued: "They see Francis as the man to get the best out of a side which promises so much, but finds consistency so elusive...". He also pointed out that Roy would have more authority than any previous Odsal coach, but that the fans would expect success.

One immediate change for the players was Roy's emphasis on speed. On 15 October, Brian Smith reported that Roy had ordered three dozen pairs of spikes and planned sprinting sessions on the speedway track on Tuesday nights. Roy was also pressing the club to be able to train on the pitch rather than using the club car park.

Northern won Roy's first game in charge at Swinton. However, he missed their next game because he had agreed to choose the 'man-of-the-match' award at the Wales versus Australia World Championship game at Swansea. It does seem surprising that his Bradford Northern commitments did not take priority.

The team's one point defeat away to Hull KR was the start of a dreadful run of results. Of the next nine games, only two were won – at home to Dewsbury and at Warrington on Boxing Day.

Roy had problems with a couple of good players who no longer wanted to play for the club. In November, they reduced the transfer fee on Phil Jackson, who had been staying away from the club. Roy told Brian Smith that "Jackson has tremendous potential. It's a shame he hasn't got sufficient nous to capitalise on it. He has been approached in a proper manner but has been totally unresponsive."

Roy and Harry Womersley were also hoping to meet Ken Kelly, who was also staying away from the club. Once again, Roy was frustrated with a relatively young player with a lot of potential not being available.

Roy's team was now in a potential relegation fight. After a 3–2 home defeat on 16 November to Keighley, he said that the performance was "pathetic … a whole month's training went to waste." He said that he was not disappointed with the physical effort, and said "there was a lot of good defensive play." However, he was not happy with the players' ability to read the game, and play as a team, rather than as "thirteen individuals". He added "I said when I arrived it would be hard work and I anticipated problems because a lot of players have been here a long time and it is not easy to introduce new systems into any institution." Brian Smith also pointed out that there was criticism from some of the supporters who only a few weeks earlier had welcome Roy to the club. Roy said that he was not worried about being booed and his priority remained to develop a good team.

In early December, Smith reported that two of the coaches at the club were to change roles. John Sykes, who had worked with Roy at Leeds, took over the 'A' team, while Garth Budge was to work with the Colts. Despite the run of poor results, Harry Womersley told Brian Smith after a 12–11 loss to Salford at Odsal that "It was very heartening. Roy Francis is clearly getting his message over to the players now and considering how many key men were missing, it was a very good display."

However, Roy was "bitterly disappointed" at a third one-point defeat in his time at the club. He did say it was the best display from the team so far, and added "our defence was good enough to restrict them to two tries despite all the possession they had and our attack was good enough to score three. If we go on playing like this the results must come."

Just before Christmas, Roy missed a 21–3 defeat at Wakefield because of a fire at the Kirkgate Market in Leeds which badly damaged the café that he and Renee ran there. Renee told Brian Smith that the family had also had a break-in at home a few weeks earlier.

Roy had a meeting with the board after the Wakefield game, but it does not seem that his position was in danger. Just before Christmas, Roy spoke at an open forum following the club's AGM. He was given an "enthusiastic reception", according to the report in the *T&A*,

and said that he thought the club would finish in the top eight in the league. He also said that "Ten weeks is no time to build a team. It took me time when I was at Hull and when I was at Leeds, but I believe there is more enthusiasm here than there was at Hull or Leeds." He continued: "Remember I have a reputation too and I value that reputation highly. It goes down on to that field every game. We have got to be patient for a while. I am not a patient man but I know football and I know footballers."

Roy also pointed out that he did not have a contract with the club, but worked on a week-to-week basis. He said that he was confident in his ability to do the job with the support of the board. He also said that the club were looking to bring in new players, and that some of the talented young players at the club needed time to mature.

Any hopes that the team had turned the corner with the Boxing Day win at Wilderspool were shattered with a 33–0 home defeat against mid-table Castleford. Northern were in an injury crisis, and had to cancel the 'A' team game because they could not raise a side, but Roy accepted that that issue could not explain a "feeble performance". He told the *T&A;* "I am always reluctant to criticise my players in public, but it's unbelievable how they could serve up such tripe yesterday after the way they played at Warrington and Salford. I felt sorry for the fans. They have supported us so well and they deserved a better present on New Year's Day. We were bad tactically and played down 25 yards in the middle of the field with two centres and two wingers virtually unemployed. Obviously, this reflects on me, but they can be better as they have shown only a week ago. Anyone who just watches at home must be baffled by the praise they have earned at Warrington, Wigan and Salford."

Four more league defeats followed, including the return match against Castleford. One player who was signed in an exchange deal with York was experienced goalkicking forward Terry Clawson. In his autobiography, Clawson recalls meeting Roy at Odsal for training. He says that Roy was in a smart tracksuit, and had a clipboard and stopwatch. He recalls that Roy said: "I hope we're going to get along Terry. We've both got reputations but I hope that won't stop us working well together." Clawson agreed, but said that one thing bothered him. Roy asked what it was. Clawson replied: "It's the stopwatch. In my case you'll need a calendar." He did say in his book that he had "a lot of admiration for the man ... He certainly knew his rugby league inside out."

Clawson was only available for a limited time because he had a player-coach position in Australia and left Bradford in mid-March. However, he did help improve the team's fortunes.

Roy was now clearly in a relegation fight. As most of his coaching had been under the 'one division' system, this was a new experience for him. Towards the end of January, after the defeat at Castleford, he told Brian Smith: "The only time you're out is when you're unconscious. There's still a long way to go and the possibility of a lot of funny results. Last night didn't help, but I am not resigning myself to relegation yet." Having played on the Friday night, Roy was holding a light training session on the Sunday before going with the team to watch their Challenge Cup opponents Rochdale at Bramley.

The board showed confidence in Roy by investing in new players. Apart from Clawson, Graham Evans, Gordon Pritchard, Peter Roe and John Wolford were all signed. The Challenge Cup provided some relief with a win at Rochdale. Roy told Brian Smith that he was pleased: "It went according to plan. We knew what had to be done and the players did it well."

This was followed by the first league win of 1976 at Huddersfield. In the league, Northern were still five points behind Dewsbury. Roy outlined: "It's obviously going to be hard to stay in the First Division, but Dewsbury have some tough games left and we must keep on trying to catch them." The Challenge Cup run ended at Headingley with a 30–12 defeat.

At the beginning of March, Bradford were still in the bottom four, and faced a busy schedule with four games in March and five in April. A draw at Wigan, and home win over Hull KR, combined with Dewsbury losing to Keighley, made things look better, particularly because five of the team's last seven games were at Odsal. Before the return match with Huddersfield on 14 March, with the gap with Dewsbury at two points, Roy told Brian Smith: "We must concentrate on playing football and winning our remaining games. I don't want ifs and buts, I want performance."

Bradford beat Huddersfield 26–7, and moved out of the bottom four on points difference. Roy told Brian Smith: "I as pleased with the result but only with threequarters of the performance. At times we were rubbish and were far too relaxed and careless."

Another problem Roy faced was the state of the Odsal pitch. A stock car meeting before the St Helens games at the end of March had damaged the edges of the pitch. The problem was resolved, but it showed the problems the club experienced with the stadium.

Approaching Easter, Bradford were still in the bottom four. A win at Oldham, who were one place above them in the table, was crucial. Three wins in six days finally pulled the club clear of the relegation zone. Roy was delighted with the win at Watersheddings: "This was the best football they have played for me. Their attitude was right before the game and their football was right all the way through … We scored nine tries and it delighted me that seven of them could have been scored by any one of two or three players who were positioned right after good build up."

Bradford's final match of the season was a 25–12 win at Odsal against Leeds. Roy got a "hero's reception" according to Brian Smith, who also said that it was now almost certain that he would be offered the post for the 1976–77 season.

Roy told Smith that he was planning a visit to Canada to see an old friend, and was going to have a full medical check-up. He said "No decision has been taken about next season, but I have had talks with the chairman." After an EGM which agreed to increase the club's share capital, it was announced that Roy was being given a one-year contract for the 1976–77 season, with a new title as 'football manager'

Bradford finally finished the season in 11th place in the table, with 27 points. They were six clear of Dewsbury, who were the highest team to be relegated, but only seven points behind Hull KR, who were in eighth place.

1976–77

Roy now had the chance to build on the successful period in the last couple of months of the previous season. Having signed several new players in the second half of the previous campaign, Bradford did not make any signings for the new season. Various players with long term injuries were now available. Roy told the *T&A*: "In my opinion the pattern of football at the end of last season does not merit any signings. All we need is consistency and consolidation."

The season opened with a Yorkshire Cup tie at home to Leeds. Bradford were winning ss the game entered injury time, but a try by Alan Smith, converted by John Holmes, saw Leeds win 11–9. Roy told Brian Smith that "We played a lot of good football, but lost our rhythm in the second half by trying to go down the middle instead of stretching them and getting the ball to the flanks ... in general after yesterday's performance we have a lot to look forward to this season...".

This left Bradford without a game the following week. However, before the next game, at Workington, came the shock news that Roy had to go into hospital for a knee operation. He expected to be absent for three weeks. 'A' team coach John Sykes was going to manage the training sessions, while David Stockwell, who had joined the coaching staff, and captain Barry Seabourne, would look after the first team at Workington. Brian Smith reported on 1 September that Roy "...has had knee trouble for some time and recently had a short stay in hospital for manipulative operations but the trouble has persisted and he was due to have a further operation today."

Roy kept in touch with his coaches by telephone. Bradford started the best run of his time at the club with a win over Rochdale, and in the next nine games won seven, drew one and lost one. The defeat was at Hull in the second round of the John Player No.6 Trophy. By mid-September, Roy was out of hospital and convalescing at home. He still had the final say on team selection.

However, on 24 September, Brian Smith reported that Roy had "temporarily relinquished his duties at Odsal.". He told Smith: "For the past few weeks I have been running a football team by proxy and picking teams by proxy and I don't want to do it this way. It's not fair to the players or the spectators." He said that he had been told to leave football alone until he was fit. He said that the coaches were welcome to telephone him but that he would not be running the team.

In mid-October, Roy called in to Odsal to congratulate the players on their performances in his absence. He said that he did not expect to be back in action before Christmas. He told Brian Smith: "There is no point in coming back before I am absolutely right."

On 24 October, Roy watched the John Player match against Huddersfield. He also had been to some of the recent training nights, but was still not prepared to give a date for his return. However, the following week he resumed control with a 20–10 win at Oldham. Roy said that he was "delighted to be back."

Roy's second game back in charge took him to the Boulevard. Hull were leading the Second Division, which they went on to win, and won 19–5. Roy told Brian Smith that "We are still a developing side and yesterday's defeat should not detract from the performances we have put together since February, many against sides who ae a lot better than Hull." He also said that Hull had a lot of possession in the first half and "We had so much tackling to do then that when we did get the ball, we just didn't seem capable of finding a rhythm."

Bradford kept their place at the top of the table with what Roy called "brilliant football" in a 30–10 win against Workington. He was also pleased how the players had bounced back from the defeat at Hull. Defeat at Featherstone the following week was followed by home wins against Salford and Warrington at Christmas.

One issue Roy was always strict on was that players had to train if they wanted to play. This was not always easy in a part-time sport with players having shift work or working far away from their club. In December, Roy left out Colin Forsyth from the first team because work commitments had stopped him attending training. The player attended training the following week and got his place back.

A poor performance at Castleford started the New Year with a defeat. Two defeats in Lancashire followed, at Widnes and Rochdale. Bradford fell to sixth place in the table, and Roy was concerned about complacency after the Rochdale result. He told Brian Smith: "I cannot find excuses for men with ability who fail to do the basics and we just didn't do the simple things right yesterday." He was also concerned about a lack of spirit in the side and said this had to be sorted out.

One new recruit was forward Bob Haigh who had been not playing, initially due to injury, at Leeds. Roy said that he "...was a good forward who knew the game." February saw Bradford win four consecutive matches, two in the league and two in the Challenge Cup. After winning at Barrow, Bradford won at Blackpool in the Cup. Their 38–8 win was their biggest win in the competition for 40 years, and biggest ever away win. Their previous best result had been against Streatham & Mitcham in 1937. Roy was "extremely pleased" with the team's performance.

Commenting on the home win against Leeds, Roy said that in coming back from 10–2 down, "We not only showed a lot of character, but continued to play the sort of football everybody wants to see. Once you start playing the sort of football I believe in, you can't suddenly change because of the conditions. We showed that you can play with a wet ball and the crowd obviously loved it."

The Leeds match was followed by a home win against Featherstone in the Challenge Cup. Roy discouraged talk about Wembley, pointing out that the team was sixth in the league, with games in hand, and had to continue to press for as high as possible a place for the Premiership. However, he did say that he was "delighted" to beat Featherstone.

In March, two defeats followed, both to Widnes, at home in the league and at Naughton Park in the Challenge Cup. Roy said to Brian Smith about the 19–5 Challenge Cup defeat that he was "... bitterly disappointed. We have played a certain style consistently and successfully for some time now but it just never came through yesterday. Winning at Widnes may have put some things right, but it wouldn't have answered all the problems and we now have to play the game we have shown we can play against good sides."

On 19 March, the day before league leaders Featherstone came to Odsal, Bradford were eighth in the league, but with between two and four games in hand on the teams above them. Their 21–5 win against Featherstone was an excellent result. However, only four more league games were won and Bradford ended the season in eighth place, with 32 points from their 30 matches. They had to play nine matches in April, almost a third of their league fixtures in one month. After a 29–13 defeat at home to Castleford, Roy refused to blame injuries. He told Brian Smith: "We got it back together again for a while in the second half yesterday, but the spirit has really sunk and we have just got to try and pick ourselves up off the floor."

After the team's defeat at Warrington, Roy did say that "We are suffering at the moment because of the rush of matches...". However, on 14 April, Roy was taken ill, which led to speculation about his future at Odsal. However, within five days, Roy had been told that he would be out of action for a month, which would take him to the end of his contract.

Roy explained to Brian Smith: "My doctor advised me to have a month off after falling ill last week and as that takes me past the end of my contract, I feel this is the right time to step down rather than carry on and cripple myself. I had intended to finish coaching at the end of the season and would like to have ended on a happier note, but I have enjoyed my time at Odsal and leave on good terms. I have had the best possible backing from the board – the best I have ever worked with – and there is a strong playing register and a great group of supporters. I am disappointed that we fell away after going so well earlier in the season, but I am convinced the series of postponements just before Christmas were a big factor. As it is, I feel I've left a legacy of a style of play which has been appreciated and there is plenty of potential for whoever takes over."

On behalf of the board, Geoff Cooper, who had replaced Harry Womersley as chairman, said that Roy "... had intimated to the board before Christmas that he intended to retire at the end of the present season and his ill health has hastened that decision. During his time at Odsal he has been a very popular figure and he produced an exciting style of football. He has had 40 glorious years in the game as an outstanding player and coach and we wish him a speedy return to health."

The Bradford directors moved quickly to appoint Peter Fox as the club's new coach. He went on to build on the squad Roy had left, and won two Championships with Bradford Northern.

Roy making a point from the touchline during his time at Hull. This photo is often used in articles about Roy. There is a story that the players knew that if he was sitting in this position, with his legs apart, they should attack. If his legs were closed, they should defend. Is this a myth? Who knows?
(Courtesy *Rugby League Journal*)

19. The first modern coach

In his foreword for this book, Jim Mills says that Roy was 'The first modern coach'. This chapter will look at some of the ideas and approaches to coaching and player management that Roy developed.

When he was appointed as Bradford Northern's new coach in October 1975, he outlined his approach to the role. Brian Smith reported the meeting in the *T&A*. He said that "Francis is known throughout the game for his elaborate planning and attention to detail in dealing with both the opposition and his own players.

And his speech last night was not an off-the-cuff affair. He spoke in front of huge sheets of paper which carried 'headlines' of his talk and further helped to drum home his message, which was populated with words like 'respect, loyalty, devotion, dedication determination and pride.'"

Smith said that Roy "promised nothing, other than a guarantee of hard work, but he had some of his audience believing that success is inevitable if only his philosophy is followed."

Roy said that this was a time to move on from the past, and that he wanted to work with the club directors to build a stable club.

He told the players and staff: "It's time to stand up and be counted and to be aware of what true success means. It means earning respect and we can only do that by giving everything on the training field and everything on a Sunday. "We don't want to be looked on as a middle of the table team or a team that is weak up front or cannot last the pace. I want a team that is going better in the last 20 minutes than when the game started."

Roy said that he would pick the team after consulting assistant coaches Garth Budge and John Sykes and emphasised: "The final decision is absolutely mine". He continued: "If you disagree, rightly or wrongly, with any selection or any decision I make, don't try to go to the directors. If you feel you should have been in the team, there is only one man to come and see and that is me. I will give you an answer and it will be straight."

He talked about the need for discipline on the field: "At Swinton on Sunday we were penalised four times for 'talking' and whether the complaint was right or wrong, it gives a bad impression of Bradford Northern and the players involved. Cut it out."

He stressed the importance of communication on the field and told them: "Try different things and get the man beside you to help you. Work for each other at all times, back up, do your tackling, cover the gaps ... and never take your eye off the ball."

So, what ideas did Roy bring to rugby league coaching? The first was the importance of fitness. He started pre-season training earlier than other clubs, and held three sessions a week. As a player, he had done sprint training, and he now applied this to the whole team, not just the backs. Players recall using spikes for the first time. Roy would keep records of sprint times and stress to all the players the importance of improvement. Bev Risman says how he struggled to keep up at Leeds in training when he joined the club from Leigh.

Interviewed by Phil Hodgson for his book *Headingley Heroes*, Alan Smith said that Roy's "training techniques were phenomenal. Nobody had experienced training like he put us through. Other clubs used to come and watch...".

Roy saw having a strong pack as the basis of a team in rugby league. Unlike later coaches such as Peter Fox, who developed 'moves' for players, Roy seems to have given his teams freedom to play, but this was built on a solid defence. Particularly at Hull, the team's success was based on the pack. At Leeds, a strong pack was complemented by talented and fast backs.

John Atkinson recalled to Phil Hodgson that Roy "introduced a level of fitness that [players] had not been used to before." Steve Pitchford recalls long runs round Headingley in training and that "I had the stamina because he made us have the stamina and I never quit on the guy." Ray Batten says that training was "harder than the game on the Saturday." Graham Eccles recalls Roy using a stopwatch all the time in training.

Alan Smith told Trevor Watson in the *Evening Post's* obituary: "His [coaching] methods were awesome ... I am convinced that all my hard work under his direction enabled me to play on until the relatively late age of 39. It cannot be coincidence that so many of us lasted so long. He was also a great psychologist, an expert who moulded Leeds into a perfect team."

Roy's son Geoff attended the training sessions at Hull from when he was aged 15. He was involved in athletics. He says that the sessions were tough, and the indoor sessions were exercises designed to build up strength and stamina. He says that Roy always had a clipboard to take notes during the sessions. One session would be at the ground and the other one indoors.

Another point was the importance of training. This was the era of part-time players, who could be working away from their home base, or on shifts. Roy would try to avoid picking a player, even an international, if they had not been able to attend training in the week before the game. Particularly at Hull, he would organise extra day-time training before cup matches. This was done even if the opposition were from the lower reaches of the league. This stressed the importance of the match, and meant that 'giant-killings' involving Roy's teams were rare.

Roy also organised for his team to go away for a day or two before big cup or play-off matches. This allowed the players to be out of the limelight of being at home, and meant they could focus on preparing properly for the match.

Another strength of Roy's was to be able to encourage players to change to a different position. In the early 1950s at Hull, the Drake twins were transformed from unsuccessful backs to legendary forwards. Mick Clark told Phil Hodgson that Roy "... transformed my career by switching me from second row to prop. I'd been struggling to get in the side and he must have been desperate when he came to me and said 'Mick I'm going to play you ... at number 8' ... I had a blinder." Mick Clark made over 200 appearances for Leeds and was captain in the 1968 Challenge Cup Final.

John Holmes told Phil Hodgson that Roy invited him for a drink at the Queen's Hotel and suggested to him that he move from full-back to stand-off. Holmes was a youngster at the time and went on to have a magnificent career with Leeds. Holmes also recalls Roy telling hooker Tony Crosby to stay in the middle of the pitch and Crosby scoring far more tries that season through following this advice.

Another aspect of the sport that Roy developed was attention to diet. Ken Eyre was told to go on a diet when he signed for Leeds, and the player covering him in the 'A' team was also told what he should and shouldn't eat. Later, Steve Pitchford was encouraged to lose weight.

In the late 1950s, Roy had the idea of filming matches and training so that players could watch and learn from their mistakes. Roy planned to build up a library of films, so they could be used to develop techniques and skills. No one else had done this before for a club team.

Roy also believed in involving the players' families in the sport. This certainly happened at Leeds and North Sydney. He also is said to have organised transport for the players' wives and girlfriends to big matches.

It can be argued that Roy worked best with young players. That was certainly the case at Hull and Leeds in his best periods. At Hull, Roy did not have control of choosing the team or signing the players. He did recognise the importance of bringing in more experienced players if necessary. Harry Poole's role at Leeds in the first part of Roy's time at the club shows this. It was also true when Roy was player-coach at Hull – it took time for the team to learn to play without him as he got older and played less often.

Roy was often known as a 'disciplinarian', but there was clearly respect for him from the younger players. His use of psychology and man management – areas which he had developed in the Army – were clearly important. Interviewed by Trevor Gibbons for the book *The Glory of their Times*, the late Johnny Whiteley said about Roy: "The players at Hull, we were from the back streets, with no education. He showed us the other side of the road. He said we could change and move on in life as well as sport. Instead of making do with living in a one-up one down terrace I finished up in a nice area with a three bedroomed semi. He was such a man of the world, he was unique. We players looked up to him as a father figure."

Whiteley also told Gibbons "Roy Francis took over the lives of 30 lads and we were like disciples." Gibbons also says that Roy was aware of his own image, dressing smartly and always driving a nice car, including finally at Hull driving a Jaguar. Gibbons also says that "Seeing Roy Francis turning up for training in his smart car left a deep impression on Johnny Whiteley … Francis's power and poise meant he vowed to himself that he would always have his destiny in his own hands when he left the game. When Whiteley left rugby league he was determined to become self-employed because of Roy Francis's insistence on having personal control and responsibility."

Roy also looked after the players at Hull. Three times he organised end of season benefit matches for that season's beneficiaries. He used his contacts in the game to bring big stars to Hull to support players who had earned a testimonial season from the club. This must have inspired loyalty from his players. Particularly when he lived in Beverley, injured players would be treated by Roy, who was a qualified masseur. If they had personal problems, he would also offer support.

It is also interesting to note that as Hull declined in the early 1960s, letters to the *Mail* usually blamed the directors for failing to sign better players. It was very rare for Roy to be blamed for the team's fortunes.

What Roy needed at both Hull and Leeds was time to build a team. This was very clear at both clubs, and it is to both sets of directors' credit that they stuck by Roy in the 1950s and 1960s, showing patience that is so often missing today. It is interesting to wonder what Roy might have achieved at Hull if he had been able to choose the team and control the transfers in and out of the club. In the 1970s, Leeds were impatient and let Roy go after one season. At Bradford, he inherited a struggling team, and in his second season took the team to the verge of qualifying for the Premiership when he left the club due to ill health.

One question is why Roy was never involved in the Wales international set-up. When the team returned to playing international matches in the late 1960s, he was in Australia, but in the early and mid-1970s could have made a contribution.

Roy was involved in the attempt to start an organisation for coaches in rugby league in 1974. Again, this initiative was well ahead of its time. In association football, the League Managers Association has a voice in the game, and can support its members in any disputes with the clubs who employ them. There is still no such comparable body in rugby league.

After he retired from coaching in 1977, Roy continued his business activities. His death was reported in the papers on 6 April 1989. He was aged 70. A week before he died, he had attended a function at Headingley with many of his former players. Ian Proctor said that he was pleased and proud to be included in the 'Wall of Fame' at the recently opened Headingley Social Club. Roy had defied doctor's orders to attend the event, and his wife Renee said that he had received 'enormous pleasure' from the evening. Roy was taken into hospital for a major operation, but never regained consciousness.

Trevor Watson said in the *Evening Post* that Roy was "still revered at Headingley for the style of football he developed there, in particular during his first spell as coach." The *Hull Daily Mail* carried news of his passing on the front page of the paper. Richard Tingle wrote in the *Mail* that Roy "was a legend in his own lifetime and Hull FC fans were saddened to hear of his death." Ian Proctor said in the *Leaguer* that Roy "would be sorely missed throughout the rugby league world. His was a unique talent, one which enabled so many others to fulfil their own capabilities."

In his obituary for *Code 13*, Robert Gate wrote that Roy's "prowess on the playing field, however, has tended to be overshadowed by his success as a coach. In this latter field he was certainly far-seeing, innovative and usually triumphant. In modern parlance Roy's coaching would be termed 'state of the art'. Even now he has probably never been accorded the credit he deserved for revolutionising the science of coaching. He was undoubtedly the antecedent of the modern breed of coach and was one of the most profound, albeit unacknowledged, influences in the coaching revolution which permeated Australia in the late 1960s and early 1970s following his three year period as coach to North Sydney.

Professionally qualified as a masseur, an expert on physical fitness, a remedial instructor during the war, deeply interested in psychology and motivation and a great player in his own right, Roy Francis was singularly well equipped to coach rugby footballers. His insistence on athleticism, high levels of skills and willingness to give talented individuals their head were embodied in his magnificent Leeds teams of the 1963 to 1968 period which dominated the earliest days of limited tackle rugby league."

For some time, Roy was quietly forgotten, except among the Hull and Leeds supporters who had watched his teams. He was included in Robert Gate's *Gone North* (Volume 1), published in 1986, along with Welsh legends such as Jim Sullivan, Trevor Foster and Billy Boston. Also included was Tommy Harris, who Roy had developed at Hull. Phil Caplan and Peter Smith included Roy in their *Leeds RLFC 100 Greats* in 2001, rating him in the top 20 in the book. He was the only person included solely as a coach. Five other coaches in the book also played for the club.

Raymond Fletcher included Roy in his *Hull RLC 100 Greats* in 2002. In 2004, the late Phil Melling and Tony Collins had a chapter on Roy in their *The Glory of their Times*, covering 17 black or Asian players from British rugby league. In 2015, David Bond included a chapter on Roy in his *Hull FC 20 legends* book.

In 2018, Roy was chosen to be included in the Welsh Sports Hall of Fame. His son Geoff and daughter-in-law Anne attended the ceremony in Cardiff. And maybe in the future there will be a place for Roy in the Rugby League Hall of Fame. The Leeds Rhinos website says that Roy was "A superb motivator and man-manager, Francis was widely acknowledged as the greatest coach and thinker in the sport in the modern era." Surely that merits wider recognition for his contribution as a player and coach.

The Black Lives Matter movement saw a growing interest and concern about racial issues and diversity in sport. This led to a greater interest in Roy and his achievements. There was a piece about Roy during one of the BBC's televised Challenge Cup matches, and a major piece on the BBC sports website. In Brynmawr, there are plans to mark Roy's origins in the town with a blue plaque. And hopefully the publication of this book will bring to more rugby league followers the achievements of this remarkable man.

Appendix 1: Statistics & records

Playing:

Rugby league

Appearances and tries

Club	Season	App	Tries	Goals	Points
Wigan	1936–37	5	7	0	21
	1937–38	3	1	0	3
	1938–39	4	1	0	3
	Total	**12**	**9**	**0**	**27**
Barrow	1938–39	18	8	0	24
	1939–40	8	5	0	15
	1943–44	2	2	0	6
	1945–46	25	16	1	50
	1946–47	33	28	1	86
	1947–48	26	12	0	36
	Total	**112**	**71**	**2**	**217**
Dewsbury (guest)	1940–41	1	1	0	3
	1941–42	27	29	0	87
	1942–43	18	19	1	59
	1943–44	11	9	0	27
	Total	**57**	**57**	**0**	**171**
Warrington	1948–49	29	22	0	66
	1949–50	8	5	0	15
	Total	**37**	**27**	**0**	**81**
Hull	1949–50	2	0	0	0
	1950–51	29	12	0	36
	1951–52	36	16	0	48
	1952–53	20	9	0	27
	1953–54	12	11	0	33
	1954–55	22	9	0	27
	1955–56	6	3	0	9
	Total	**127**	**60**	**0**	**180**
Great Britain	1947–48	**1**	**2**	**0**	**6**
Wales	1946 & 1947	**5**	**1**	**0**	**3**
Northern Command	1942	**2**	**1**	**0**	**3**
Lancashire	1942	**1**	**0**	**0**	**0**
Career	**Totals**	**354**	**228**	**2**	**688**

Club honours

Dewsbury:
1941–42 War Emergency League Champions
1942–43: Yorkshire Cup winners
1942–43: War Emergency League Championship finalists (no title awarded due to dispute over player eligibility)
1943–44: War Emergency League Championship runners-up

Warrington:
1948–49: Championship runners-up (1 try in final)

Hull:
1954–55: Yorkshire Cup runners-up

Representative honours:

Rugby League:

1941–42: Northern Command vs Rugby League XIII Won 22–18 (1 try)
1941–42: Lancashire XIII vs Yorkshire XIII Lost 13–2
1942–43: Northern Command vs Rugby League XIII Won 14–10
1945–46: France vs Wales 24/3/46 Bordeaux Lost 19–7
1946–47: Wales vs England Swinton 12/10/46 Won 13–10 (1 try)
1946–47: France vs Wales 18/1/1947 Marseilles Lost 14–5
1947–48: Great Britain vs New Zealand 20/12/1947 Odsal Won 25–9 (2 tries)
1947–48: Wales vs England 6/12/1947 Swansea Lost 18–7
1947–48: Wales vs France 20/3/1948 Swansea Lost 12–20

Rugby Union:

England Services internationals:
27/2/1943: Scotland won 29–6 at Inverleith (1 try)
20/3/1943: Wales lost 34–7 at Gloucester (1 try)
10/4/1943: Scotland won 24–19 at Leicester (1 try)
20/11/1943: Wales lost 11–9 at Swansea
26/2/1944: Scotland won 23–13 at Murrayfield
18/3/1944: Scotland won 27–15 at Leicester (2 tries)
8/4/1944: Wales won 20–8 at Gloucester (1 try)

Other matches:
1942–43: Northern Command XV vs Northern Command Rugby Union XV
1943–44: Rugby League Combined Services vs Rugby Union Combined Services
1943–44: Army XV vs Civil Defence XV at Castleford
1943–44: Army vs RAF at Richmond
1943–44: Ireland XV v Army XV at Ravenhill, Belfast
1943–44: Northern Command v Combined Universities at Leicester

1944–45: South Wales XV v Army XV at Swansea
1944–45: Northern Command Scots & Welsh v Northern Command English*
1944–45: Army versus RAF*
* Selected, not confirmed if played.
There may be more matches that Roy played in. Complete records for these matches are very difficult to compile.

Coaching:

Finals and trophies:

Hull:
1953–54: Yorkshire Cup runners-up to Bradford N 7–2 at Headingley
1954–55: Yorkshire Cup runners-up to Halifax 22–14 at Headingley
1955–56: Yorkshire Cup runners-up to Halifax (after replay), 7–7 at Headingley, 7–0 in
    replay at Odsal
1955–56: **Championship winners 10–9 vs Halifax at Maine Rd**
1956–57: Championship runners-up 15–14 vs Oldham at Odsal
1957–58: **Championship winners 20–3 vs Workington Town at Odsal**
1958–59: Challenge Cup runners-up 30–13 to Wigan at Wembley
1959–60: Challenge Cup runners-up 38–5 to Wakefield Trinity at Wembley
1959–60: Yorkshire Cup runners-up to Featherstone 15–14 at Headingley

Leeds:
1964–65: Yorkshire Cup runners-up to Wakefield Trinity 18–2 at Fartown
1966–67: **Championship League Leaders Trophy & Yorkshire League winners**
1967–68: **Challenge Cup winners 11–10 vs Wakefield Trinity at Wembley**
    Championship League Leaders Trophy & Yorkshire League winners
1968–69: **Yorkshire Cup winners vs Castleford 22–11 at Wakefield**
1974–75: **Premiership winners 26–11 vs St Helens at Wigan**

League results

Season	Table place	Played	Points	Percentage
Hull				
1951–52	3	36	53	74
1952–53	15	36	36	50
1953–54	5	36	50	69
1954–55	19	36	35	49
1955–56	4	36	51	71
1956–57	2	38	60	79
1957–58	4	38	56	74
1958–59	7	38	51	67
1959–60	3	38	57	75
1960–61	11	36	41	57
1961–62	16	36	37	51

1962–63	14	30	22	37
1963–64 (part)		10	2	10
Leeds				
1963–64 (part)		20	14	35
1964–65	10	34	40	59
1965–66	6	34	48	71
1966–67	1	34	58	85
1967–68	1	34	56	82
1968–69 (part)		14	23	82
North Sydney				
1969	7	22	21	48
1970	9	22	15	34
Hull				
1972–73 (part)		11	8	36
Leeds				
1974–75	3	30	39	65
Bradford N				
1975–76 (part)		26	23	44
1967–77 (part)		27	28	52
Totals		**752**	**924**	**61**

Appendix 2: Wartime rugby league and union

Roy Francis played a lot of rugby during the War. The representative matches raised funds for war-related charities, and because he was a serving soldier, his Army or Services rugby union matches took priority over rugby league club or representative matches.

This may not be a complete record of his rugby union matches. Often the team selected and the one that played were different, because of military commitments and transport difficulties. It is difficult to find complete records of these matches.

Date	Match	Venue	Tries	Notes
1940–41				
12 Apr 41	Oldham 9 Dewsbury 13		1	
1941-42				
13 Sep 41	Dewsbury 34 Broughton 8		4	
20 Sep 41	Dewsbury 11 Wigan 5		1	
27 Sep 41	Batley 4 Dewsbury 5			
4 Oct 41	Dewsbury 14 Leeds 8		1	
11 Oct 41	Bradford N 17 Dewsbury 8			
18 Oct 41	Dewsbury 18 Featherstone 5		1	
25 Oct 41	Castleford 18 Dewsbury 2			Yorkshire Cup
1 Nov 41	Dewsbury 8 Castleford 5			Yorkshire Cup
8 Nov 41	Keighley 10 Dewsbury 31		2	
15 Nov 41	Dewsbury 18 Keighley 12		1	
22 Nov 41	Hull 9 Dewsbury 6			
29 Nov 41	Dewsbury 13 Batley 4		1	
20 Dec 41	Featherstone 5 Dewsbury 3			
25 Dec 41	Dewsbury 24 Wakefield 5		2	
27 Dec 41	Dewsbury 45 Bramley 8		4	
3 Jan 42	Oldham 7 Dewsbury 8		1	
10 Jan 42	Dewsbury 38 St Helens 8			
14 Feb 42	Dewsbury 22 Castleford 7		2	
28 Feb 42	Dewsbury 19 Halifax 5		1	
14 Mar 42	Dewsbury 5 Bradford N 3			
21 Mar 42	Northern Command 22 Rugby League XIII 18	Halifax	1	
28 Mar 42	Lancashire XIII 2 Yorkshire XIII 13	Dewsbury		
4 Apr 42	Dewsbury 15 Hull 7		1	
6 Apr 42	St Helens 2 Dewsbury 9		1	
11 Apr 42	Dewsbury 32 Hull 18		2	Play off
18 Apr 42	Dewsbury 13 Bradford 0	Neutral - Leeds	1	Play off final
25 Apr 42	Wigan 6 Dewsbury 4			Challenge Cup
2 May 42	Dewsbury 12 Wigan 14		1	Challenge Cup
9 May	Huddersfield 9 Dewsbury 23		2	
1942–43				
19 Sep 42	Batley 2 Dewsbury 29		2	
10 Oct 42	Northern Command 14 Rugby League XIII 10	Hull		

17 Oct 42	Leeds 15 Dewsbury 7			Yorkshire Cup
24 Oct 42	Dewsbury 18 Leeds5		1	Yorkshire Cup
31 Oct 42	Hull 12 Dewsbury 10			Yorkshire Cup
7 Nov 42	Dewsbury 23 Hull 7		3	Yorkshire Cup
14 Nov 42	Dewsbury 11 Wigan 3		1, 1 goal	Yorkshire Cup
21 Nov 42	Wigan 0 Dewsbury 6			Yorkshire Cup
28 Nov 42	Dewsbury 7 Huddersfield 0		1	Yorkshire Cup
5 Dec 42	Huddersfield 2 Dewsbury 0			Yorkshire Cup
19 Dec 42	Dewsbury 28 Batley 8		3	
25 Dec 42	Dewsbury 9 Wakefield 15			
26 Dec 42	Wakefield 3 Dewsbury 10			
16 Jan 43	Leeds 8 Dewsbury 22		4	
23 Jan 43	RU XV 11 RL XV 18	Leeds		Northern Command RU match
6 Feb 43	Featherstone 11 Dewsbury 3			
20 Feb 43	Dewsbury 5 Leeds 5			
27 Feb 43	Scotland 6 England 29	Inverleith	1	RU Services International
6 Mar 43	Huddersfield 9 Dewsbury 15		2	
20 Mar 43	England 7 Wales 34	Gloucester	1	RU Services International
10 Apr 43	England 24 Scotland 19	Leicester	1	RU Services International
6 May 43	Dewsbury 3 Bradford 8			Play off
13 May 43	Dewsbury 11 Halifax 3		2	Play off final
1943–44				
18 Sept 43	Dewsbury 48 St Helens 16		3	
25 Sept 43	Hunslet 14 Dewsbury 17			
13 Nov 43	Dewsbury 2 Wakefield 4			
20 Nov 43	Wales 11 England 9	Swansea		RU Services International
27 Nov 43	Dewsbury 16 Oldham 3		1	
4 Dec 43	Halifax 15 Barrow 10		2	
18 Dec 43	Northern Army XIII 4 RL XIII 11	Halifax		Roy listed in programme but did not play
25 Dec 43	Batley 16 Dewsbury 19		1	
27 Dec 43	Dewsbury 21 Batley 2		1	
15 Jan 44	Bradford 21 Barrow 3			
22 Jan 44	Northern Command XV v Civil Defence XV	Castleford		RU representative match
29 Jan 44	Army XV 8 RAF XV 11	Richmond		RU representative match
Feb 44	Northern Command v Combined Universities XV	Leicester		RU representative match
12 Feb 44	Irish XV v British Army XV	Ravenhill Belfast		RU representative match
19 Feb 44	Dewsbury 6 Hunslet 5			
26 Feb 44	Scotland 13 England 23	Murrayfield		RU Services International
4 Mar 44	Northern Command 37 Scottish Services 5	Leeds	2	RU representative match
18 Mar 44	England 27 Scotland 15	Leicester	2	RU Services International
8 Apr 44	England 20 Wales 8	Gloucester	1	RU Services International
10 Apr 44	Wakefield 2 Dewsbury 9		1	

29 Apr 44	RL XV 15 RU XV 10	Odsal		Combined Services RU match
6 May 44	Wakefield 5 Dewsbury 11		1	Play off
13 May 44	Wigan 13 Dewsbury 9			Play off final
20 May 44	Dewsbury 5 Wigan 12		1	Play off final
1944-45				
21 Oct 44	British Army XV 24 S Wales 8	Swansea		
28 Oct 44	Northern Command Scots & Welsh XV v Northern Command English XV			Not confirmed if Roy played
4 Nov 44	Army XV 18 RAF XV 15	Richmond		Not confirmed if Roy played

Bibliography

Newspapers and journals

Barrow News
Bradford Observer
Bradford Telegraph & Argus
Code 13
Dewsbury Reporter
Halifax Evening Courier
Huddersfield Daily Examiner
Hull Daily Mail
Merthyr Express
North Sydney Herald
North-Western Evening Mail

Rugby League Gazette
Rugby League Review
Rugby Leaguer
The Times
Warrington Guardian
Warrington RLFC club programmes
Western Mail
Wigan Express
Wigan Observer
Yorkshire Evening Post / Evening Post
Yorkshire Post

Websites
Brynmawr History Society

Books
John Bale & Joseph Maguire (Editors) *The Global Sports Arena*
Maurice Bamford *Memoirs of a Blood and Thunder Coach*
David Bond *Hull FC 20 Legends*
Stephen Bourne *The Motherland Calls*
Phil Caplan *Shoey the Lionheart – The Mick Shoebottom Story*
Phil Caplan and Peter Smith *Leeds Rugby League Football Club 100 Greats*
Ken Dalby *The Headingley Story (Volume 2)*
Ken Dalby with 'George' Hirst *Exodus – In Quest of Silver (Volume 5)*
Howard Evans & Phil Atkinson *War Games – Rugby Union during the Second World War*
Raymond Fletcher *Hull Rugby League Football Club – 50 of the finest matches*
Raymond Fletcher *Hull Rugby League Club 100 Greats*
Simon Foster, Robert Gate and Peter Lush *Trevor Foster – The life of a Rugby League Legend*
Peter Fryer *Staying Power*
Robert Gate *Gone North* (Volume 1)
Robert Gate *Rugby League Lions*
Tony Hannen *Being Eddie Waring*
Phil Hodgson *Headingley Heroes – Leeds RLFC in the 60s and 70s*
Dave Huitson, Keith Nutter & Steve Andrews *"Keeping the Dream Alive" – Barrow Rugby Football Club*
Joe Latus *Hard Road to the Top – The Clive Sullivan Story*
RE Lee and JA Saville *Hull FC Ltd Centenary 1865–66 to 1964–65*
Joe Mercer *The Great Ones*
Phil Melling and Tony Collins (Editors) *The Glory of their Times*
Andrew Moore *The Mighty Bears!*
Graham Morris *Grand Final*
Graham Morris *Wigan RLFC - 100 Greats*
Bev Risman *Both sides of the fence*
Irving Saxton *History of Rugby League (various seasons)*
Michael E Ulyatt *Hull: A Divided City*
Michael E Ulyatt *Old Faithful – A History of Hull FC 1865–1987*
Gareth Williams *1905 and all that*
Nigel Williams *Bradford Northern – The History 1863–1989*
Jack Winstanley *The Illustrated History of Wigan RLFC*

Papers
Huw Richards *Roy Francis, White Australia and the 1946 Indomitables*

A Northern Union Man
The life of Harold Wagstaff

By Robert Gate & Graham Williams

Harold Wagstaff, known as the 'Prince of Centres', was one of the key players in the development of rugby league in the early twentieth century.

He made his debut for the Huddersfield first team in November 1906, at the age of 15, having previously played for Underbank. He joined the professional game at an important time for the sport. The number of players had been reduced to 13, and other rule changes made, including the introduction of play-the-ball after a tackle. This made Northern Union rugby a more open game, and Wagstaff and the Huddersfield team took full advantage of the changes.

He played for Yorkshire in 1908, and in January 1909 made his Great Britain debut against Australia, the first player aged under 18 to play for his country. He was made captain of Huddersfield in 1911, and under his direction the club won the Challenge Cup three times, the Northern Rugby League Championship three times, the Yorkshire League six times and the Yorkshire Cup five times. They won 'All Four Cups' in 1914–15, and were known as the 'Team of all the Talents'.

For Great Britain, Wagstaff captained the 1914 and 1920 Lions tours to Australia and New Zealand. This included the 1914 'Rorke's Drift' test, when a Great Britain team reduced to 10 men through injuries hung on to beat the Australians and win the Ashes.

However, it was not just his success that made him one of the sport's greatest players. It was the way he played the game, seeing the sport as a passing and handling game, rarely kicking the ball. He was made a founder member of the Rugby League Hall of Fame in 1988.

This book, as well as contributions from the two authors, includes an autobiographical newspaper series that Wagstaff wrote in the 1930s, excerpts from an autobiographical series published in 1921 and contributions from other rugby league writers, including Tony Collins and Harry Edgar. It is book that every rugby league fan will enjoy.

Published in July 2019 at £12.95. Special offer: £12.50 post free in the UK available direct from London League Publications Ltd. Also available on Amazon and Abe Books.

Also available as an E-Book for Kindle from Amazon.